C++ Programming
with CORBA®

ANDREAS VOGEL
BHASKAR VASUDEVAN
MAIRA BENJAMIN
TED VILLALBA

WILEY COMPUTER PUBLISHING

John Wiley & Sons, Inc.

New York • Chichester • Weinheim • Brisbane • Singapore • Toronto

Publisher: Robert Ipsen
Editor: Robert Elliott
Assistant Editor: Pam Sobotka
Managing Editor: Angela Murphy
Electronic Products, Associate Editor: Mike Sosa
Text Design & Composition: North Market Street Graphics

This book is printed on acid-free paper. ⊚

Published by John Wiley & Sons, Inc.

Published simultaneously in Canada.

This publication is designed to provide accurate and authoritative information in regard to the subject matter covered. It is sold with the understanding that the publisher is not engaged in professional services. If professional advice or other expert assistance is required, the services of a competent professional person should be sought.

Library of Congress Cataloging-in-Publication Data:

ISBN 0-471-28306-1

Printed in the United States of America.

10 9 8 7 6 5 4 3 2 1

Contents

CHAPTER 3

OMG IDL to C++ Mapping   107

CHAPTER 4

ORB Runtime System 167

CHAPTER 5

CHAPTER 6

CHAPTER 7

Foreword

While it may seem somewhat retrograde in 1999 to publish a book which centers on C++ (rather than the hot C-based language, Java), this book will find an important place in the library of programmers everywhere. Even as Java turns 35 in dog years (oops, I guess I mean Internet years!), or about five in human reckoning, according to most surveyors of the programming scene C++ is still the primary C-based language, especially in mission-critical, high-performance systems. Fortunately, the CORBA technology discussed in this tome (as was discussed in its predecessor Java-based version) excels at solving cross-language integration problems. In fact, the de facto standard CORBA architecture provides interoperability in thousands of distributed, heterogeneous enterprise-wide applications worldwide today; heterogeneous not just in programming language but in operating system, underlying network connection, and hardware platforms as well. This C++ revision of the book provides another strong platform for understanding and implementing CORBA technology with confidence.

Richard Mark Soley, Ph.D.
Chairman and CEO,
Object Management Group, Inc.

Acknowledgments

First of all, we want to thank those people who assisted us in writing this book. These are our editors at John Wiley and Sons, Robert Elliott, Pam Sobotka, Angela Murphy, and the Wiley production team.

Thanks to Keith Duddy, who wrote many CORBA-related sections of Java Programming for CORBA which have been the base of this book and to Michael McCaffrey, who helped with some of the POA examples.

Special thanks to Inprise's Visibroker team, specifically to Prasad Mokkapati, Jon Goldberg, Tom Casaletto, Vijay Natarajan, Nick Trown and Vishy Kasar, which made an early Visibroker release, which supported the POA, available to us and gave support and guidance for using the POA features. We also thank Peter Holzwarth for his help with the Visibroker Trader implementation.

We acknowledge the corporation of the OMG, and in particular Richard Soley.

Thanks to Meta and Dorit for letting me work on evenings and weekends instead of going out or to the beach. I promise the next book will be the last one, for a while.

Also a word of thanks to Mike Cook of Bellcore who I helped designing and building a cool CORBA-controlled, Java-implemented IP telephony system. Mike always teased me that my CORBA books don't have any comics featuring out-of-space characters. Well, Mike, this one doesn't have any comics either, but I recommend as a supplement publications by Hank Hill which are of great educational value specifically when you raise an American boy as you do.

—Andreas

I am extremely grateful to Prasad Mokkapati, Jon Goldberg, Ke Jin, Nick Trown, and Vijay Natarajan, to whom I owe all I have learnt about the ORB so far. I am grateful to my family and friends to whom I owe all I am today.

—Bhaskar

To Jazzy and Scott for giving me the love, support, and understanding that I needed to get this book done and to all of my friends and family that believed in me—you know who you are! I truly believe that without the support of the people that you care for, you cannot achieve any of the goals that you are passionate about.

—Maira

I would also like to thank my mother for her amazing patience and unconditional love, thank my father for his guidance and dedicate my efforts to my sister Elena for teaching me that recycling is a way of life: paper, plastic, aluminum, code . . .

—Ted

About the Authors

Andreas Vogel is a Principal Consultant with Inprise Corporation since January 1997. In this position he works with customers, mostly Fortune 500 companies, on CORBA solutions for their distributed computing needs. More recently, he is also involved in strategy and product development.

Prior to this appointment, Andreas worked at the Distributed Systems Technology Centre (DSTC) in Brisbane, Australia in the position of a Principal Research Scientist, working on various aspects of distributed systems including CORBA2.0 Interoperability, OMG's Object Trader specification, CORBA-DCE interoperability, Web and middleware integration, and distributed multimedia systems. From 1993 to 1994, he worked as a Research Scientist for the University of Montreal, Canada, on quality of service issues of multimedia applications.

Andreas has co-authored *Java Programming with CORBA* (John Wiley & Sons, 1998), and is now working on a new book on Enterprise JavaBeans, the Java Transaction Service, and the CORBA Object Transaction Service. Andreas is Java Report Online's CORBA columnist and is a contributor to the Middleware Spectra. He also serves on program committees and advisory boards of a number of international conferences, workshops, and journals devoted to different aspects of distributing computing. Andreas holds a PhD and MSc in Computer Science from Humboldt-University at Berlin, Germany.

Andreas lives with his wife Dorit G. Hillmann and daughter Meta J.D. Hillmann in San Francisco. When not being at customer sites, he enjoys the 35 km commute to the San Mateo office on his bicycle.

Bhaskar Vasudevan, a Software Engineer with Inprise Corporation, is part of the VisiBroker for C++ team. Prior to this, he was a Member of Technical Staff with the Networking Products Development group at Oracle Corporation. He earned his Masters degree in Computer Science from the Rensselaer Polytechnic Institute, New York. He is interested in distributed computing and object-oriented programming. He currently lives in San Mateo, California.

Maira Benjamin, a Senior Support Engineer with CrossWorlds Software, has extensive expertise in educating and supporting customers and consultants to use complex business solutions. She uses her knowledge of originating technologies such as CORBA, Java, C++, Message Queuing, RDBMs, and data mapping tools to support interchange of data between the companies' solutions and other business solutions such as PeopleSoft and SAP.

Maira enjoys a successful career in high tech that included time at well-known companies including ASK, Sybase, UNIFACE, and Visigenic Software. She's held various engineering posts from porting and development to manager of maintenance, QA, and code management. Maira has also lent her talents to the consulting arena.

Maira enjoys the company of her husband Scott and her daughter Jasmine in their home located in the San Francisco Bay Area. Maira would like more opportunities to practice her Spanish, French, Japanese, and Sign Language. Some of her other passions are dancing, fashion, and going out with her friends.

Ted Villalba lives in San Francisco, works at Broadvision in Redwood City, and spends as much time as possible on a mountain bike in the mountains between the two.

How to Read This Book

This book introduces C++ Object Request Brokers (ORBs) to an audience familiar with the basic concepts of object-oriented programming and distributed systems. It contains chapters that fall into three categories: introduction and background, tutorial, and reference.

Chapter 1 gives motivation for the use of C++ ORBs, as well as an introduction on CORBA programming in C++. Chapter 2 is a solid introduction to CORBA. Chapters 3 and 4 explain the complete mapping from IDL to C++ and the C++ mapping of all CORBA interfaces. The new Portable Object Adapter is explained and many examples, specifically for the non-trivial memory management in C++, are given.

Chapter 5 introduces two fundamental CORBA Services, the Naming and the Trading Service, and demonstrates their use. This chapter also covers the bootstrap mechanisms for CORBA applications. Chapter 6 shows how to build applications with C++ ORBs using a room booking example. Advanced features are explained in Chapter 7. They include the Any type and TypeCodes, the Dynamic Invocation Interface and the Dynamic Skeleton Interface, the Tie mechanism, and Contexts.

Besides the default approach of reading the book front to back, we suggest the following paths through the book. Beginners should start with Chapter 1 and then continue with Chapters 5 and 6 and eventually 7. Chapters 2, 3 and 4 can be used as references as needed.

Advanced programmers will have experience with C++ and CORBA and may be most interested in the POA features and examples that are distributed throughout the book.

We recommend the book for self-teaching as well as source material for training and university courses. In any case, it is recommended that users work through the examples provided. The source code can be obtained from the John Wiley & Sons web site at http://www.wiley.com/compbooks/vogel. The web site is organized according to chapters, and should be easy to navigate.

Please note that the sample code in the book was tested against a beta of VisiBroker 4.0, but should work with any ORB that includes the Portable Object Adapter (POA). Please check our companion web site for updates reflecting new ORB releases.

1

Introduction

1 Benefits of C++ Programming with CORBA

This book brings together C++, the most widely used object-oriented programming language, and the Common Object Request Broker Architecture (CORBA), the most popular object-based distributed middleware. CORBA, a standard produced by the Object Management Group (OMG)—the world's largest industry consortium—defines an infrastructure that enables invocations of operations on objects located anywhere on a network as if they were local to the application using them. Although CORBA is defined to support many programming languages, C++ is the most popular language for implementing CORBA objects.

The OMG Interface Definition Language (IDL) is a language which allows you to specify the interface of objects in an implementation and programming language independent manner. Conceptually and syntactically, the OMG IDL uses many C++ language conventions, so the mapping from IDL to C++ is a very natural progression.

Throughout this chapter, we look at the advantages of using CORBA for C++ users and the advantages of using C++ for programming distributed systems with CORBA. Similarly, we provide some explanation of the object-

1

oriented concepts of C++ in the context of CORBA. We will also give an introduction to CORBA and C++ Object Request Brokers (ORBs). Finally, we explain how to program with C++ ORBs by introducing a simple example.

1.1 What Does CORBA Offer C++ Programmers?

The major advantages of using CORBA to build distributed applications with C++ are

♦ Interoperability across programming languages and operating systems
♦ Open standardization of CORBA
♦ Vendor independence
♦ Legacy integration
♦ Location transparency
♦ Programmer productivity
♦ Reusing CORBA services and facilities

1.1.1 Interoperability across Programming Languages and Operating Systems

CORBA defines an architecture for building distributed systems (for details see Chapter 2). One of the core pieces of CORBA is the OMG IDL, a language used to define interfaces to potentially distributed objects. IDL is program language independent and there are a growing number of specifications that define the mapping from IDL into programming languages. Currently there are mappings defined for the following languages: C++, Java, C, Smalltalk, Ada, and COBOL. Products implementing the CORBA architecture provide IDL compilers that generate code into a programming language for your IDL specification.

The benefit of IDL is that you can choose the most appropriate programming language for a certain task. This allows you to choose Java to implement applets, and thus provides access to applications from within a web browser. On the other hand, you can choose to use C++ to implement your objects on the server side.

Similarly you can have multiple clients to an application using different presentation models. This means that you can have an applet as well as a spreadsheet as a front end in the same application.

1.1.2 Open Standardization of CORBA

The OMG is defining the standard for CORBA, which in turn is implemented by companies, also known as ORB vendors. Since the OMG is a vendor consortium that is open to everyone, you can participate in the process of what is defined by the OMG. A specification adopted by the OMG must be implemented by the submitters.

1.1.3   Vendor Independence

Since CORBA is an open standard, anyone can implement it without having to obtain a license from the OMG or anyone else. Hence there are lot of vendors providing CORBA implementations. However, there are only a handful of companies providing full-featured, industrial-strength CORBA implementations, including support for multiple programming languages and a rich set of CORBA services and facilities. In addition, there are many companies that have CORBA-enabled their products. Examples of such products are Web servers, databases, operating systems, and networks. Finally, there are a number of research institutions that provide free CORBA implementations, often including the source code.

You can choose an appropriate ORB vendor depending on your requirements. You can write code so that it can be easily ported to a different ORB product, just in case you decide to switch products or your ORB vendor goes out of business. To achieve this portability, you must restrict yourself to the application programming interfaces (APIs) defined by the CORBA specifications. However, ORB vendors often provide a value-added feature set that makes the programming easier. Essentially it's a trade-off.

Besides the portability, you must also consider the interoperability of different components or subsystems that are implemented with different ORB products. CORBA specifies a hierarchy of interoperability protocols: the General Inter-ORB Protocol (GIOP), which is transport independent, and the Internet Inter-ORB Protocol (IIOP), which is the TCP/IP implementation of GIOP. These protocols are a mandatory part of the CORBA specification (since version 2.0). Details are given in Chapter 2. The protocols ensure interoperability between components implemented with different products. You can see a live demonstration of CORBA interoperability at the CORBAnet website (www.corba.net).

1.1.4   Legacy Integration

There are two reasons to use CORBA. One is to build new distributed applications with an object-based architecture. The other is to integrate existing systems into new applications. The way CORBA integrates legacy system implementations is to wrap those systems into a layer of IDL interfaces. You only need to write a layer of code which, in turn, makes the wrapper IDL interface call functions on the legacy APIs. That can be rather straightforward for libraries written in C, C++, or COBOL for which there are existing IDL mapping standards. If you have code in other legacy languages, for example, in FORTRAN or PL/1, you can wrap it using a C or C++ layer between the CORBA interfaces and the legacy code. The glue layer becomes more complex when the legacy system does not support the notion of a functional API. For example, a CICS interface to a mainframe application could require parsing screens to extract data. However, once the legacy system has been wrapped with a layer of IDL interfaces, it becomes very easy to enhance it with additional functionality, to integrate it with another application, or to expose its functionality in a web browser.

1.1.5 Location Transparency

If you build distributed systems with simpler mechanisms than CORBA, such as remote procedure calls (RPCs) or transport protocol APIs such as sockets, you typically need to know exactly where a server is located. For example, when using TCP/IP networking, a client needs the IP address and port number of a server.

CORBA provides the notion of an object reference, a concept known from C++ and other object-oriented programming languages. But while a C++ object reference is only valid in the address space of a program, a CORBA object reference is valid across processes, machines, programming languages, and ORB products. CORBA object references are often abbreviated as interoperable object references (IORs). Once a component has obtained an IOR it creates a client proxy which encapsulates all of the complexity of networking, and a developer only needs to write code against the signature of this local object, in our case C++.

CORBA goes even further. IORs and client proxy objects are still valid in the case that the object implementation changes its location. The ORB's communication infrastructure forwards your invocations to the relocated object.

1.1.6 Programmer Productivity

The CORBA environment maximizes programmer productivity. As you have just seen, CORBA frees a developer from most of the complexity of network programming. There is no need to deal with address information, network connections, or writing code for marshaling and unmarshaling your application data structure in byte streams. CORBA gives you the freedom to choose the programming language that is most appropriate for your task and that best fits the skill set of your developers.

CORBA is not the only core component that can handle your invocations on potentially remote objects. There is an increasing number of services and horizontal and vertical facilities that are specified by the OMG and implemented by ORB and component vendors. There are a good number of such services available today. In the next section we provide more details.

The encapsulation of code in objects enables reusability. This is a benefit you probably won't see when you implement your first CORBA application. But with a second application, you will find that certain business objects you built in the first application are reusable in the second one.

1.1.7   Reusing CORBA Services and Facilities

As mentioned earlier, the OMG has specified a growing set of services and facilities for common horizontal and vertical tasks. Following is a list of the most common and widely used services:

Naming Service.   White pages for CORBA objects (see Chapter 5).

Object Trading Service.   Yellow pages for CORBA objects (see Chapter 5).

Event Service.   An asynchronous, subscription-based messaging service.

Security Service.   Securing CORBA applications.

Object Transaction Service.   Transaction processing for distributed objects.

There are a number of Domain Task Forces (DTFs) within the OMG which actively work on vertical services and facilities. In particular, the Telecom DTF and the CORBAmed DTF have produced a number of services and facilities. For details and activities of other DTFs, see Chapter 2 and the OMG web site for the latest updates.

1.2   What Does C++ Offer CORBA Programmers?

The main reason for using a C++ language mapping of the OMG IDL is to take advantage of the following C++ features:

- ♦ Performance that is closely tied to the machine
- ♦ Ties to legacy systems/architectures
- ♦ Low-level programming

1.2.1   System Performance

C++ was designed with a strong focus on the performance of executables. C++ compilers provide various levels of sophistication for optimizing executable code. The target of a C++ compiler is typically the native instruction set of a specific platform. The design of other object-oriented languages such as Java and Smalltalk has followed other priorities, mostly productivity and portability. The compilers for these two languages produce platform-independent, intermediate code, which is then executed by an interpreter.

Although many attempts are ongoing to improve the performance of code, particularly that written in Java, executables generated by highly optimized C++ compilers are still more efficient.

1.2.2 Legacy Systems/Architectures

Today we face quite a bit of legacy code, which if it had to be rewritten would be quite expensive. However, as explained, CORBA provides an excellent way of making this code available through object wrapping. The C++ language mapping is a key CORBA feature that makes this happen. The wrapping of C and C++ code is straightforward. For almost any programming language, there exists an API into the C/C++ world that allows access to libraries written via CORBA through the C++ mapping.

You might ask, why not use the IDL/C mapping instead of C++? Although this works, the IDL/C mapping is not as natural as the C++ one, since C does not have all of the object-oriented features, making the mapping somewhat awkward. The call of C APIs from a C++ class, however, is straightforward.

1.2.3 Low-Level Programming

C++ has, through its C inheritance, the capability to write low-level code. This is hard or impossible to do with languages such as Java or Smalltalk. Combined with the natural IDL mapping, this makes C++ the language of choice for implementing CORBA interfaces to low-level tasks, for example, controlling interfaces for device drivers.

2 C++ Overview

C++ supports object-oriented programming. This section discusses object-oriented principles within C++ that have significance to CORBA. There may be occasional references to CORBA. Please note that this is not meant to serve as a tutorial. For detailed discussions and observations concerning the language, please refer to one of the many books on C++.

The central proposition of object-oriented design is the definition of objects and the operations that are invoked by them. Object-oriented design uses the following ideas:

- ◆ Encapsulation
- ◆ Modularity
- ◆ Abstraction/Interfaces
- ◆ Inheritance
- ◆ Exceptions/Overloading

Throughout this section we use C++ coding samples to help explain the concepts. We will end the section with a Hello World example. Although it is simple, it does help to illustrate some of the concepts presented. Later in this chapter we will distribute this example using CORBA.

2.1 Objects and Classes

There is a differentiation between objects and classes within the object-oriented design concept. A *class* is a type and an *object* is an instance of a class. That means a class is a static entity described in your code and an object is a runtime representation of this code. There can be many objects/instances of the same class/type. For example, you can declare a class *bridge* which is a type describing the concept of a bridge in generic terms. We can have bridge objects that are instances of the class bridge, for example, the Bay Bridge, the Tri-Borough Bridge, the London Bridge, etc.

Classes in C++ can be virtual or concrete. A virtual class defines only the signature. A *signature* is the syntax of the type. This is also known as an *interface* in generic object-oriented terms. Java and OMG IDL rely heavily on the concept of an interface. In our bridge example, a virtual class defines the signature of a bridge with members such as `int yearCompleted`, `int length`, and methods like `payToll()`.

A virtual class must be fully implemented to make a program that contains objects of this class executable. The concrete class is also known as the implementation. It completely defines the behavior of the class. A C++ convention is to define a class virtually in a header file and provide the implementation of the methods in an implementation file.

OMG IDL is only concerned with the definition of interfaces that are mapped to virtual classes. It is the application programmer's responsibility to provide implementations of the methods of the virtual classes.

2.2 Encapsulation

Encapsulation builds on the concept of abstraction (or hiding) of implementation details. The idea is to show and provide access to a number of member variables and methods to an outside entity. Variables and methods can be declared `private` or `public`. The concept of `friend` weakens the clarity of this concept for pragmatic reasons. Generally only member variables and methods declared as `public` can be accessed or invoked from the outside of the object.

OMG IDL is only concerned with the definition of the publicly available attributes and operations. Attributes and operations are mapped to public C++ methods.

2.3 Modularity and Scoping

Modularity simply means that a program can be separated into various parts. Scoping means that these parts have separated namespaces. That means you use the same identifiers in various parts. C++ contains better facilities than C for modular programming. C++ does this through the mechanism known as `namespace`. The concept of `namespace` allows you to group related data, functions, and the like.

Although C++ defines `namespaces` to separate namespaces of different components, only recently have C++ compilers supported this concept. The scope of nested classes can be used to a certain extent as an alternative scoping mechanism.

OMG IDL uses the concept of module to separate different namespaces. The IDL/C++ mapping defines two alternatives: a mapping to C++ namespaces where available and to the nested classes otherwise.

2.4 Inheritance

C++ supports the concept of inheritance of classes. A class, known as the derived class, can inherit from another class, known as the superclass. That means that the derived class will have all of the member variables and methods of the superclass and can define additional ones. For our bridge example we can define a class `TrainBridge` which inherits attributes from the superclass `Bridge` and adds a member variable `int numberOfTracks`. Inheritance can be applied recursively. For example, we can define a class `AmericanTrainBridges` that will inherit attributes from the class `TrainBridge`.

C++ also supports the notion of multiple inheritance. This means that a class can inherit any number of superclasses. Multiple inheritance of concrete classes has a potential problem. When a class inherits the methods with the same signature from different superclasses, they can have different implementations. The behavior of this method in the derived class is undefined.

OMG IDL also supports the inheritance of interface, including multiple inheritance. The problem described above does not apply because there is no behavior associated with methods in IDL.

2.5 Method Overloading

C++ provides method overloading. This means there can be multiple definitions of methods with the same method in a class as long as the method result type and the parameter types allow distinguishing between the various methods. This concept also applies to multiple classes that are in an inheritance relationship.

OMG IDL does not allow the overloading of operations. The motivation is in the mapping of IDL to programming languages that do not provide the concept of method overloading.

2.6 Exceptions

Exceptions provide an alternative termination of a method. Exceptions are often used to handle errors or other exceptional conditions. C++ defines exceptions as classes and hence allows inheritance of exceptions.

An entity can invoke methods that can raise exceptions. The entity can then decouple the exception handling from the unexceptional behavior by encapsulating the method invocations into a try-catch block. When a method raises an exception, it triggers the catch block in the invoked program.

OMG IDL also defines exceptions. However, exceptions are datatypes similar to structures and not objects. Hence inheritance does not apply to exceptions in IDL.

2.7 Hello World Example

We will introduce a simple C++ example, a Hello World program. We show the optional definition of a C++ virtual class and its implementation. We then explain how to build a C++ application. The object of the implementation class is created and a method is invoked on the object. We return to the same example later in the chapter where we will distribute the components.

The Hello World example contains an object of a class `GoodDay` that provides a method `hello()`. This method returns a string containing the message, "Hello World, from *location*," where location is the name of a geographical location, for example, Brisbane.

2.7.1 Defining the Signature and Implementation Class

A C++ interface defines the signature of an object, its types, fields, and methods. Hence it allows various substitutable implementations. For our example we define the interface `GoodDay`, which has one method, `hello()`. This is defined in the header file, `GoodDay.h`, for this example.

```
// GoodDay.h

class GoodDay {

    char * hello();
};
```

2.7.2   Implementing the Class

As we noted before, we need to create an implementation class which we will use to execute the hello() operation. The hello() operation will return the locality which we set in the constructor of the object. This implementation of the class we put in the GoodDayImpl.cpp file.

```
// GoodDayImpl.cpp

#include "fstream.h"
#include "GoodDay.h"

class GoodDayImpl : public GoodDay {
private:
    char* _locality;
public:
    GoodDayImpl (char *locality) : _locality(locality){}

    char *hello() {
        return(_locality);
    }
};
```

2.7.3   Creating and Invoking the Object

We create a GoodDay object in the main() routine of our program. We initialize with the location "Brisbane." We then invoke the hello() method on the GoodDay object and print out the result.

```
// GoodDayServer.C

#include <GoodDayImpl.cpp>

int main(int argc, char* const* argv) {

  // Create a GoodDay object.

  GoodDayImpl goodDayImpl( "Brisbane" );

  // invoke method hello() and print result
  cout << "Hello World, from " << goodDayImpl.hello() << endl;

 return(0);
}
```

2.7.4   Build and Execute

The final step in order for us to execute the Hello World program is to build the executable. We compile the two C++ files and link them. Now we can run the executable, which prints the following message:

```
Hello World, from Brisbane
```

3   *Overview of C++ ORBs*

A C++ ORB is an ORB that supports a C++ language mapping for OMG IDL. This language mapping, or language binding, allows clients and objects to be implemented in C++. A C++ ORB must offer a complete implementation of the CORBA specification.

This section introduces the architecture of the C++ ORB. First, we examine some necessary terminology. We then discuss the requirements for C++ applications to communicate with CORBA objects. Specifically, we cover the following topics:

♦ C++ ORB features
♦ C++ applications as clients and servers
♦ Clients and servers implemented using other programming languages

3.1   Terminology

In this section and throughout the rest of the book we will use a number of terms that have specific technical meanings. Because both CORBA and C++ are object-oriented and have similar object models at the interface level, some terms will apply to both. However, most of the time we will use different language to refer to concepts in each domain. Here is the way in which we will differentiate:

Object.   Refers to some program component that has a well-defined interface. We usually refer specifically to CORBA objects, whose interfaces are represented in OMG IDL, and C++ objects, whose interfaces are represented by C++ variables and method declarations.

Operation.   An action that can be invoked on a CORBA object, as defined in IDL.

Method.   An action that can be invoked on a C++ object, as defined in that object's public class declaration. C++ objects can implement CORBA interfaces. Methods on these objects correspond to operations in the CORBA interface.

Client.   A role that is played by a program in the context of an invocation.

Server.   A role that is played by a CORBA object in the context of an invocation. Many programs that are servers are also clients to other servers.

CORBA Server.   An operating system process that is hosting one or multiple objects and object adapters.

Object Adapter. A component of the ORB which connects CORBA objects with the ORB runtime system. It can make CORBA objects accessible to clients, activate or deactivate CORBA objects, control threading policies, etc.

3.2 Clients and Servers as C++ Applications

Figure 1.1 illustrates the simplest scenario involving C++ ORBs: a client interacting with a server. Client and server are both implemented in C++. Figure 1.1 is an abstract representation of the client-server model in C++ ORBs. We see three components in the figure: the client, the server, and the ORB. The client communicates with the ORB in order to convey a request for an operation invocation to the server, which then sends results via the ORB back to the client. The interfaces these components use are defined by the CORBA standard and by the application-specific IDL definitions that the object at the server supports.

Figure 1.2 shows a more concrete view of how the ORB performs the task of conveying an invocation from client to server. Most C++ ORBs are implemented as libraries that are linked into a program. The lightly shaded objects in Figure 1.2 are provided by the ORB (compare with Figure 2.4). The following sections describe the functionality of each of these components.

3.2.1 Stub and Skeleton Code

The IDL compiler generates a number of C++ classes known as stub classes for the client and skeleton classes for the server. The role of the stub class is to provide proxy objects that clients can invoke methods on. The proxy object method implementations invoke operations on the object implementation, which may be located remotely. If the object implementation is at a remote location, the proxy object marshals and transmits the invocation request. That is, it takes the operation name and the types and values of its arguments from language-dependent data structures and places them into a linear representation suitable for transmitting across a network. The code to marshal programmer-defined datatypes is an essential part of the stub

FIGURE 1.1 Client-server model with C++ ORBs: abstract view.

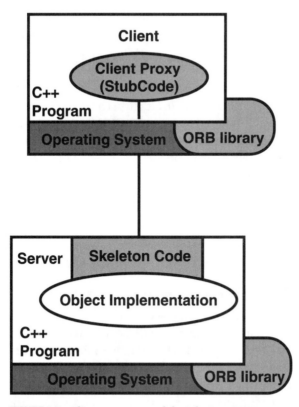

FIGURE 1.2 Client-server model with C++ ORBs: concrete view.

code. The resulting marshaled form of the request is sent to the object implementation using the particular ORB's infrastructure. This infrastructure involves a network transport mechanism and additional mechanisms to locate the implementation object, and perhaps to activate the CORBA server program that provides the implementation.

The skeleton code provides the glue between an object implementation, a CORBA server, and the ORB, in particular the object adapter (OA). The original CORBA specification defined the basic object adapter (BOA). This specification left many of the interfaces between the ORB core, BOA, and server program partially or totally unspecified. For this reason, different ORBs have different mechanisms for use by the BOA to activate servers and for use by servers to inform the BOA that their objects are ready to receive invocation requests. In the meantime, the OMG has adopted the specification of the portable object adapter (POA), which overcomes the shortcomings of the BOA.

The POA was designed to provide a standard portable interface that CORBA objects can use to communicate with the ORB runtime. The key differentiation between the POA and the BOA is that the POA provides a layer of abstraction between the object and the ORB, allowing an object implementation to be portable across multiple vendor implementations. In contrast, the BOA is very tightly coupled with a particular ORB implementation and object implementations written with one vendor's ORB will not work with another vendor's ORB. In either case, the build process for the object is effectively the same. When developing a CORBA object implementation, the class must access either the BOA skeleton class or the more portable POA skeleton class. The access can be via inheritance (inheritance approach) or by delegation (tie approach).

The skeleton class for either the BOA or POA implements the mechanisms by which invocation requests coming into a server can be directed to the right method of the right implementation object. The implementation of those methods is the responsibility of the application programmer.

3.2.2 *ORB and Object Adapter*

The BOA has a proprietary interface to the ORB that is not standardized in CORBA. This generally means that BOA functionality is implemented as part of the same code as the ORB, partially in libraries, partially in stub and skeleton code, and partially in a runtime daemon (background task or process). The marshaling routines in both the stub and skeleton code exchange invocation requests and results via a network connection that is set up using ORB library code that must be linked into CORBA servers and clients. This code also communicates with the ORB runtime daemon which knows which servers implement which objects and can locate and/or activate servers when requests are made to them. The POA provides the same functionality, but now the interfaces between the OA, the ORB, and the skeleton are defined.

Unlike the BOA, the POA provides a well-published interface for objects to code directly to, independent of the underlying vendor implementation. The POA introduces new terminology, defining CORBA object implementations as *servants*. In the POA model, an object implementation registers itself with the POA as a servant and the POA maintains a mapping of object references to servant implementations. Further, the POA allows activation of these servants based on the definition of various types of *policies*.

The information about how objects and servers are associated with idle or running C++ code files is stored in the Implementation Repository. This is a component of CORBA that is assumed to exist, but its interface is not specified and is different in each ORB.

Figure 1.3 presents a simplified view of the interactions between server programs, the objects they support, the ORB, and the OA. As the figure shows, a CORBA server usually supports a number of CORBA objects. The server's main routine is used to create CORBA object instances and to notify the OA of their availability to CORBA clients.

The BOA provides the operations `obj_to_ready()` and `impl_is_ready()`. They are supported by library methods on a BOA pseudo-object in an implementation of a CORBA pseudo-IDL interface specification in an ORB-dependent manner (usually as library code).

The POA provides a richer interface that is explained in more detail in Chapter 2. Typically the POA is implemented in the same manner as the BOA, as part of the ORB library. The POA's policies can be configured to make it behave like most vendors' BOA implementations. This allows programmers to continue writing code against the convenient BOA interface, which, in fact, will be just an API on top of the POA with some default policies. The POA will require different operations to be used to activate servants based on the activation policy.

3.3 Clients and Servers Implemented with Non-C++ ORBs

Since CORBA provides multiple programming language mappings for OMG IDL, clients and servers can be implemented in a wide variety of languages. There are many reasons for using other languages, for example, to deploy clients on the Internet as Java applets, to integrate legacy code, or to exploit

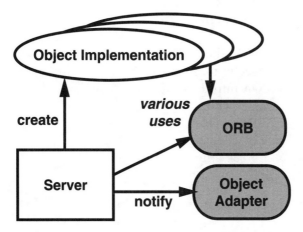

FIGURE 1.3   C++ ORB server side: simplified view.

specific skills of a software engineering team. Other programming languages are made available by ORB vendors in the following ways:

Within the same ORB or ORB family. This requires an IDL compiler that generates the stub and skeleton code in the required programming language. The implementation of the ORB and OA pseudo-objects must be accessible via an API wrapper in this programming language or they must be reimplemented in this language. The ORB runtime system, including daemons and configuration files, can be shared. The objects implemented in different languages can use an ORB's proprietary protocol.

With different ORBs using CORBA 2.0 interoperability. Implementations in different languages using the development and runtime environments of different ORBs can communicate using IORs. This is often referred to as communication across ORB domain boundaries.

The trend is clearly going toward the second approach. Today we see more and more ORB implementations choosing IIOP as their native or primary communication protocol. Figure 1.4 illustrates the interworking between clients and servers implemented in different programming languages using IIOP as the communication protocol. Besides the C++ client and server, we show Java clients and servers because they are very popular. A typical example of clients and servers in other programming languages are those implemented in Smalltalk.

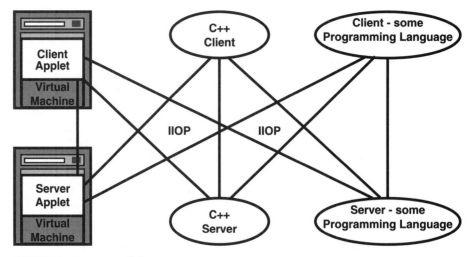

FIGURE 1.4 Interoperability.

4   Building a First C++ ORB Application

In this section we use another simple Hello World example (see Figure 1.5) to introduce the principles of building distributed applications with C++ ORBs. This example expands the Hello World example introduced above. We will implement a client, a C++ application, and a server supporting an object implementation. Figure 1.5 illustrates the components of our example.

All code is available in electronic form from www.wiley.com/compbooks/vogel. We used Visibroker for C++ to develop and run our examples. The code is available for Solaris and Windows 95/NT and is easily portable to other platforms. As long as standard CORBA features are used, the ORB you choose does not matter. However, there are a few portability issues for CORBA/C++ code. We have already mentioned the incomplete BOA specification and how the POA overcomes it.

The various ORB products, which conform to the CORBA specification, differentiate themselves with implementation details that have an impact on performance and scalability. Most also have extensions to the CORBA core.

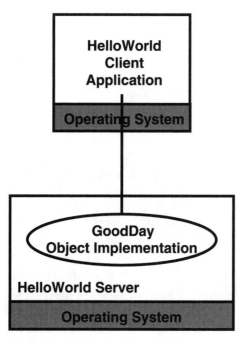

FIGURE 1.5   Hello World application.

The section starts with a summary of the development process for CORBA applications in C++. We then give detailed explanations for the development of a simple example application and subsequently extend this to include more features. In Chapter 6 we return to application development with a more substantial example.

4.1 Summary of the CORBA Development Process

The examples presented in this section will follow these steps:

1. Write some IDL that describes the interface to the object or objects that we will use or implement.
2. Compile the IDL using the IDL compiler provided by the particular ORB. This produces the stub and skeleton code. It will convert an object reference into a network connection to a remote server and then marshal the arguments we provide to an operation on the object reference, convey them to the correct method in the object denoted by our object reference, execute the method, and return the results.
3. Identify the classes (header and implementation files) generated by the IDL compiler that we need to use or specialize in order to invoke or implement operations.
4. Write code to initialize the ORB and inform it of any CORBA objects we have created.
5. Compile all the generated code and our application code with the C++ compiler.
6. Run the distributed application.

Figure 1.6 shows the use of IDL and the IDL compiler when building the application.

Executing the IDL compiler for the C++ ORB that you have installed typically creates two sets of C++ files. The files contain the following information:

The client files (2).   These files contain C++-type definitions for the client structure as well as C++ definitions for the client classes. They also contain the various C++ implementation methods for use by the client application. The methods generated by the IDL are stub code methods.

The server files (2).   These files contain C++ definitions for classes that contain skeleton methods. The ORB uses skeleton methods

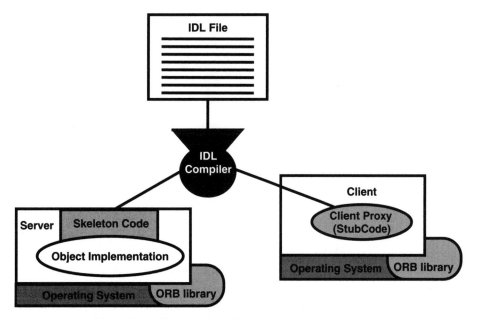

FIGURE 1.6 Building the Hello World application.

to unpack parameters from the client application's request. They will invoke the actual method on the server object.

4.2 Environment Setup

Before we can start with the examples we have to set up a working environment. We implemented the examples using Visibroker for C++ on a Sun/Solaris platform and ported the code to Microsoft's Windows operating system. For setups in other environments, the reader is referred to the installation manuals for the particular products and platforms.

4.3 Interface Specification

Our first example provides the same functionality as the one introduced in section 3. However, a client invokes an operation hello() on the interface of a potentially remote object GoodDay. The result of the invocation is a message that is printed by the client.

For any CORBA application we must write an IDL specification that defines datatypes and interfaces, including attributes and operations. For our example, we defined an IDL file called SimpleHelloWorld.idl, which resembles the C++ class of the Hello World example from section 3.

```
// SimpleHelloWorld.idl

module SimpleHelloWorld {
 interface GoodDay {
  string hello();
 };
};
```

The file contains the specification of a module SimpleHelloWorld. It is good specification style to

♦ Use modules to create a separate namespace for an application or its major components.
♦ Have one file per module.
♦ Name the file after the module.

Within the module we define one interface: GoodDay. The interface is not in an inheritance relationship. It provides one operation: hello(). This operation does not have any parameters and returns a result of type string.

As we will see in the implementation, the object returns a string describing its locality as part of the result of the operation hello(). The operation returns a message saying: "Hello World, from *location*."

4.4 Compiling the IDL

The next step in the application development is to compile the IDL to generate the client code stub and server skeleton code. The compiler for Visibroker for C++ is idl2cpp. The compile command is

```
prompt> idl2cpp SimpleHelloWorld.idl
```

The following four files are generated by the IDL compiler:

♦ SimpleHelloWorld_c.hh
♦ SimpleHelloWorld_c.cpp
♦ SimpleHelloWorld_s.hh
♦ SimpleHelloWorld_s.cpp

The SimpleHelloWorld_c.* files comprise the client side of the application. The SimpleHelloWorld_s.* files comprise the object server side of the application. The suffixes .cpp and .hh help you distinguish between these generated files and the files you will need to create to complete the example. The .hh files are the generated header files for the application. The .cpp files are the generated source files for the application. Note that you will not need to modify these generated files.

4.5   A Client as a C++ Application

A client implementation follows these steps:

1. Initialize the CORBA environment, that is, initialize the ORB.
2. Obtain an object reference for the object on which it wants to invoke operations.
3. Invoke operations and process the results.

4.5.1   Generated C++ Interfaces

Let's look at the C++ definitions that correspond to the interface defined in the IDL. All these classes extend a virtual base class for the CORBA object. Corresponding to our IDL interface definition, the class GoodDay defines a method hello() which returns a pointer to char. Here we present only an incomplete part of the code for clarity. This is coming from the generated SimpleHelloWorld_c.hh header file:

```
class SimpleHelloWorld {
public:
 ...
 class GoodDay : public virtual CORBA_Object {
 private:
  static const CORBA::TypeInfo classinfo;
  GoodDay(const GoodDay&) {}
  void operator=(const GoodDay&) {}
  ...
  virtual char* hello()
```

4.5.2   Initializing the ORB

The client program is essentially a main() function. Initializing an ORB means obtaining a reference to an ORB pseudo-object. The ORB is called a pseudo-object because its methods are provided by a library, and its pseudo-object reference cannot be passed as a parameter to CORBA interface operations. Excluding that restriction, however, a reference to an ORB looks like any other object reference.

The reference to the ORB object is obtained by calling the static method CORBA::ORB_init().

```
#include "SimpleHelloWorld_c.hh"

int main(int argc, char* const* argv) {

  CORBA::String_var stringifiedIor;

  try {
    // Initialize the ORB
    CORBA::ORB_var orb = CORBA::ORB_init(argc, argv)
```

4.5.3 *Obtaining an Object Reference*

References to objects can be obtained by various means, as explained in depth in Chapter 5. Here we use a rather unsophisticated method. Object references are opaque data structures. However, an object reference can be made persistent by converting it into a string (as we show when explaining the server). This is known as stringifying an object reference. The resulting string is called a stringified object reference. Stringified object references are reconvertible into "live" object references. This is done using the two corresponding operations object_to_string() and string_to_object() defined in the CORBA::ORB interface. Stringified interoperable object references can be converted into working object references by any CORBA 2.0–compliant ORB.

```
// get stringified IOR from command line
if( argc >=2 )
  stringifiedIor = (const char *) argv[1];
else {
  cerr << argv[0] << ": Missing IOR" << endl;
  return 1;
}
// get object reference from command-line argument
CORBA::Object obj = orb::string_to_object( stringifiedIor );
```

For this example client, we assume that a stringified object reference is provided as the first argument to the client program. It is then provided as the argument to the method string_to_object(), which is invoked on the ORB pseudo-object. The method returns an object reference of type CORBA::Object_ptr, the base type of all **CORBA** objects. To make use of the object, it needs to be narrowed to the appropriate type. Narrowing is equivalent to downcasting in some object-oriented programming languages. The narrow operation is type safe. It returns a null reference if the object is not of the expected type, but make sure that you test for null references. In addition, the narrow operation can raise a CORBA system exception.

```
// narrow it down to GoodDay
SimpleHelloWorld::GoodDay_var goodDay =
SimpleHelloWorld::GoodDay::_narrow( obj );
if( goodDay == null ) {
  cout << "Good day is null" << endl;
  return(1);
  }
```

4.5.4 *Invoking the Operation*

Once the ORB is initialized and an object reference is obtained, CORBA programming looks very much like standard object-oriented programming.

One invokes methods on objects, and it looks exactly the same for remote and local objects.

```
//invoke the operation and print the result
cout << "Hello World, from " << goodDay->hello() << endl;
```

Our simple client invokes the method `hello()` on the object `goodDay` and the result is printed to standard output.

The last thing to consider is handling exceptions that might occur. Since there are no user exceptions raised by the `hello()` operation, we only have to catch and process CORBA system exceptions which can be raised during the initialization of the ORB, the `narrow()` and the invocation of the `hello()` operation.

```
  //catch CORBA system exceptions
  catch(const CORBA::Exception& e) {
    cerr << e << end;
    return(1);
  }
 return(0);
 }
}
```

4.6   Object Implementation

Now we turn to the implementation of the object whose interface has been specified in IDL. The object implementation class must be associated with the skeleton class generated by the IDL compiler. This can be done by inheritance or by delegation.

The skeleton class is an implementation of the C++ interface, which corresponds to the IDL interface. The object implementation is an extension of this class. This is known as associating the skeleton with its implementation by inheritance.

Another way to associate the skeleton class with the inheritance implementation is to use the Tie method. The Tie method associates the skeleton with its implementation by delegation. That is, there are separate skeleton and implementation objects, and the skeleton is given a reference to the implementation object. This is explained in detail in Chapter 7 using the same example.

In our example, we have an implementation class `SimpleGoodDayImpl` that extends the POA skeleton class (`POA_SimpleHelloWorld::POA_GoodDay`). As in the implementation of the equally named class shown in section 2, we locally declare a private variable that holds a string identifying the location of the service. Here we mean the geographic location, as shown in the client example.

We also have to implement the constructor of the class. The constructor has one parameter that is assigned to the private variable `_locality`.

```
class SimpleGoodDayImpl : public POA_SimpleHelloWorld::POA_GoodDay {

// variable declaration
private:
 CORBA::String_var_locality;

// constructor
public:
 SimpleGoodDayImpl( const char *locality,
     Const char *object_name = NULL) :
     _locality( locality ),
     _sk_SimpleHelloWorld::_sk_GoodDay ( object_name ) {}

 char *hello() {
  CORBA::strdup(_locality);
  }
}
```

We implement the method `hello()`, which returns a `*char` holding the value of the variable `_locality`. We have to duplicate the string value, otherwise the ORB releases the memory.

4.7 A Server as a C++ Application

Now we have to implement a server executable. This executable initializes the environment, creates the implementation object, makes it available to clients, and then listens for events.

The server executable for our example is called `SimpleHelloWorldServer`. Since it is a stand-alone program, we need to have a `main()` routine. We check for the right number of arguments: one argument that indicates the locality of the server.

A server is responsible for the following tasks:

♦ Initializing the ORB and the POA
♦ Creating the object/servant
♦ Using the POA to activate a servant

4.7.1 Initializing the ORB and POA

We initialize the ORB in the same way we did on the client side, by calling `CORBA::ORB_init()`, which returns a reference to the ORB pseudo-object. For the POA, we will call `resolve_initial_references()` in order to obtain a reference. This will return a `CORBA::Object`, which must be narrowed to the appropriate POA type.

```
try {
  // Initialize the ORB
  CORBA::ORB_var orb = CORBA::ORB_init(argc, argv);

  //Initialize Portable Object Adapter
  // Get the Root POA object reference
    CORBA::Object_var obj =
             orb->resolve_initial_references ("PersistentPOA");

  //Narrow the object reference to a POA reference
  PortableServer::POA_var root_poa =
        PortableServer::POA::_narrow (obj.in());
```

4.7.2   Creating the Object

We create our implementation object and supply one parameter for the constructor, which we copy from the command line argument.

```
// Create a new GoodDay object.
    GoodDayImpl goodDayImpl( argv[1] );
```

4.7.3   Using the POA to Activate a Servant

Once we create the implementation object we notify the POA that this object is available and that it must map the object reference to a POA servant by calling the method `activate_object()`. When using the POA instantiating a POA manager is also required. A POA manager provides the ability to utilize multiple POAs, each with different policies. We also print out the stringified version of the object reference, which we obtain by calling `servant_to_reference()` to get the standard reference, and then pass this to the ORB operation `object_to_string()`. This is the object reference we used in the client to establish a connection with a server.

```
// Allocate a POA Object id and map it to the servant
    PortableServer::ObjectId_var oid =
root_poa->activate_object(&goodDayImpl);

    // Activate a POA Manager for our POA.
    root_poa->the_POAManager()->activate();

    // Get a stringified IOR to our Servant
    cout << orb->object_to_string
(root_poa->servant_to_reference(&goodDayImpl)) << endl;
```

```
orb->run();
}
 catch(const CORBA::Exception& e) {
  cerr << e << endl;
  return(1);
 }
 return(0);
}
```

4.8   Compiling the Server and the Client

To compile the server and the client source code and make them executable, it is best to create a makefile that will also compile the IDL file. We are responsible for the following files:

- ♦ SimpleHelloWorld.idl
- ♦ SimpleHelloWorldClient.C
- ♦ SimpleHelloWorldServer.C

The makefile needs to take these files into account as well as the IDL-generated compiled files:

- ♦ SimpleHelloWorld_c.cpp
- ♦ SimpleHelloWorld_c.hh
- ♦ SimpleHelloWorld_s.cpp
- ♦ SimpleHelloWorld_s.hh

Here are the specific makefile rules for our SimpleHelloWorld application:

```
SimpleHelloWorld_c.cpp: SimpleHelloWorld.idl
     idl2cpp SimpleHelloWorld.idl

SimpleHelloWorld_s.cpp: SimpleHelloWorld.idl
     idl2cpp SimpleHelloWorld.idl

SimpleHelloWorldClient.exe: SimpleHelloWorld_c.o SimpleHelloWorldClient.o
     $(CC) -o SimpleHelloWorldClient SimpleHelloWorldClient.o \
     SimpleHelloWorld_c.o $(LIBPATH) $(LIBORB) $(STDCC_LIBS)

SimpleHelloWorldServer.exe: SimpleHelloWorld_s.o SimpleHelloWorldServer.o
     $(CC) -o SimpleHelloWorldServer SimpleHelloWorldServer.o \
     SimpleHelloWorld_s.o $(LIBPATH) $(LIBORB) $(STDCC_LIBS)
```

The definitions of the global variables that we are referring to in this makefile are contained in a standard makefile. It is best to distinguish platform-specific makefiles from each other.

4.9   Running the Application

After the successful compilation of the files you have created, you will need to run the resulting executable files—SimpleHelloWorldClient and SimpleHelloWorldServer—to test the validity of the application. Start the application server:

```
prompt> SimpleHelloWorldServer Brisbane
```

The server will then display a stringified IOR that we will need to reference when executing the client:

```
IOR:012020202100000049444c3a53696d706c6548656c6c6f576f726c642f476f6f64446179
3a312e3000020202001000000000000000540000000010100200b00000031302e312e332e313434
0020170e20203800000001504d4301000000210000049444c3a53696d706c6548656c6c6f57
6f726c642f476f6f644461793a312e30000202020200000000059810c35
```

We execute the client by typing the client application name and the stringified object reference that was obtained from the execution of the server:

```
prompt> SimpleHelloWorldClient IOR:012020202100000049444c3a53696d706c6548656
6c6c6f576f726c642f476f6f644461793a312e3000020202001000000000000000540000000101
00200b00000031302e312e332e3134340020170e20203800000001504d430100000021000000
49444c3a53696d706c6548656c6c6f576f726c642f476f6f644461793a312e3000202020200000
000059810c35
```

The client then prints the expected message:

```
Hello World, from Brisbane
```

CORBA Overview

This chapter contains detailed information, from a CORBA application developer's perspective, about the OMG and the architecture documents and specifications it has produced. Section 1 is an overview of the history, goals, organizational structure, and processes of the OMG. It provides descriptions of all the committees, task forces, and special interest groups within the consortium.

Section 2 is a detailed summary of the contents of the *Object Management Architecture Guide* and includes the changes made to the OMA since the third revision in mid-1995. There are two main topics in this section, the Core Object Model (section 2.2) and the OMA Reference Architecture (section 2.3).

The third, and longest, section summarizes the CORBA 2.1 specification. This section attempts to balance conciseness and detail, and covers all of the content of the July 1995 *Common Object Request Broker: Architecture and Specification* document that is relevant to ORB users while briefly introducing the material relevant to ORB implementers. The major topics covered include

- CORBA Object Model (section 3.2)
- ORB Structure (section 3.3)
- OMG IDL (section 3.4)
- ORB and Object Interfaces (section 3.5)
- Basic Object Adapter (section 3.6)
- Portable Object Adapter (section 3.7)
- Language mappings (section 3.8)
- Interoperability Architecture (section 3.9)
- TypeCode, Any, and Dynamic Any (section 3.10)
- Dynamic Invocation and Dynamic Skeleton Interfaces (section 3.11)
- Interface Repository (section 3.12)

1 The Object Management Group

The Object Management Group (OMG) is the world's largest computer industry consortium, with over 750 members in 1997. It is a nonprofit organization that began in 1989 with eight members: 3Com, American Airlines, Canon, Data General, Hewlett-Packard, Philips Telecommunications N.V., Sun Microsystems, and Unisys. The organization remains fairly small and does not develop any technology or specifications itself. It provides a structure whereby its members specify technology and then produce commercial implementations that comply with those specifications. The OMG's processes emphasize cooperation, compromise, and agreement rather than choosing one member's solution over another's.

1.1 OMG's Goals

The goals of the OMG are promotion of the object-oriented approach to software engineering, and development of a common architectural framework for writing distributed object-oriented applications based on interface specifications for the objects in the application.

1.2 The Organizational Structure of the OMG

The OMG Board administers the organization and ratifies the activities of the other groups within the OMG (see Figure 2.1). Most positions in the OMG are unpaid and are held by representatives of member companies.

The technical group of the OMG is overseen by the Architecture Board (AB), whose members are experienced system architects. The AB is elected by the OMG membership. It reviews all technology proposals and specifica-

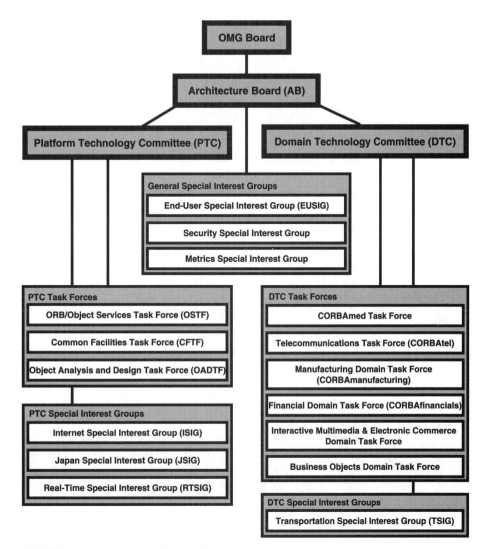

FIGURE 2.1 Organization of the OMG.

tions for consistency and conformance with the Object Management Architecture (OMA).

The structure of the committees, task forces, and other groups within the OMG reflect the structure of the OMA. Two committees oversee the technology adoption of a number of task forces (TFs) and special interest groups (SIGs).

> **Platform Technology Committee (PTC).** This committee is concerned with infrastructure issues: the Object Request Broker,

Object Services, and the relationship of the OMA to object-oriented analysis and design.

Domain Technology Committee (DTC). This committee is concerned with technologies to support application development, in particular vertical markets such as manufacturing, electronic commerce, or health care.

Task forces may issue requests for proposals (RFPs). These are detailed statements of a problem that needs to be solved. Responses are solicited in the form of IDL specifications with object semantics explained in English. Two rounds of submissions are taken, usually 3 months apart, and then the most suitable specification is selected by a vote of members and presented to the task force's controlling committee.

Special interest groups may not issue RFPs directly or adopt technology specifications, but may do so with the support of a task force. Usually special interest groups discuss areas of common interest and report their findings to their controlling committee via documents and presentations. A number of special interest groups do not belong to either the PTC or the DTC. Instead they report directly to the Architecture Board.

1.2.1 PTC Task Forces and Special Interest Groups

The following are the task forces and special interest groups that report to the Platform Technical Committee:

ORB/Object Services Task Force (OSTF). This task force is responsible for specifying the ORB, which is published as the Common Object Request Broker Architecture and Specification (CORBA). The task force also specifies general purpose Object Services (published as CORBAservices). This is the area which supports the basic infrastructure of object interaction. This task force has adopted the largest number of specifications.

Common Facilities Task Force (CFTF) (disbanded). This task force specified technologies that provided services to applications at a high level. Its specifications were published as CORBAfacilities. It was disbanded in June 1997 because most of the work it undertook was undertaken by the Domain Task Forces. The distinction between the remaining "horizontal" facilities and Object Services has long seemed too subtle, and so future work will take place in other task forces.

Object Analysis and Design Task Force (OADTF). This task force is concerned with applying widely used object-oriented analysis and design methodologies to distributed object-oriented application development using CORBA. It is a new task force which has published some white papers but as yet no specifications.

Internet Special Interest Group (ISIG). The ISIG is concerned with the convergence between distributed objects and the Internet, both as a distribution mechanism and as a growing area of commercial activity.

Japan Special Interest Group (JSIG). The JSIG is a focus for Japanese developers of distributed objects and is particularly concerned with internationalization issues across the OMG.

Real Time Special Interest Group (RTSIG). The RTSIG is concerned with issues of guaranteed performance of requests to distributed objects, embedded systems, and fault tolerance.

1.2.2 DTC Task Forces and Special Interest Groups

The following are the task forces and special interest groups that report to the Domain Technical Committee.

CORBAmed Task Force (Healthcare). The CORBAmed Task Force is concerned with adopting specifications that meet the vertical domain requirements of the health care sector. It also promotes the use of object-oriented technology in the medical field.

Telecommunications Task Force (CORBAtel). CORBAtel is working toward adoption of specifications that meet the needs of telecommunications providers. It also promotes the OMG and liaises with relevant telecommunications industry bodies.

Manufacturing Domain Task Force (CORBAmanufacturing). The MDTF promotes the use of CORBA technology in manufacturing industry computer systems and is adopting technology specifications tailored to that broad sector.

Financial Domain Task Force (CORBAfinancials). This task force promotes the use of financial services and accounting software based on OMG standards. They are adopting specifications for standard interfaces to this kind of software.

Interactive Multimedia and Electronic Commerce Domain Task Force. The IMCDTF is interested in on-line commerce, including rights and royalties, and electronic payment for media services.

Business Objects Domain Task Force (BODTF). The BODTF covers a broad area: it includes any standard objects used in business processes. This covers such areas as workflow, document processing, task scheduling, etc. The first RFP issued by the BODTF was controversial in that it did not solicit a single well-focused specification, but rather invited submitters to specify anything that they considered to be a Business Object. In the end a framework for business objects was adopted.

Transportation Special Interest Group (TSIG). The TSIG examines the requirements of the transportation industry in the development of Distributed Object Applications.

1.2.3 Architecture Board Special Interest Groups

The following special interest groups that report directly to the Architecture Board.

End User Special Interest Group (EUSIG). The EUSIG is becoming increasingly important as the OMG membership shifts from representing mainly technology vendors to including a large number of users of the technology. The EUSIG seeks to emphasize the usability of the specifications adopted throughout the OMG from the point of view of application builders in business, the military, and government.

Security Special Interest Group. This SIG is similar to the EUSIG in that it feeds the security requirements of end users into the OMG-wide technology adoption process.

Metrics Special Interest Group. This SIG investigates the measurement of the performance of object technology and the processes by which the technology is developed.

Inactive SIGs. The following SIGs still exist but are not meeting or currently developing documents:

♦ Database Special Interest Group
♦ Smalltalk Special Interest Group
♦ Parallel Object Systems Special Interest Group
♦ Class Libraries Special Interest Group

1.3 OMG Technology Adoption Process

The process, in brief, is as follows:

A task force puts out a Request for Information (RFI) on a particular technology area.

RFI submissions are considered in the process of drawing up an RFP, which solicits submissions addressing its proposal from contributing members of the OMG.

Any member company that wishes to respond to an RFP must submit a letter of intent (LOI) stating that they are willing to release a commercial implementation of their submitted specification within one year of its adoption, should it be chosen.

A voting list is established from OMG members who express an interest in selecting from the submissions.

A first submission takes place, usually about 3 months after the issue of the RFP. Typically there are three to six submissions.

The task force session at one of the six annual OMG meetings asks questions and provides feedback on the initial submissions.

The submitters consider each other's specifications, and frequently some or all of them decide to produce a consensus merger of specifications which align fairly closely.

Second (final) submissions are made, usually after another 3 months, and if there is more than one submission the choice of which to adopt is put to a vote.

The adopted specification is presented to a technical committee plenary session and a yes/no vote to adopt the chosen submission is put to the entire OMG membership. This usually passes without problem.

The Architecture Board then considers the broader implications of the new specification on the whole OMA. They may approve the specification unequivocally, suggest revisions, or reject the specification and issue a new RFP. Reissue of the RFP is not likely to occur.

Once the Architecture Board is happy with the specification, it is ratified by the OMG Board based on a further vote by members.

The form of submissions to the OMG's task forces and technical committees is usually a specification detailing the problem area that is being solved and proposing a number of interface definitions (in OMG IDL). The IDL is accompanied by English text describing the semantics of the objects and the roles and relationships to other objects in the specification and outside of it. The interfaces are described in terms of the actions of their operations and not in terms of a particular underlying implementation.

2 *The Object Management Architecture*

This section introduces the OMA and provides a summary of the technical parts of the third edition of the OMG publication *Object Management Architecture Guide,* which consists of two main parts: the Core Object Model (described in section 2.2) and the Reference Model (described in section 2.3).

2.1 Overview of the OMA

The OMA is the framework within which all OMG adopted technology fits. It provides two fundamental models on which CORBA and the other standard interfaces are based: the Core Object Model and the Reference Model.

The Core Object Model defines the concepts that allow distributed application development to be facilitated by an Object Request Broker (ORB). The Core Object Model is restricted to abstract definitions which do not constrain the syntax of object interfaces or the implementation of objects or ORBs. It then defines a framework for refining the model to a more concrete form. The model provides the basis for CORBA, but is more relevant to ORB designers and implementers than to distributed object application developers.

The Reference Model places the ORB at the center of groupings of objects with standardized interfaces that provide support for application object developers. The groups identified are Object Services, which provide infrastructure; Domain Interfaces, which provide special support to applications from various industry domains; Common Facilities, which provide application-level services across domains; and Application Interfaces, which is the set of all other objects developed for specific applications. Since the disbanding of the Common Facilities Task Force (see section 1.2.1), the OMA Reference Model has not been redefined, and a number of specifications still populate this space in the OMA.

The Reference Model is directly relevant to CORBA programmers because it provides the big picture from which components and frameworks can be drawn to support developers of distributed applications. The Reference Model also provides the framework for OMG's technology adoption process. It does this by identifying logical groupings of interface specifications that are provided by organizational groups (TFs and SIGs) which specify and adopt them.

2.2 Core Object Model

This section provides a detailed explanation of the theoretical underpinnings of CORBA. These specifics will not be of interest to everyone. We have tried to provide a readable summary of the contents of the OMG's *Object Management Architecture Guide*, but section 3 of this chapter on CORBA is written without assuming that the reader is familiar with the details of the Core Object Model. This section will mostly be of interest to readers with a background in object-oriented theory, but it starts with principles and so is readable by anyone with a somewhat broader interest than simply using CORBA as an application development platform.

2.2.1 Scope of the Core Object Model

The main goals of the Core Object Model are portability and interoperability. The most important aspect of portability to consider is *design portability*. This means knowledge of an object's interface and the ability to create applications whose components do not rely on the existence or location of a particular object implementation. The core does not define the syntax of interface descriptions, but does describe the semantics of types and their relationships to one another.

Interoperability means being able to invoke operations on objects regardless of where they are located, which platform they execute on, or what programming language they are implemented in. This is achieved by the ORB, which relies on the semantics of objects and operations described in the Core Object Model. The ORB also requires some extensions to the core which provide specifications for specific communication protocols, an interface definition syntax, and basic services to object implementations. CORBA provides these extensions.

The Core Object Model is not a meta-model. This means that it cannot have many possible concrete instances of the basic concepts. It consists of an abstract set of concepts that allow understanding of objects and their interfaces. However, these concepts cannot be redefined or replaced, only extended and made more concrete. The Core Object Model is specialized using components and profiles to provide a concrete architecture for an ORB.

2.2.2 Components and Profiles

A *component* is an extension to the abstract Core Object Model that provides a more concrete specialization of the concepts defined in the core. The core together with one or more components produces what is called a *profile*. CORBA is a profile that extends the core with several components which provide specializations such as a syntax for object interfaces and a protocol for interoperation between objects implemented using different ORBs.

Figure 2.2 shows how components and profiles are used to add to the Core Object Model.

2.2.3 Concept Definitions

The Core Object Model is a classical object model. This means that actions in the system are performed by sending request messages to objects. The

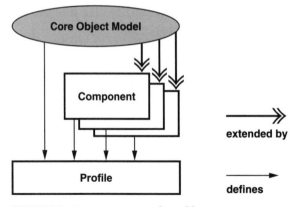

FIGURE 2.2 Components and profiles.

request will identify an operation and its parameters. The object will then interpret the message and perform some actions, and then possibly send a return message to the caller containing resulting values. The concepts defined in the Core Object Model are objects; operations, including their signatures, parameters, and return values; nonobject types; interfaces; and substitutability.

Objects. Objects are defined simply as models of entities or concepts. For example, an object can model a document, a date, an employee, a subatomic particle, or a compiler. The important characteristic of an object is its identity, which is fixed for the life of the object and is independent of the object's properties or behavior. This identity is represented by an object reference.

Operations, signatures, parameters, and return values. An operation is an action offered by an object which is known to the outside world by its signature. The notion of sending a request to an object is equivalent to the notion of invoking an operation on an object.

An operation's signature has the following components: a name, a set of parameters, and a set of result types. Operation names are unique within a particular object. No syntax for describing operations and their types is provided.

When a request is sent to an object it nominates an operation and provides arguments matching the parameters in that operation's signature. The operation then performs some action on those arguments and returns zero or more results. It is important to note that object references may be returned as part of the result of an operation.

Operations may cause some side effects, usually manifested as changes in the encapsulated state of the object. When an object cannot process a request it will typically return an exception message, but exceptions are defined in a separate component that is part of CORBA, not in the Core Object Model.

The Core Object Model does not specify whether or not requests are accepted by an object in parallel or what the consequences of parallel execution would be if they were. An implementation of objects could choose to provide atomic operations or a sequence of operations for transaction management.

Nonobject types. Unlike the object models of Smalltalk and Eiffel, there are types in the OMA core that are not objects. These are usually called datatypes. The set of objects and nonobject types makes up the whole of the denotable values in the OMA.

While the Core Object Model does not specify a set of nonobject types, another component of CORBA does. Even though the OMA core is designed to be extensible into several profiles via different sets of components, the likelihood of an alternative profile to CORBA being specified in the OMA is almost nonexistent. This design decision has been made so that new components can be added to CORBA in a consistent manner, and so that new versions of CORBA can be defined in terms of the makeup of its components and their versions.

2.2.4 *Interfaces and Substitutability*

An *interface* is a collection of operation signatures. Typically the interface to an object is the set of operations offered by that object, but this is left, once again, to CORBA to specify. Interfaces are related to one another by substitutability relationships. This means that an object offering an interface can be used in place of an object offering a "similar" interface. The Core Object Model simply defines substitutability as being able to use one interface in place of another without "interaction error." However, it is useful to examine a more concrete definition.

The simplest form of substitutability is when two interfaces offer exactly the same operations. Generally, if an interface A offers a superset of the operations offered by another interface B, then A is substitutable for B. Substitutability is not symmetrical, except in the simple case where A and B offer the same operations. However, it is transitive. That is, if A is substitutable for B and B is substitutable for a third interface C, then A is also substitutable for C.

2.2.5 Inheritance

Since interfaces may offer operations with the same signatures that have different purposes and semantics, it is useful to have an assertion of compatibility between them. In order to ensure a semantic relationship, the model introduces inheritance. If interface A inherits from interface B, then A offers all of the operations of B, and may also offer some additional operations. The set of operations of A is therefore a superset of the operations of B, and hence A is substitutable for B. However, because the relationship between A and B is explicit, we can be certain that the operations they have in common serve the same purpose, and A and B don't merely coincidentally share signatures. Figure 2.3 shows this example in a graphical form.

The Core Object Model defines *subtyping* as a form of substitutability dependent on inheritance of interfaces. That is, an interface A that inherits from an interface B is a subtype of B. We can also say that B is a supertype of A. In the Core Object Model, subtyping is the only acceptable form of substitutability.

The supertype of all objects in the Core Object Model is an abstract type Object that has an empty set of operations. The inheritance hierarchy places Object at the root and all other objects as its subtypes and is also called the type graph.

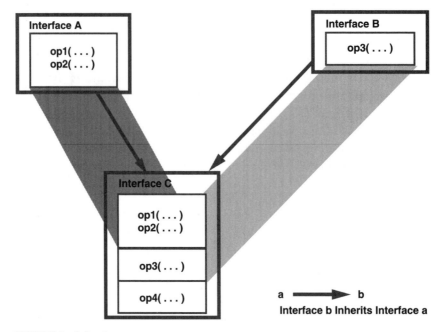

FIGURE 2.3 Inheritance.

2.3 The Reference Model

The OMA Reference Model is an architectural framework for the standardization of interfaces to infrastructure and services that applications can use. The object-oriented paradigm emphasizes reusability of components that perform small, well-defined parts of an application's functionality. The Reference Model allows users of components to understand what support they can expect in what areas from ORB vendors and third-party component providers.

The Reference Model is shown in Figure 2.4, which identifies five main components of the OMA:

- ♦ Object Request Broker
- ♦ Object Services
- ♦ Common Facilities
- ♦ Domain Interfaces
- ♦ Application Interfaces

Only the last of these is not intended to have interfaces specified through OMG processes. Application objects are the project-specific part of an integrated application.

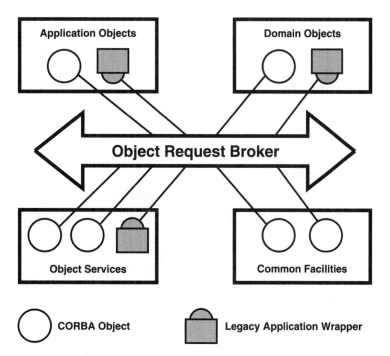

FIGURE 2.4 The OMA Reference Model.

2.3.1   Object Request Broker

The ORB is defined in the *Common Object Request Broker Architecture (CORBA) and Specification* document. CORBA builds on the **OMA** Core Object Model and provides

- ♦ An extended CORBA core including syntax and semantics for an IDL
- ♦ A framework for interoperability, including two specific protocol definitions
- ♦ A set of language mappings from IDL to implementation languages (C, C++, Smalltalk, Ada'95)

The ORB is situated at the conceptual (and graphical) center of the Reference Model. It acts as a message bus between objects which may be located on any machine in a network, implemented in any programming language, and executed on any hardware or operating system platform. The caller only needs an object reference and well-formed arguments in the language mapping of choice to invoke an operation as if it were a local function and receive results. This is called location and access transparency.

At the heart of CORBA is the Interface Definition Language (IDL), which is covered in detail in section 3.4. It provides a way of defining the interfaces of objects independent of the programming language in which they are implemented. It is a strongly typed declarative language with a rich set of datatypes for describing complex parameters. An IDL interface acts as a contract between developers of objects and the eventual users of their interfaces. It also allows the user of CORBA objects to compile the interface definitions into hidden code for the transmission of invocation requests across networks and machine architectures without knowledge of the network protocol, the target machine architecture, or even the location of the object being invoked.

2.3.2   Object Services

This set of interface specifications provides fundamental services that application developers may need in order to find and manage their objects and data, and to coordinate the execution of complex operations. Object Services are the building blocks from which other components of the **OMA** can be constructed and which application objects may require. The **OMG** brand name for these services is CORBAservices. The published services include

- ♦ Naming
- ♦ Events
- ♦ Life Cycle

- Persistent Object (deprecated)
- Relationships
- Externalization
- Transactions
- Concurrency Control
- Licensing
- Query
- Properties
- Security (including IIOP over SSL)
- Time
- Collections
- Trading

Some of these are simply framework interfaces that will be inherited by applications or other objects, for example, the Life Cycle Service. Others represent low-level components on which higher level application-oriented components can be built, for example, Transaction Service. Others provide basic services used at all levels of applications, such as the Naming and Trading Services. These last two services provide a means of locating objects by name or by type and properties for late binding in an application. See Chapter 8 for a detailed description of these services.

2.3.3   Common Facilities

Common Facilities are those end-user-oriented interfaces that provide facilities across application domains. The first such specification adopted, published by the OMG as CORBAfacilities, is the Distributed Document Component Facility, based on OpenDoc. Work has been completed on Internationalization and Time Facilities, Data Interchange, and Mobile Agent Facilities, as well as a Printing Facility. A Meta-Object Facility, which is a way of defining repositories for IDL and non-IDL types, and a Systems Management Facility have also recently been adopted.

2.3.4   Domain Interfaces

The OMG contains a large number of special interest groups and task forces which focus on particular application domains such as telecommunications, Internet, business objects, manufacturing, and health care. This area of standardization was separated from the Common Facilities in early 1996 where it was called Vertical Facilities. Several Requests for Information RFIs and Requests for Proposals RFPs are in progress in the Domain Task Forces. Some examples are the Common Business Object Facility, Product Data Management Enablers, and a Healthcare Patient Lexicon Service.

2.3.5 *Specification Adoption in the OMG*

Technology adoption in the OMG emphasizes the use of existing technologies and rapid market availability. To this end, submitters of specifications must vouch that an implementation of the specification exists and that, should their submission be adopted, they will make an implementation commercially available within 1 year of adoption. The adoption process is detailed in section 1.3.

3 *Common Object Request Broker Architecture*

This section provides a summary of the Common Object Request Broker Architecture and Specification, version 2.0.

3.1 Overview

CORBA is the specification of the functionality of the ORB, the crucial message bus that conveys operation invocation requests and their results to CORBA objects resident anywhere, however they are implemented. The CORBA specification provides certain interfaces to components of the ORB, but leaves the interfaces to other components up to the ORB implementer.

The notion of transparency is at the center of CORBA. *Location transparency* is the ability to access and invoke operations on a CORBA object without needing to know where the object resides. The idea is that it should be equally easy to invoke an operation on an object residing on a remote machine as it is to invoke a method on an object in the same address space.

Programming language transparency provides the freedom to implement the functionality encapsulated in an object using the most appropriate language, whether because of the skills of the programmers, the appropriateness of the language to the task, or the choice of a third-party developer who provides off-the-shelf component objects. The key to this freedom is an implementation-neutral interface definition language, OMG IDL, which provides separation of interface and implementation.

IDL interface definitions inform clients of an object offering an interface exactly what operations an object supports, the types of their parameters, and what return types to expect. A client programmer needs only the IDL to write client code that is ready to invoke operations on a remote object. The client uses the datatypes defined in IDL through a language mapping. This mapping defines the programming language constructs (datatypes, classes, etc.) that will be generated by the IDL compiler supplied by an ORB vendor.

The IDL compiler also generates stub code that the client links to, and this translates, or *marshals,* the programming language datatypes into a wire format for transmission as a request message to an object implementation. The implementation of the object has linked to it similar marshaling code, called a *skeleton,* that unmarshals the request into programming language datatypes. The skeleton can be generated by a different IDL compiler with a different language mapping. In this way the object's method implementation can be invoked and the results returned by the same means. Figure 2.5 illustrates the use of stub, skeleton, and ORB code to make a remote invocation.

IDL and IDL compilers allow programs providing and using object interfaces to agree on the form of their exchanges, even though they may be developed completely independently, in different languages, and on different ORB technologies. This means that objects offering the same interfaces are substitutable, and that clients can decide which object to use at runtime with the assurance that there will be no interaction mismatches. Because the implementation of a particular object offering an interface is hidden, there may be quality of service differences, or even differences in the semantics of operations. The Trading Service allows clients to find the most appropriate object that matches their particular performance, location, cost, or other criteria.

The interfaces to components of the ORB are all specified in IDL. This provides a language-neutral representation of the computational interface

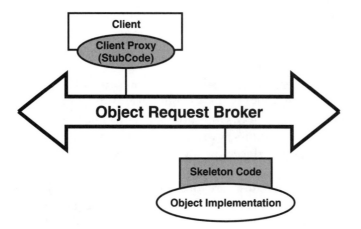

FIGURE 2.5 Stub, ORB, and skeleton.

of the ORB. However, certain parts of these definitions are designated as pseudo-IDL (PIDL), which means that their implementations are not necessarily CORBA objects and datatypes. Any interface definition that is commented as pseudo-IDL may be implemented as a pseudo-object. This usually means that it is a library that is linked into the application using it. Although operations on pseudo-objects are invoked in the same way as operations on real CORBA objects, their references and pseudo-IDL datatypes cannot be passed as parameters to real CORBA objects.

3.2   Object Model

The OMA Core Object Model provides some fundamental definitions of concepts that are extended by the CORBA specification. CORBA uses the same concepts as the OMA core, but makes them more specific and concrete. The definitions here refer to the way in which these concepts are declared, but do not provide syntax for declarations. The syntax is provided by IDL (see section 3.4).

3.2.1   Object Implementations and Object References

It is necessary to distinguish between object implementations and object references. The former is the code that implements the operations defined by an IDL interface definition, while the latter is the object's identity, which is used by clients to invoke its operations.

An object implementation is the part of a CORBA object that is provided by an application developer. It usually includes some internal state and will often cause side effects on things that are not objects, such as a database, screen display, or telecommunications network elements. The methods of this implementation may be accessed by any mechanism, but in practice most object implementations will be invoked via the skeleton code generated by an IDL compiler.

Object references are handles to objects. A given object reference will always denote a single object, but several distinct object references may denote the same object. Object references can be passed to clients of objects, either as an operation's parameter or result, where the IDL for an operation nominates an interface type, or they can be passed as strings which can be turned into live object references that can have operations invoked on them.

Object references are opaque to their users. That is, they contain enough information for the ORB to send a request to the correct object implementation, but this information is inaccessible to their users. Object references contain information about the location and type of the object denoted, but do so in a sophisticated manner so that if the object has migrated or is not active at the time, the ORB can perform the necessary tasks to redirect the request to a new location or activate an object to receive the request.

Unless an object has been explicitly destroyed, or the underlying network and operating system infrastructure is malfunctioning, the ORB should be able to convey an operation invocation to its target and return results. The ORB also supports operations that interpret the object reference and provide the client with some of the information it contains.

3.2.2 Types

Types are defined using predicate logic in the CORBA specification. Object types are related in an inheritance hierarchy, with the type Object at the root. An object type derived from another can be substituted for it. Object types may be specified as parameters and return types for operations, and may be used as components in structured datatypes. A set of nonobject types are defined with specific properties in CORBA. These are represented by constructs in OMG IDL. The usual kind of basic numeric, string, and boolean types are defined. A type called Any is also given as a basic type. It can store any legitimate value of a CORBA type in a self-describing manner. See Chapter 6 for detailed descriptions of Anys and Chapter 10 for examples using Anys.

The basic types can be used as components for a rich set of structured types, including structures, arrays, variable length sequences, and discriminated unions. The syntax and specifications of CORBA types are given in the OMG IDL description.

3.2.3 Interfaces

An *interface* is a description of the operations that are offered by an object and can also contain structured type definitions used as parameters to those operations. Interfaces are specified in OMG IDL and are related in an inheritance hierarchy. In CORBA, interface types and object types have a one-to-one mapping. This is a restriction of the OMA Core Object Model, which implies that objects have single interfaces but does not state that this must be the case. The term *principal interface* is used to indicate the most specific (most derived) interface type that an object supports. The Multiple Interfaces RFP is currently soliciting submissions in the OMG, and a model for objects with multiple interfaces will probably be introduced in a revised CORBA specification.

3.2.4 Operation Semantics

There are two kinds of operation execution semantics defined for static (stub code) invocations:

At-Most-Once. An operation is a named action that a client can request an invocation of. The invocation of an operation results in the ORB conveying the arguments to the object implementation and returning the results (if any) to the requester, which is blocked and waiting for a successful termination or an exception. The semantics of the invocation are "at-most-once." That is, the operation will execute exactly once if a successful completion takes place, or if an exception is raised it will have executed no more than once.

Best-Effort. If an operation is declared using the oneway keyword then the requester does not wait for the operation to complete and the semantics is "best-effort." Both these kinds of requests can be made using the generated stubs or using the Dynamic Invocation Interface (DII), but the DII also offers a third type of execution semantics—*deferred-synchronous*. This allows the requester to send the request without blocking and at some later time to poll for the results.

3.2.5 *Operation Signatures*

Each operation has a signature, expressed in IDL, which contains the following mandatory components:

- ♦ An operation identifier (also called an operation name).
- ♦ The type of the value returned by the operation.
- ♦ A (possibly empty) list of parameters, each with a name, type, and direction indication. The direction will be one of in, out, or inout, stating that the parameter is being transmitted from the client to the object, is being returned as a result from the operation, or is client data to be modified by the operation, respectively.

An operation signature may also have the following optional components:

- ♦ A raises clause that lists user-defined exceptions that the operation may raise. Any operation may raise system exceptions.
- ♦ A oneway keyword that indicates "best-effort" semantics. The signature must have a void return type and may not contain any out or inout parameters or a raises clause.
- ♦ A context clause that lists the names of operating system, user, or client program environment values that must be transmitted with the request. Contexts are transmitted as sets of string pairs and are not type safe. Contexts are intended to play a similar role to environment variables known from various operating systems.

3.2.6 *Attributes*

An interface may contain *attributes*. These are declared as named types, with a possible readonly modifier. They are logically equivalent to a pair of operations. The first, an accessor operation, retrieves a value of the specified type. The second, a modifier operation, takes an argument of the specified type and sets that value. Readonly attributes will only have an accessor. Attributes cannot raise user-defined exceptions.

The execution semantics for attributes are the same as for operations. Attributes do not necessarily represent a state variable in an object, and executing the modifier operation with a particular argument does not guarantee that the same value will be returned by the next accessor execution. Section 3.4.6 contains a full syntax for operation and attribute declarations.

3.2.7 *Exceptions*

An *exception* is a specialized nonobject type in OMG IDL. It is declared with the keyword exception and has a name and optional fields of named data values that provide further information about what caused the abnormal termination of an operation.

The standard IDL module, CORBA, contains declarations for 26 standard exceptions to address network, ORB, and operating system errors. These exceptions may be raised by any operation, either implicitly by the ORB or explicitly in the operation implementation. Each standard exception, also known as a system exception, has two pieces of data associated with it:

◆ A completion status, an enumerated type with three possible values— COMPLETED_YES, COMPLETED_NO, and COMPLETED_MAYBE—indicating that the operation implementation was either executed in full, not at all, or that this cannot be determined

◆ A long integer minor code which can be set to some ORB-dependent value for more information

Further user-defined exceptions may be declared in IDL and associated with operations in the raises clause of their signatures. An operation may only raise user exceptions that appear in its signature.

3.3 ORB Structure

As we have mentioned, OMG IDL provides the basis of agreement about what can be requested of an object implementation via the ORB. IDL, however, is not just a guide to clients of objects. IDL compilers use interface definitions to create the means by which a client can invoke a local function and an invocation then happens, as if by magic, on an object on another machine. The code generated for the client to use is known as stub code, and the code generated for the object implementation is called skeleton code. Figure 2.6 shows the ORB core, stub and skeleton code, and the interfaces to the ORB.

These two pieces of generated code are linked into the respective client and object implementations, and they interface with the ORB run-time system to convey requests and results for static invocations. Static means that the IDL is statically defined at compile time, and only operations on known interface types can be invoked.

The CORBA standard also defines an interface to allow requests to be built dynamically for any operation by a client. This is known as the Dynamic Invocation Interface (DII). A symmetric interface is defined for responding to arbitrary requests, called the Dynamic Skeleton Interface (DSI).

CORBA defines an interface for communicating with the ORB from either client or server. This interface deals mainly with ORB initialization and object reference manipulation.

Finally, object implementations need extra facilities for managing their interactions with the ORB. A component called an object adapter (OA) fills this role and is responsible for operating system process management for implementations on behalf of the ORB and for informing the ORB when implementations are ready to receive requests.

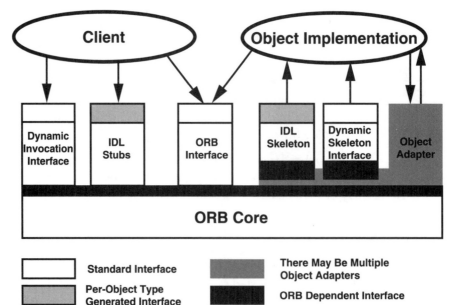

FIGURE 2.6 ORB interfaces.

3.3.1 Client Stubs

When a client wishes to invoke an IDL-defined operation on an object reference as if it were a local method or function call, it must link in stubs for the IDL interface which convey that invocation to the target object. In object-oriented implementation languages the stubs are instantiated as local proxy objects that delegate invocations on their methods to the remote implementation object. The stubs are generated from an IDL compiler for the language (and ORB environment) the client is using.

3.3.2 Dynamic Invocation Interface

A *request* is a notional message that is sent to an object denoted by an object reference to request the invocation of a particular operation with particular arguments. The DII defines the form of such a message so that clients that know of an object by reference, and can determine its interface type, can build requests without requiring an IDL compiler to generate stub code. A request interface is defined in pseudo-IDL. It provides operations to set the target object for the invocation, name the operation to be invoked, and add arguments to send to it. It also provides operations to invoke the operation and retrieve any resulting values. As noted earlier, the implementation of pseudo-IDL is provided as a library and the operations map to local methods on a non-CORBA object.

The DII defines various types of execution semantics for operations invoked using request pseudo-objects. The usual synchronous at-most-once semantics are available, as well as a deferred-synchronous option which sends the request and immediately returns to the client code to allow further processing while waiting for a response.

3.3.3 Implementation Skeleton

Once a request reaches a server that supports one or more objects, there must be a way for it to invoke the right method on the right implementation object. The translation from a wire format to in-memory data structures (unmarshaling) uses the language mapping to the implementation language. This is achieved by the skeleton code generated by an IDL compiler.

3.3.4 Dynamic Skeleton Interface

Implementation code may be written that deals with requests in a generic manner, looking at the requested operation and its arguments and interpreting the semantics dynamically. This is called the Dynamic Skeleton Interface (DSI) and is realized by allowing the implementer access to the request in the form of a ServerRequest pseudo-object, which is the same as the DII request, except for the invocation operations.

An example use of the DSI is a minimal wrapper around some legacy command processing code which accepts each request it receives with a single string argument. It then parses the string for a numeric value and sets this in a register before passing the operation name to an interpreter. It then checks the contents of the register, and unless an error bit is set, encodes the rest of the register as a numeric string and passes it back as the result. Clients can then write IDL that matches the expected pattern and use the generated stubs in a type-safe way to invoke the server which was implemented before the IDL was written.

3.3.5   Object Adapters

An object adapter is a component that an object implementation uses to make itself available through an ORB and which the ORB uses to manage the run-time environment of the object implementations. An adapter is used, rather than extending the interface to the ORB, so that different object adapters suitable for different implementations can be used for greater efficiency.

Currently CORBA defines two such interfaces, the basic object adapter (BOA) and the portable object adapter (POA). Their purpose is to generate and interpret object references, and to activate and deactivate object implementations. The interface to the BOA is described in detail in section 3.6, and the interface to the POA is described in section 3.7.

3.4   OMG Interface Definition Language

OMG IDL is a declarative language for defining the interfaces of CORBA objects. It is a language-independent way in which implementers and users of objects can be assured of type-safe invocation of operations, even though the only other information that needs to pass between them is an object reference. IDL is used by ORB-specific IDL compilers to generate stub and/or skeleton code that converts in-memory data structures in one programming language into network streams and then unpacks them on another machine into equivalent data structures in another (or the same) language, makes a method call, and then transmits the results in the opposite direction.

The syntax of IDL is drawn from C++, but it contains different and unambiguous keywords. There are no programming statements, as its only purpose is to define interface signatures. To do this a number of constructs are supported:

Constants—to assist with type declarations

Data type declarations—to use for parameter typing

Attributes—which get and set a value of a particular type

Operations—which take parameters and return values

Interfaces—which group datatype, attribute, and operation declarations

Modules—for namespace separation

All of the declarations made in IDL can be made available through the Interface Repository (IR). This is part of the CORBA specification and its interfaces are explained in section 3.12.

3.4.1 Lexical Analysis

OMG IDL uses the ISO Latin-1 character set.

Identifiers. Identifiers must start with a letter and may be followed by zero or more letters, numbers, and underscores. The only strange feature of the lexical analysis of IDL is that identifiers are case sensitive but cannot coexist with other identifiers that differ only in case. To put it another way, to identify the same entity the identifier must use the same case in each instance, but another identifier with the same spelling and different case may not coexist with it. For example, short DisplayTerminal and interface displayTerminal denote different entities, but may not both be declared in the same IDL. The reason for this is that language mappings to case-insensitive languages could not cope with both identifiers.

Preprocessing. The standard C++ preprocessing macros are the first thing to be dealt with in lexical analysis. They include #include, #define, #ifdef, and #pragma.

Keywords. Keywords are all in lowercase and other identifiers may not differ only in case.

Comments. Both styles of C++ comments are used in IDL. The "/*" characters open a comment and "*/" closes it. These comments cannot be nested. The characters "//" indicate that the rest of a line is a comment.

Punctuation. The curly brace is used to enclose naming scopes, and closing braces are always followed by a semicolon. Declarations are always followed by a semicolon. Lists of parameters are surrounded by parentheses with the parameters separated by commas.

3.4.2 Modules and Interfaces

The purpose of IDL is to define interfaces and their operations. To avoid name clashes when using several IDL declarations together a *module* is used as a naming scope. Modules can contain any well-formed IDL, including nested modules. Interfaces also open a new naming scope and can contain constants, datatype declarations, attributes, and operations.

```
// RoomBooking.idl
module RoomBooking {
  interface Room {};
};
```

Any interface name in the same scope can be used as a type name, and interfaces in other name scopes can be referred to by giving a scoped name that is separated in C++ style by double colons. For example, RoomBooking::Room is the name of the empty interface declared above. This name can also be written ::RoomBooking::Room to explicitly show that it is relative to the global scope.

Modules may be nested inside other modules and their contents may be named relative to the current naming scope. For example,

```
module outer {
  module inner { // nested module
    interface inside {};
  };

  interface outside { // can refer to inner as a local name
    inner::inside get_inside();
  };
};
```

The get_inside() operation returns an object reference of type ::outer::inner:inside, but may use the relative form of the name due to its position in the same scope as the inner module.

Interfaces may be mutually referential. That is, declarations in each interface may use the name of the other as an object type. To avoid compilation errors, an interface type must be forward declared before it is used. That is,

```
interface A; // forward declaration

interface B { // B can use forward-declared interfaces as type names
  A get_an_A();
};

interface A {
  B get_a_B();
};
```

The preceding example declares the existence of an interface with name A before defining interface B, which has an operation returning an object reference to an A. It then defines A, which has an operation returning an object reference to B. Forward declaration of interfaces is often used for formatting and readability rather than mutual recursion.

When a declaration in a module needs some mutual reference to a declaration in another module, this is achieved by closing the first module and reopening it after some other declarations. This is shown in the following declaration:

```
module X {
  // forward declaration of A
  interface A;
}; // close the module to allow interface A needs to be declared

module Y {
  interface B { // B can use X::A as a type name
    X::A get_an_A();
  };
}

module X { // reopen module to define A

  interface C { // C can use A unqualified as it is in the same scope
    A get_an_A();
  };

  interface A { // A can use Y::B as a type name
    Y::B get_a_B();
  };
};
```

Reopening modules is a recent addition to OMG IDL, and as yet many IDL compilers do not accept it as valid syntax. This is mainly due to the lack of such flexible name scoping mechanisms in programming language compilers. Java is one language that can support this correctly.

3.4.3 *Inheritance*

The set of operations offered by an interface can be extended by declaring a new interface that inherits from the existing one. The existing interface is called the *base interface* and the new interface is called the *derived interface*. Inheritance is declared by using a colon after the new interface name, followed by a base interface name, as the following example shows:

```
module InheritanceExample {

  interface A {
    typedef unsigned short ushort;
```

```
        ushort op1();
    };

    interface B : A {
      boolean op2(ushort num);
    };
};
```

In this example, interface B extends interface A and offers operations op1() and op2(). The datatype declarations are also inherited, allowing the use of ushort as a parameter type in op2(). All interfaces implicitly inherit from CORBA::Object. This becomes clear when looking at the language mapping. In Java, for example, interface A will map to a Java interface A, which extends a Java interface called org.omg.CORBA.Object provided by the ORB. In the same manner interface B will map to a Java interface B which extends A.

CORBA IDL allows any nonobject types declared in an interface to be redefined in a derived interface. We consider this to be an oversight, and it is not recommended that this feature ever be used. The beauty of inheritance is that it is a clean mechanism for determining subtyping and substitutability of interfaces. An object implementing interface B would be able to be used where an object of type A was required, as B is a subtype of A.

3.4.4 Multiple Inheritance

An interface may inherit from several other interfaces. The syntax is the same as single inheritance, and the base interfaces are separated by commas. For example,

```
interface C : A, B, VendorY::interfaceX {
  ...
};
```

The names of the operations in each of the inherited interfaces (including the operations they inherit from other interfaces) must be unique and may not be redeclared in the derived interface. The exception to this rule is when the operations are inherited into two or more classes from the same base class. This is known as *diamond inheritance* (the inheritance graph is in the shape of a diamond). For example,

```
module DiamondInheritanceExample {

  interface Base {
    string BaseOp();
  };
```

```
interface Left:Base {
  short LeftOp(in string LeftParam);
};

interface Right:Base {
  any RightOp(in long RightParam);
};

interface Derived:Left,Right {
  octet DerivedOp(in float DerivedInParam,
      out unsigned long DerivedOutParam);
};
};
```

Figure 2.7 shows the IDL in graphical form. Both interfaces Left and Right contain the operation BaseOp(), but they can both be inherited by Derived because BaseOp() comes from the same base interface.

3.4.5 *Types and Constants*

The name of any interface declared in IDL becomes an object type name that may be used as the type of any operation parameter or return value or as a member in a structured type declaration; for example, to declare the length of an array. The basic types are rich enough to represent numerics, strings, characters, and booleans. The definitions of these are very precise to allow unambiguous marshaling. The structured types available in IDL are structures, discriminated unions, arrays, and sequences. Exceptions can be considered to be a special case of structures that are only used in raises clauses of operations.

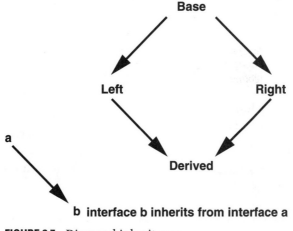

FIGURE 2.7 Diamond inheritance.

The set of basic types provided by IDL and their required characteristics are as follows:

Type keyword	*Description*
[unsigned] short	Signed [unsigned] 16-bit 2's complement integer
[unsigned] long	Signed [unsigned] 32-bit 2's complement integer
float	16-bit IEEE floating point number
double	32-bit IEEE floating point number
char	ISO Latin-1 character
boolean	Boolean type taking values TRUE and FALSE
string	Variable-length string of characters whose length is available at run time
octet	8-bit uninterpreted type
enum	Enumerated type with named integer values
any	Can represent a value from any possible IDL type, basic or constructed, object or nonobject

The keyword typedef allows aliases to be created for any legal type declaration. In the case of template types (types that require a parameter to determine their length or contents) a typedef is required before the type can be used in an operation or attribute declaration. See the following string example.

Strings may be bounded or unbounded. Bounded strings are a template type. That is, their declaration contains a maximum length parameter in angle brackets. For example,

```
interface StringProcessor {
    typedef octstring string <8>;
    typedef centastring string <100>;

    //...
    octstring MiddleEight(in string str);
    centastring PadOctString(in octstring ostr, char pad_char);
};
```

Enumerated types are declared with a name, which can be used as a valid type thereafter, and a comma-separated list of identifiers. The identifiers used in an enum declaration must be unique within a namespace. For example,

```
enum glass_color {gc_clear, gc_red, gc_blue, gc_green};
```

Any. The Any type has an API defined in pseudo-IDL which describes how values are inserted and extracted from it and how the type of its contained value may be discovered. This is addressed in Chapter 6.

Structures. Structures are declared with the keyword struct, which must be followed by a name. This name is usable as a valid type name thereafter. This is followed by a semicolon-separated list of named type fields, as in C and C++. For example,

```
interface HardwareStore {
  struct window_spec {
      glass_color color;
    height   float;
    width    float;
};
```

Discriminated unions. Discriminated unions are declared with the keyword union, which must be followed by a name. The name, once again, becomes a valid type name for use in subsequent declarations. The keyword switch follows the type name and it is parameterized by a scalar type (integer, char, boolean, or enum) which acts as the discriminator. The body of the union is enclosed in braces and contains a number of case statements followed by named type declarations. For example,

```
enum fitting_kind {door_k, window_k, shelf_k, cupboard_k};

union fitting switch (fitting_kind) {
  case door_k:   door_spec    door;
  case window_k:window_spec win;
  default:          float           width;
};
```

The default case is optional, but may not appear more than once. In each language mapping there is a means of accessing the discriminator value by name in order to determine which field of the union contains a value. The value of a union consists of the value of the discriminator and the value of the element that it nominates. If the discriminator is set to a value not mentioned in a case label, and there is no default case, then that part of the union's value is undefined.

Sequences. Sequences are template types. That means that their declarations nominate other types which will be contained within the sequence. A sequence is an ordered collection of items that can grow at run time. Its elements are accessed by index. Sequences may be bounded or unbounded. All sequences have two characteristics at runtime, a maximum and a current length. The maximum length of bounded sequences is set at compile time. The advantage of sequences is that only the current number of elements is transmitted to a remote object when a sequence argument is passed.

Sequence declarations must be given a typedef alias in order to be used as types in operation parameters or return types. Here are some example sequences of hardware fittings used to convey orders to a hardware store:

```
// union type "fitting" declared above.

typedef sequence <fitting> HardwareOrderSeq;
typedef sequence <fitting, 10> LimitedHWQrderSeq;

typedef sequence <sequence <fitting>, 3> ThreeStoreHWOrderSeq;
typedef sequence <sequence <fitting> > ManyStoreHWOrderSeq;
```

Sequence is the only unaliased complex type that may be used in angle brackets. All other types must be typedefed before sequences of them can be declared. Note that there is a space between the two closing angle brackets in the final declaration. If these were put side by side they would be parsed as the operator >>, which can be used when declaring integer constants. A better style would be to declare ThreeStoreHWOrderSeq as a sequence of HardwareOrderSeq.

Arrays. Arrays are also usually declared within a typedef, as they must be named before using them as operation parameter or return types. However, they may be declared as an element type of a union or member type of a struct.

Arrays at runtime will have a fixed length. The entire array (regardless of useful content) will be marshaled and transmitted in a request if used in a parameter or return type. In contrast, sequences passed as arguments or returned as results will only be transmitted up to their length at the time of the invocation.

Arrays are declared by adding one or more square-bracketed dimensions containing an integer constant. For example,

```
typedef window[10] WindowVec10;
typedef fitting[3][10] FittingGrid;

struct bathroom {
    float       width;
    float       length;
    float       height;
    boolean     has_toilet;
    fitting[6]  fittings;
};
```

Exceptions. Exceptions are declared in exactly the same manner as structures, using the keyword exception in place of struct. A set of standard exceptions, also known as system exceptions, is declared in the CORBA module. Here are some examples of user-defined exceptions:

```
exception OrderTooLarge {
  long max_items;
  long num_items_submitted;
};

exception ColorMismatch {
  sequence <color> other_window_colors;
  color        color_submitted;
};
```

It is good style to include values of arguments that are relevant to the cause of a failure in an exception. That way exception handling can be done by a generic handler that does not know what arguments were given that may have caused the exception. The handler can determine the context of the operation that raised the exception from the values in the exception.

Constants. Constant values can be declared at global scope or within modules and interfaces. The declaration begins with the keyword const, followed by a boolean, numeric, character, or string type name, an identifier, and then an equals sign and a value. Numeric values can be declared as expressions, with the full range of C++ bitwise, integer, and floating point mathematical operators available. For example,

```
const short max_storage_bays = 200;
const short windows_per_bay = 45;
const long max_windows = max_storage_bays * windows_per_bay;
const string initial_quote = "fox in socks on knox on blocks";
const HardwareStore::CashAmount balance = (max_storage_bays – 3) / 1.45
```

3.4.6 *Operations and Attributes*

Operation declarations are similar to C++ function prototypes. They contain an operation name, a return type (or void to indicate that no value is expected), and a parameter list, which may be empty. In addition, an operation may have a raises clause, which specifies what user exceptions the operation may raise, and it may have a context clause, which gives a list of names of string properties from the caller's environment that need to be supplied to the operation implementation.

Lists of parameters to operations are surrounded by parentheses and the parameters are separated by commas. Each parameter must have a directional indicator so that it is clear which direction the data travels in.

These are in, out, and inout, indicating client to object, return parameter, and client value modified by object and returned, respectively. These points are shown in the IDL that follows:

```
// interface HardwareStore cont..
    typedef float CashAmount;
    typedef sequence <window_spec> WindowSeq;

    CashAmount OrderFittings(in HardwareOrderSeq order)
      raises (OrderTooLarge);

    void OrderWindows(
        in WindowSeq     order,
        in CashAmount    willing_to_pay,
        out CashAmount  total_price,
        out short          order_number)
      raises (OrderTooLarge, ColorMismatch)
      context ("LOCAL_CURRENCY");
```

Operations can be declared oneway if it is desirable for the caller to send some noncritical message to an object. Oneway operation invocations will use best-effort semantics. The caller will get an immediate return and cannot know for certain if the request has been invoked. For obvious reasons there can be no out or inout parameters declared on oneway operations. There must be no raises clause and the operation must have a void return type. The following declaration illustrates this.

```
// interface HardwareStore cont...

    oneway void requestAccountStatement(in short customer_id);
```

An attribute is logically equivalent to a pair of accessor functions, one to access the value, the other to modify it. Read-only attributes require only an accessor function.

Attributes are simpler to declare than operations. They consist of the keyword attribute followed by the type of the attribute and then an attribute name list. The optional keyword readonly may precede the attribute declaration.

```
// interface HardwareStore cont...
    readonly attribute CashAmount min_order, max_order;
    readonly attribute FittingSeq new_fittings;
        attribute string quote_of_the_day;
```

The previous attributes could be replaced by the following IDL:

```
CashAmount min_order();
CashAmount max_order();
```

```
FittingSeq new_fittings();
string get_quote_of_the_day();
void set_quote_of_the_day(in string quote);
```

As declared, the operations and attributes are equivalent. The actual names chosen for the methods in the object implementation are determined by the language mapping. Attributes and operations can both raise standard exceptions. However, operations can be given raises clauses, allowing better handling of error conditions.

3.4.7   *Contexts*

Contexts provide a way of passing string-to-string mappings from the computing environment of the client to the object implementation. The specification does not define the way in which an ORB populates contexts to pass to objects. Some ORBs treat contexts as equivalent to UNIX or DOS environment variables. Others require users to build context objects explicitly. The string literals within a context clause must start with a letter and may end with "*", the wild card matching character. The matching character will cause the ORB to find all context items with the leading characters in common.

Contexts are a powerful concept but must be used with care. For example, the use of wild card pattern matching is especially dangerous, as the IDL author has no way at specification time of knowing what names will be defined in the context of all callers. A broad pattern match may cause many kilobytes of strings to be transmitted unnecessarily for an otherwise lightweight operation invocation. In general, contexts are a hole in an otherwise type-safe interface definition language.

3.5   ORB and Object Interfaces

The ORB interface is available directly to clients and object implementations for several object management reasons. These include creating string representations of object references, and transforming them back again, copying and deleting object references, and comparing object references against the empty, or nil, object reference.

As already mentioned, there are a number of interfaces defined within the CORBA standard that use the IDL syntax for programming-language-neutral API definitions. They are interfaces to ORB components that are implemented as libraries or in whatever way ORB implementers see fit. The IDL is commented as pseudo-IDL.

3.5.1   Stringified Object References

As object references are opaque, the only way to correctly make an object reference persistent is to stringify it. A stringified object reference can be passed by means such as email, web sites, or pen and paper, and when supplied as an argument to the string_to_object() operation it will produce a valid object reference that can be invoked. In order to use generated stubs to do this, the returned object reference must be passed to the `narrow()` method of the appropriate interface stub to cast the object reference into a reference to a more specific interface than Object.

```
module CORBA { //PIDL

  interface ORB {
    string object_to_string(in Object obj);
    Object string_to_object(in string obj);

    // several other operations are defined here but used in
    // other contexts, such as the ORB initialization and the DII
  };
};
```

The object_to_string() operation takes an object and produces a string. This string may be passed to the converse operation, string_to_object(), to generate a new object reference that can be invoked and will send its requests to the same object passed to object_to_string().

3.5.2   Managing Object References

This subsection addresses the pseudo-IDL for the CORBA::Object interface. This is the base interface for all CORBA objects and its operations can be invoked on any object reference. However, the functionality is implemented in the libraries provided by the ORB and results are not obtained by sending a request to the object implementation.

Object references, although opaque to their users, always contain certain information that can be extracted by using appropriate operations. The main components in an object reference are

- ◆ Abstract information about the name and location of the object implementation
- ◆ The interface type of the object
- ◆ Reference data, that is, a unique key that differentiates this object from other objects in the same implementation (server)

The get_implementation() and get_interface() operations provide access to the first two components, and the get_id() operation on the BOA interface provides access to the third. Many ORBs provide this information in other forms by additional operations not required by the standard.

```
module CORBA {

  interface Object { // PIDL
    implementationDef    get_implementation();
    interfaceDef         get_interface();
    boolean              is_nil();
    Object               duplicate();
    void                 release();
    boolean              is_a(in string logical_type_id);
    boolean              non_existent();
    boolean              is_equivalent(in Object other_object);
    unsigned long        hash(in unsigned long maximum);

    // the create_request operation used by the DII is defined here
  };
};
```

The get_implementation() operation returns an ORB-dependent interface called ImplementationDef, which the standard does not specify. This interface should provide information about how the object adapter launches implementations of objects. Usually the object adapter does this by starting a new process or task running from a particular executable file with certain arguments.

The get_interface() operation returns a standard interface from the Interface Repository. This allows a client to investigate the IDL definition of an interface via calls to objects that represent the IDL in the Interface Repository. This approach can be used to discover the operations available on an object reference when its type is unknown at compile time. The DII can then be used to invoke these operations.

The is_nil() operation returns TRUE if this object reference denotes no object. Object implementations that return object references as output parameters or return values may choose to return a nil object reference rather than raise an exception. Different language bindings implement object references differently and an invocation on a nil object reference may result in a fatal error.

The duplicate() and release() operations are very important in programming languages where programmers do explicit memory management (such as C and C++). Luckily in Java this is done for us automatically. These operations ensure correct management of copies of an object reference. When an object reference is to be passed to another object, or thread of control, the opaque type which implements the object reference *must not* be copied by using features of the implementation language. The duplicate() operation must be used instead. The reason is that when a remote client uses an object reference, a proxy object is created locally for the client to invoke operations on directly. The proxy, in concert with the ORB, creates the request which ends up at the object implementation.

A proxy object keeps a counter of all object references that refer to it. This is called a reference count. If a copy of a reference to that proxy is created without the knowledge of the proxy, it cannot increase its reference count. When the counted references are released the proxy assumes that no other references to it exist and it will deallocate its resources and delete itself. Now the reference copied without using duplicate() refers to a deleted proxy and invocations made on it will incur a run-time error. This is illustrated in Figure 2.8.

When duplicate() is called to obtain a new copy of the object reference, the proxy will increase its reference count and wait for all references to call release() before cleaning up and going away. This makes the importance of using release() equally clear. If the last reference to a proxy is deleted without calling release() the proxy will continue to consume memory, and probably

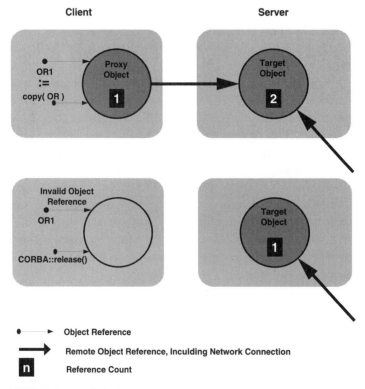

FIGURE 2.8 Invalid object reference copy.

network resources, until the process or task in which it executes dies. Figure 2.9 illustrates this case. Figure 2.10 shows the correct use of duplicate() and release() where the reference count in the proxy reflects the actual number of references to it.

Figure 2.11 shows what occurs when an object reference is duplicated for passing across machine boundaries. The figure does not show the temporary increase in the reference count on proxy object B before the skeleton code does a release() when passing the reference back to the client.

The is_a() operation returns TRUE if the Interface Repository identifier passed to it refers to a type of which this object is a subtype. It is mainly used in dynamically typed languages that cannot support a narrow() method. We recommend the use of narrow(), which can be attempted for various object types. It will return a valid object reference if it is of a compatible type. Otherwise it will return a nil object reference or raise an exception.

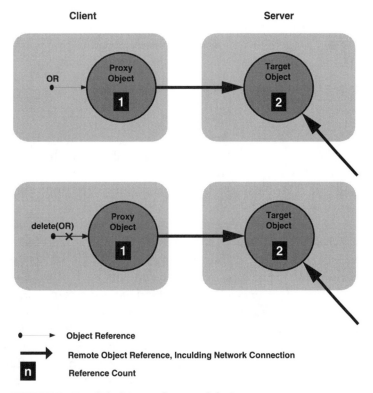

FIGURE 2.9 Invalid object reference deletion.

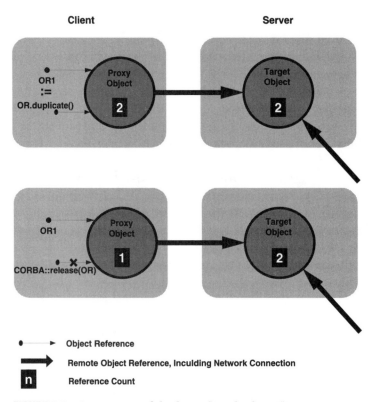

Client   **Server**

● ────►   Object Reference

━━━━►   Remote Object Reference, Incuding Network Connection

n   Reference Count

FIGURE 2.10   Correct use of duplicate() and release().

The non_existent() operation returns TRUE if the object implementation denoted by this reference has been destroyed. The ORB will return FALSE if the object exists or if it cannot determine the answer definitively.

The is_equivalent() operation is the only way within CORBA of determining whether two object references denote the same object. All references that are created by calling duplicate() on a single object reference will be equivalent to the original reference and with each other. Even so, it is possible that two references that actually denote the same object may return a FALSE result from this operation. That is, a TRUE result guarantees that the object denoted is the same, but a FALSE result does not guarantee that two references denote different objects. String representations obtained from object_to_string() are ORB dependent and often are different every time they are generated. Hence they do not offer a means of comparing references.

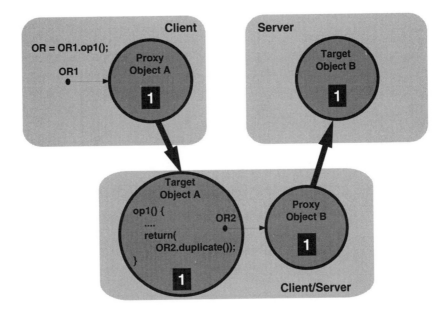

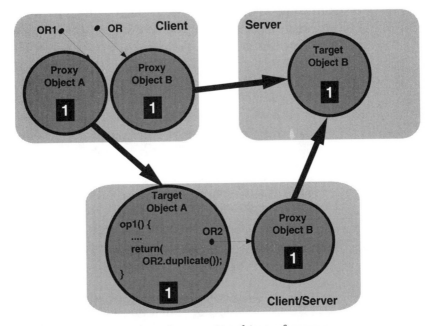

FIGURE 2.11 Proxy creation when passing object references.

The hash() operation provides a way of searching for an equivalent object reference that is more efficient than comparing a reference against every object reference in a list. The same object reference will return the same hash value each time. This provides a way of selecting a small number of possibly identical references in a chained hash table, which can be compared pairwise for a match. Most **CORBA** application programmers will never need to use is_equivalent() or hash().

3.5.3 *Initialization*

The CORBA module contains a pseudo-IDL operation ORB_init() for bootstrapping the ORB.

```
module CORBA { // PIDL
    typedef string ORBid;
    typedef sequence <string> arg_list;
    ORB ORB_init(inout arg_list argv, in ORBid orb_identifier);
};
```

ORB_init() is provided to obtain a reference to an ORB pseudo-object. Ordinarily operations must be associated with an interface, but ORB_init() is freestanding. ORB_init() takes the command line arguments from a UNIX shell-style process launch and removes any that are intended for the ORB. It also takes the name of the **ORB** to be initialized in the form of a string.

The ORB interface supports some further operations to allow any ORB user to get access to fundamental object services and/or facilities by name. The most important of these for object implementations is an object adapter. The following IDL shows the signature of BOA_init(), which is the way to obtain a reference to a BOA pseudo-object.

```
module CORBA {
  interface ORB { // PIDL
    typedef string OAid;
    typedef sequence <string> arg_list;

  BOA BOA_init(inout arg_list argv,
        in OAid boa_identifier);
```

As with the **ORB** initialization, the argument list may be scanned for BOA-specific arguments and it will be returned with these removed. The object adapter identifier parameter, boa_identifier, must be passed a string specified by the particular **ORB** vendor.

The declarations following allow the **ORB** user to find out which basic services and facilities the **ORB** supports and obtain references to their objects. This mechanism is also used to obtain a POA reference. The list_initial_services() operation provides a list of the strings that identify the services and facilities, and the resolve_initial_references() operation takes these strings as an argument and returns an object reference.

```
// interface ORB cont ...
    typedef string ObjectId;
    typedef sequence <ObjectId> ObjectIdList;

    exception InvalidName {};

    ObjectIdList list_initial_services();

    Object resolve_initial_references (in ObjectId identifier)
        raises (InvalidName);

    }; // interface ORB
}; // module CORBA
```

The resolve_initial_references() operation is a bootstrap to get object references to the POA and CORBAservices, such as the Naming Service, Interface Repository, and Trading Service. The argument is a string specified in each CORBA service specification, for example, "NameService" for the Naming Service and "TradingService" for the Trader.

The type of interface expected as a return type is well known, and the object reference returned can be narrowed to the correct object type: CosNaming::NamingContext for the Naming Service and CosTrading::Lookup for the Trading Service. See Chapter 8 for a full explanation of how to obtain these references using the Java language binding and how to use them to obtain references to application objects.

3.6   Basic Object Adapter

For the object implementer, the BOA is the interface used to inform the ORB when objects come into existence and when running processes or tasks are ready to accept incoming requests on those objects. However, for the client the BOA is the component of the ORB that ensures that an invocation on an object reference always reaches a running object that can respond to it. That is, the BOA is capable of launching processes, waiting for them to initialize, and then dispatching requests to them. To do this it needs access to the Implementation Repository—a component proprietary to each ORB which stores information about where the executable code that implements objects resides and how to run it correctly.

The CORBA specification lists the creation, destruction, and lookup of information relating to object references as one of the BOA's primary functions. It provides pseudo-IDL (PIDL) descriptions of interfaces to do this.

These will be described later for completeness. However, in effect, creation and destruction of object references is managed by code that is generated by IDL compilers as part of the implementation skeleton. When implementation objects are created their object references are usually created with them.

3.6.1 Registration, Activation, and Deactivation of Implementations

Let's look at what a program that implements some objects needs to do to allow the skeletons for those objects to be called and cause the methods of the objects to be invoked.

```
module CORBA { // PIDL

  interface BOA {
    void impl_is_ready (in ImplementationDef impl);
    void deactivate_impl (in ImplementationDef impl);
    void obj_is_ready (in Object obj, in ImplementationDef impl);
    void deactivate_obj (in Object obj);

    // continued ....
  };
};
```

The program implementing an object may have been started by some external means or by the BOA using the information in the Implementation Repository. The BOA should use policy information in the Implementation Repository to determine how to start the program (or server process) and what registration calls to expect. Four policies are explained in the CORBA specification:

Shared server activation policy. According to CORBA, each object should register itself with an obj_is_ready() operation if the process it runs in supports many objects. This is called the shared server activation policy. The obj_is_ready() operation is invoked to associate a running object implementation with an entity in the Implementation Repository. When an object can no longer respond to requests it should inform the BOA using the deactivate_obj() operation. Most ORBs provide automatic deregistration of objects in the destructor of the generated skeleton code.

Unshared server activation policy. In the unshared server activation policy the process encapsulates an application that supports only one object interface. In this case, when all the other initialization has been completed, the impl_is_ready() operation should be invoked. This associates the single object with an entity in the Implementation Repository. The deactivate_impl() operation informs the BOA that the server can no longer service requests.

Server-per-method activation policy. In the server-per-method activation policy a new process is started for each request received by the BOA. The standard says that no registration call is needed in this case, but ORBs that support this policy often require an impl_is_ready() call to notify the ORB that requests can be served.

Persistent server policy. A persistent server is a process that is started by some means other than BOA activation. Typically an operating system script or user command starts the server. In this case the impl_is_ready() operation should be used to register the server with the BOA.

Some ORBs' BOAs support only impl_is_ready() and don't allow objects to be activated individually, while others support both approaches, even in programs that use the shared activation policy. Some offer the above activation policies explicitly, but not necessarily using the registration operations specified. Others support orthogonal policies which consider the caller's identity. Most ORBs implement impl_is_ready() as a dispatch loop that doesn't return while the server is accepting requests and which calls deactivate_impl() if interrupted.

In short, BOA implementations vary a great deal, and object implementers should not only be aware of their responsibilities when initializing implementations, but they should be aware of the peculiarities of their ORB. See Chapter 7 for details of what Java ORBs require.

3.6.2 BOA Implementation

The BOA is a logical component of the ORB, but its implementation is usually divided between the ORB daemon, the BOA pseudo-object, and the generated code from the IDL compiler. As one would expect, the ORB daemon takes responsibility for launching processes. The BOA pseudo-object provides the interface that is invoked to register the objects.

Two common strategies are used by ORBs for object-oriented languages when incorporating the skeleton code into the object implementation. The first is to inherit the generated skeleton class into each implementation of an interface described in the IDL file. The base class is then responsible for supporting interactions between the ORB and the implementation methods. The second approach is to generate a proxy class that implements the same functionality as the skeleton class, but is not inherited by the class that implements the object's application semantics. When a logical CORBA object is instantiated, the application implementer must actually instantiate two objects, the proxy object and an implementation object. The proxy object must then be given a reference to the implementation object so that it can delegate incoming requests there. This is called the *Tie* approach, as the application developer must "tie" the proxy and implementation objects together when they are created.

In the programming chapters of this book we use the inheritance approach, but the Tie approach is covered in Chapter 10.

3.6.3 *Other Functions*

The BOA interface description provided in the CORBA module contains several additional operations that are seldom used by any ORB implementation. The generation of object references is usually done implicitly when a programming language reference to an implementation object is passed as a parameter. The handling of authentication and access control is done by a higher level service. The reference data in an object reference may be used for many purposes, among them retrieval of persistent state. The following IDL supports object reference creation for non-object-oriented languages and retrieval of information from object references.

```
// interface CORBA::BOA PIDL cont ...

    interface Principal;
        typedef sequence <octet, 1024> ReferenceData;

    Object create(
        in ReferenceData        id,
        in InterfaceDef  intf,
        in ImplementationDef impl);

    void dispose(in Object obj);
    ReferenceData get_id (in Object obj);

    void change_implementation (
        in Object        obj,
        in ImplementationDef impl);

    Principal get_principal (
        in Object        obj,
        in Environment ev);

    }; // interface BOA
}; // module CORBA
```

Generation of object references. As explained in section 3.5.2, an object reference has three main components: a unique key within the server implementation, the object's interface type, and a way of locating its implementation, for example, an IP address and port number. Not surprisingly, these are the parameters that the create() operation needs to create a new object reference. It is unlikely that this operation will actually be offered in most ORB implementations, as object references are created implicitly from implementation objects by the ORB. The way to safely delete an object reference is by passing it to the dispose() operation.

The change_implementation() operation associates a new object implementation with a particular object reference. This must be done with care, making sure to deactivate the object before switching its implementation. There are security problems with providing access to a new object implementation using an existing object reference. Most objects will be associated with a single implementation for the duration of their life span.

Access control. The get_principal() operation is used to determine the identity of a client that caused the activation of an object. It will generally be used by a higher level security service.

Persistence. The get_id() operation will return the reference data of an object reference that is guaranteed to be unique within the server that implements the object. This uniqueness means that it can be used as a key to a database table which contains a persistent state that survives between activations of a server.

3.7   The Portable Object Adapter

The semantics of the BOA specification were left intentionally vague because it was not clear which features would be required on various platforms or how implementations would be achieved. As a result, different vendors implemented different parts of the BOA with differences in their semantics. This implementation experience was used as the basis for the specification of the portable object adapter (POA), which aims to eliminate these inconsistencies and standardize some of the proprietary features that have emerged to fill the gaps in the BOA specification.

3.7.1   POA Overview

The POA aims to provide a comprehensive set of interfaces for managing object references and their implementations, now called *servants*. The code written using the POA interfaces should now be portable across ORB implementations and have the same semantics in every ORB.

The POA defines standard interfaces to

♦ Map an object reference to the servant that implements that object
♦ Allow transparent activation of objects

◆ Associate policy information with objects
◆ Make a CORBA object persistent over several server process lifetimes

The use of pseudo-IDL has been deprecated in favor of an approach that uses ordinary IDL, which is mapped into programming languages using the standard language mappings, but which is *locality constrained*. This means that references to objects defined in POA may not be passed outside of a server's address space. One addition has been made to IDL: the native keyword. Parts of the specification tagged as native may be mapped to programming languages in a manner different from the standard language mappings.

The rest of this section will explain the architecture of the POA and provide an overview of the important interfaces it provides as well as the object activation policies that the interfaces may administer.

3.7.2 POA Architecture

First it is useful to provide definitions of some key concepts used in the POA specification:

Servant. An implementation object that provides the runtime semantics of one or more CORBA objects.

Object ID. An identifier, unique with respect to a POA, that the POA uses to associate a CORBA object identity with a servant.

Active object map. A table of associations between Object IDs and servants kept by a POA to allow it to dispatch incoming requests.

Incarnate. The action of providing a running servant to serve requests associated with a particular Object ID. A POA will keep this association in its active object map.

Etherealize. The action of destroying a servant associated with an Object ID, so that the Object ID no longer identifies a CORBA object with respect to a particular POA.

Default servant. An object to which all incoming requests for Object IDs not in the Active Object Map are dispatched.

3.7.3 POA Policies

The policies used by POAs are divided into several interacting categories:

ID uniqueness. Whether more than one Object ID may refer to the same servant object. The names of the policies are UNIQUE_ID and MULTIPLE_ID.

ID assignment. Whether the POA or the programmer assigns Object IDs. The names of the policies are USER_ID and SYSTEM_ID.

Lifespan. Whether objects are transient or persistent. That is, whether the CORBA object is available to clients after the server process dies or whether it returns the OBJECT_NOT_EXIST exception when the server is reactivated. The names of the policies are TRANSIENT and PERSISTENT.

Servant retention. Whether the POA keeps Object ID/servant associations in its Active Object Map or relies on default servants or servant locators to find servants for each request. The names of the policies are RETAIN and NON_RETAIN.

Request processing. Whether the POA uses only the Active Object Map, only the default servant, only a servant locator, or some combination of these to locate the correct servant for incoming requests. The POA also relies on the value of the servant retention policy to determine its request processing behavior. The names of the policies are USE_ACTIVE_OBJECT_MAP_ONLY, USE_DEFAULT_SER-VANT, and USE_SERVANT_MANAGER.

Servant manager. A programmer-supplied object that manages servants. There are two subtypes of this abstract interface: activators and locators.

Servant activator. An object that a POA uses to incarnate objects for continued use and then to etherealize them when their life cycle is complete.

Servant locator. An object that a POA uses to obtain a servant to invoke a single operation on an object identified by an Object ID. A POA will not place this association in its Active Object Map.

The purpose of a POA is to dispatch incoming invocation requests to the correct servant object. It does so based on policies determined by the programmer of the CORBA server. This allows a range of behaviors from automatic generation of unique Object IDs, which are kept with servant references in the Active Object Map, to the use of programmer-supplied servant manager objects, which interpret Object IDs and return appropriate servants for invocations.

There can be more than one POA active in a particular server; however, there is always a root POA from which all of the other POAs are created. Each POA has a name relative to the POA in which it was created, and a find operation is defined to allow POAs to be located (and activated) by their parents. POAs themselves have manager objects which activate them and may change their processing state to allow them to suspend processing of requests or even to discard requests for some period (see Figure 2.12).

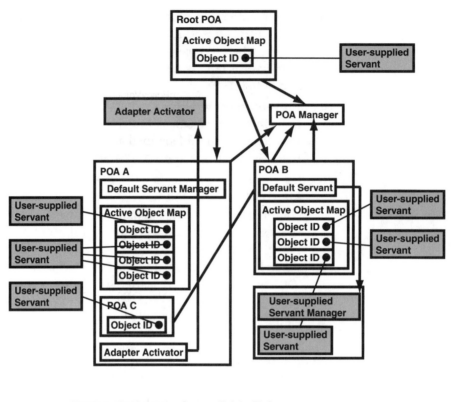

FIGURE 2.12 POA architecture.

Thread policy. Determines whether single or multiple threading is used so that safe deletion of servants may be achieved. The names of the policies are ORB_CTRL_MODEL and SINGLE_THREAD_MODEL.

Implicit activation policy. Determine whether the POA can implicitly activate a servant or whether it needs to call a servant activator to do so. The names of the policies are IMPLICIT_ACTIVATION and NO_IMPLICIT_ACTIVATION.

Policies are specified as IDL interfaces in the PortableServer module. They all derive from a base interface called CORBA::Policy. The values that the policy objects represent are specified as read-only enum attributes. There are factory operations defined in the POA interface for creating these objects. For example, the LifespanPolicy object is specified as follows:

```
enum LifespanPolicy Value {
    TRANSIENT,
    PERSISTENT
};

interface LifespanPolicy {
    readonly attribute LifespanPolicyValue value;
};
```

with the following operation defined in the POA interface to create the object:

```
LifespanPolicy create_lifespan_policy(in LifespanPolicyValue value);
```

The way in which a new POA is created and initialized is by using the root POA (or one of its extant children) to create policy objects which are then passed in a sequence to the create_POA() operation.

Following are some useful policy combinations for child POAs:

RETAIN and USE_ACTIVE_OBJECT_MAP_ONLY. This combination resembles the default situation of most ORBs implemented with the BOA. It relies on servers to explicitly activate new objects using the activate_object() or activate_object_with_id() operations.

RETAIN and USE_SERVANT_MANAGER. This is a portable way of allowing a server to implement a generic servant manager interface (namely ServantActivator). The POA uses the ServantActivator when an object is not found in the Active Object Map. Each ServantActivator supports the operation incarnate(), which takes an Object ID and returns the servant that implements the object identified.

RETAIN and USE_DEFAULT_SERVANT. This combination assumes that objects not found in the Active Object Map are to be implemented by a generic servant object (probably using the DSI), which is registered with the POA as its default servant. The POA will raise the OBJECT_ADAPTER system exception if no default servant has been registered.

NON_RETAIN and USE_DEFAULT_SERVANT. This is similar to the previous situation, except that no Active Object Map is kept, meaning that all requests are sent to the default servant.

NON_RETAIN and USE_SERVANT_MANAGER. The server will configure a POA to use this policy combination when it wishes to be in control of mapping each incoming invocation request to the appropriate servant. The servant manager used in this situation is a ServantLocator, which the POA calls using operations called preinvoke(), which obtains the servant which will service the request, and postinvoke(), which allows the server to clean up afterward.

3.7.4   POA Life Cycle

A reference to the root POA is always available from the ORB. Its name is RootPOA and it is obtained using the ORB::resolve_initial_references() operation. It has a predetermined set of policies, which can be summarized by saying that all object references are transient, mapping a single servant to an Object ID which is set by the POA and retained in the Active Object Map. When a server is being initialized it is responsible for setting up any other (descendant) POAs that it requires to support its objects.

Creating POAs manually. In order to create other POAs, the createPOA() operation must be invoked on the root POA. A hierarchy of POAs can be created by subsequently calling createPOA() on the resulting child. When a POA is no longer required its destroy() operation must be invoked. The other operation used in relation to children of a POA is find_POA(), which allows a relative name to be resolved, returning an existing or newly activated POA.

```
create_POA(in string adapter_name,
        in POAManager a_POAManager,
        in CORBA::PolicyList policies)
    raises (AdapterAlreadyExists, InvalidPolicy);
```

The create_POA() operation takes a name parameter and a POAManager parameter, which is usually a nil object reference, indicating that the ORB should assign a manager to the POA. It also requires a list of consistent policies, such as the combinations given previously.

```
find_POA (in string adapter_name, in boolean activate_it)
    raises (AdapterNonExistent);
```

The find_POA() operation may find child POAs that have been activated by create_POA() or it may be used to activate a POA using a preregistered adapter activator.

Adapter activators are associated with POAs at the time of their first creation and allow them to be made persistent when their objects are not being used and reactivated when required. The adapter activator for a POA is registered by setting the POA attribute called the_activator.

Adapter activators have a single operation:

```
boolean unknown_adapter(in POA parent, in string name);
```

This operation is called when find_POA() is invoked with the activate_it argument set to TRUE or when an invocation request is received nominating a POA that is not active. In this case the activators are called in succession from the one closest to the root to the furthest descendant. The parent parameter passes the reference of the parent POA to the activator. A typical activator implementation retrieves any stored information about the child and uses the parent POA's policy operations to create the correct policies. It then uses its create_POA() operation to instantiate the child. If it can successfully create the child, the activator returns TRUE from the unknown_adapter() call. The ORB can then call unknown_adapter() on the adapter activator of the new child to activate the next POA in the chain. For example, if the currently instantiated POA hierarchy consists only of the root POA and its child A, an incoming request for an object controlled by a POA identified as "<root>/A/B/C" will result in the following calls (in pseudo-code):

```
if (A.the_activator.unknown_adapter (A, "B"))
    then B.the_activator.unknown_adapter(B, "C")
```

POA references to other objects. Certain POA policies require the assistance of other objects, such as managers, and the POA interface provides operations to set and get references to these objects. References to other objects are implicit in the POA's position in the hierarchy or are derived from the arguments provided to its parent at creation.

There are a number of attributes that POAs support:

```
readonly attribute string the_name;
readonly attribute POA the_parent;
readonly attribute POAManager the_manager;
attribute AdapterActivator the_activator;
```

The read-only attributes allow users of the POA (ORB and server implementers) to access the name of the POA with respect to its parent, the POA's parent, and its manager. The writable attribute the_activator must be set if this POA is not always created by the server initialization code.

If the USE_DEFAULT_SERVANT policy is set, a servant must be nominated as the default using:

```
void set_servant(in Servant p_servant) raises(WrongPolicy)
```

The default servant can be retrieved using:

```
Servant get_servant() raises (NoServant, WrongPolicy);
```

The WrongPolicy exception is raised by both operations if the USE_DEFAULT_SERVANT policy is not set. NoServant is raised by get_servant() when set_servant() has not yet provided a default servant.

If the USE_SERVANT_MANAGER policy is set, the following operations are used in the same manner as set/get_servant() to initialize the ServantManager to be used by the POA:

```
void set_servant_manager(in ServantManager imgr)
    raises(WrongPolicy);
ServantManager get_servant_manager()
    raises(WrongPolicy);
```

3.7.5 Using the POA to Create Object References

The other operations of the POA interface are for mapping Object IDs to servants and for activating servants that already have Object IDs, thereby creating usable object references that can be handed to clients. If the USER_ID policy is set, servers can allocate their own Object IDs and map them to servants using the following operation:

```
void activate_object_with_id(
        in ObjectId id,
        in Servant p_servant)
    raises (ServantAlreadyActive, ObjectAlreadyActive, WrongPolicy);
```

The ServantAlreadyActive exception is raised if the servant is already mapped and the UNIQUE_ID policy is set. The ObjectAlreadyActive exception is raised when this Object ID is already in use.

When the SYSTEM_ID policy is set, activate_object_with_id() will raise the WrongPolicy exception and explicit server activation must be done using:

```
ObjectId activate_object(in Servant p_servant)
    raises (ServantAlreadyActive, WrongPolicy);
```

The return value is the POA's allocated Object ID for the new servant.

One more step is required (under the USER_ID policy) to make a usable object reference. The create_reference_with_id() operation is used to associate an object reference with an Object ID and hence with its active servant.

```
Object create_reference_with_id(
        in ObjectId oid,
        in CORBA::RepositoryId intf)
    raises(WrongPolicy);
```

The Object ID becomes associated with an object reference and conforms to the type specified in the Interface Repository using the repository ID provided as the intf argument. The association between Object IDs and object references can be made by the POA when the policy is SYSTEM_ID:

```
Object create_reference(in CORBA::RepositoryId intf)
    raises(WrongPolicy);
```

Once the object is no longer required, its Object ID is deallocated and the mapping is removed from the Active Object Map using

```
void deactivate_object(in ObjectId oid)
    raises(ObjectNotActive, WrongPolicy);
```

3.7.6 *Discovering the Mappings in a POA*

If the Active Object Map is being used (RETAIN policy is set) the following operations allow its mappings between Object ID, object reference, and servant to be interrogated:

```
ObjectId reference_to_id(in Object reference)
    raises (WrongAdapter, WrongPolicy);
Object id_to_reference(in ObjectId oid)
    raises (ObjectNotActive, WrongPolicy);
Servant reference_to_servant(in Object reference)
    raises (ObjectNotActive, WrongAdapter, WrongPolicy);
Servant id_to_servant(in ObjectId oid)
    raises (ObjectNotActive, WrongPolicy);
```

The mappings from servant to Object ID and reference can also be obtained if the UNIQUE_ID policy is set:

```
ObjectId servant_to_id(in Servant p_servant)
    raises(ServantNotActive, WrongPolicy);
Object servant_to_reference(in Servant p_servant)
    raises(ServantNotActive, WrongPolicy);
```

3.7.7 *The Current Interface*

When a servant implements methods for more than one Object ID it often needs to know which CORBA identity is associated with the request that has been dispatched to it. For this purpose an interface is defined that allows the servant to acquire information about its POA and its Object ID in that POA. The CORBA::Current interface is inherited by the PortableServer::Current interface, which adds the following operations:

POA get_POA() raises(NoContext);—this operation allows the servant to determine which POA processed the request, and to examine the policies of that POA.

ObjectId get_object_id() raises (NoContext)—this operation allows the Object ID relative to that POA to be discovered, and the servant can use this identity to access the correct state for the CORBA object it is serving for the current invocation.

3.8 Language Mappings

The OMG has standardized four language bindings and has RFPs issued to standardize several more. The current adopted specifications are C, C++, Smalltalk, Ada '95, COBOL, and Java.

3.8.1 C

The C mapping was published along with the CORBA 1.1 specification. It provides an example of how to implement CORBA clients and servers in a non-object-oriented language. Operation and interface names are concatenated to provide function names and object references are passed explicitly as parameters.

3.8.2 C++

The C++ language mapping is the most widely supported language mapping at the moment. Its syntactic resemblance to IDL provides class definitions that very closely mirror IDL interface definitions. The generated stub code can be incorporated by inheritance into object implementation classes or delegate to them. The major drawback of this mapping is that implementers of clients and servers must pay very close attention to memory management responsibilities. The rules for allocation and deallocation of data memory are just as complex as old-style Remote Procedure Call (RPC) programming. Some helper classes are defined that can deallocate memory when they go out of scope, but these must be declared and used with care because they might deallocate memory that is still being used by another object.

3.8.3 Smalltalk

Smalltalk is a dynamically typed, single-inheritance object-oriented language in which all types are first-class objects. The datatype mappings use existing Smalltalk classes and operations map to methods on classes. The way in which IDL interfaces map to Smalltalk objects is unconstrained. Explicit protocol mappings are made for some IDL types, such as unions and Anys, which provide a standard way of accessing their discriminators and TypeCodes, respectively. However, implicit mappings may be used by programmers.

3.8.4 COBOL

The IDL/COBOL mapping was adopted in 1997. Since COBOL is not object oriented the mapping is not as natural as, for example, those for C++ or

Java. In particular, IDL concepts such as name scopes, interfaces, and inheritance require complex mapping rules. The datatype mapping is based on the optional COBOL typedef construct. However, older COBOL compilers may not provide typedefs, in which case the mapping has to use COBOL copy files as an alternative.

3.9   Interoperability

The CORBA 2.1 specification has a section called Interoperability. It specifies an architecture for interoperability, as well as an out-of-the-box interoperability protocol, running over TCP/IP, and a second, optional protocol which uses the DCE RPC transport.

The specification contains a lot of technical detail about the protocols specified and about bridging between proprietary protocols. Here we will give an overview of the framework within which the two specified protocols exist and of the mandatory Internet Inter-ORB Protocol (IIOP). The rest of the standard applies to ORB implementers and will not be covered.

3.9.1   The ORB Interoperability Architecture

The architecture contains definitions of ORB domains, bridges, and interoperable object references (IORs). It defines domains as islands within which objects are accessible because they use the same communication protocols, the same security, and the same way of identifying objects. In order to establish interoperability between domains, one of these elements must be replaced with a common element or a bridge must be set up to facilitate translation of the protocol, identity, authority, etc., between domains.

The approach of the architecture is to identify the things that can be used as common representations (canonical forms) between domains and then suggest ways in which ORB domains can create half-bridges that communicate using the common representation. The first step, a common object reference format, is defined as part of the architecture. An IOR contains the same information as a single domain object reference, but it adds a list of protocol profiles indicating which communication protocols the domain of origin can accept requests in. The protocol interoperability problem is addressed in a separate component called the General Inter-ORB Protocol (GIOP). Allowance is also made for the introduction of third-party protocols, called Environment-Specific Inter-ORB Protocols (ESIOPs), within this framework. Figure 2.13 illustrates the relationships between these protocols.

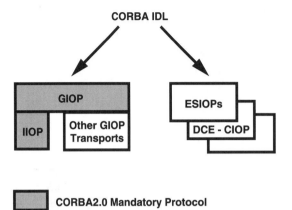

FIGURE 2.13 ORB protocols.

3.9.2 General Inter-ORB Protocol

The GIOP defines a linear format for the transmission of CORBA requests and replies without requiring a particular network transport protocol.

3.9.3 Internet Inter-ORB Protocol

The IIOP is a specialization of the GIOP which specifies the use of TCP/IP (the Internet Protocol). It defines some primitives to assist in the establishment of TCP connections. This protocol is required for compliance with CORBA 2.0 and is intended to provide a base-level interoperability between all ORB vendors' products, even though some vendors will continue to support proprietary protocols. Java ORBs are all implemented using IIOP.

3.9.4 Other Approaches

As can be seen in Figure 2.13, the interoperability architecture allows for the specification of ESIOPs, which will provide "islands of interoperability," but which should be able to be bridged to other ORBs using IIOP. The first adopted ESIOP is the DCE Common Inter-ORB Protocol (DCE-CIOP), which was already used by a number of ORBs before the introduction of GIOP/IIOP.

An alternative implementation for GIOP can be expected for 1998. There are projects in progress to implement GIOP directly over ATM protocol layers. Most likely the implementation will choose AAL5.

Before the CORBA 2.0 specification was introduced, each ORB vendor had to choose or invent a protocol for the transmission of invocation requests and responses. Most vendors have a customer base with extant objects that use a certain protocol, and so it is in their interest to continue to support old protocols alongside IIOP. However, leading ORB products now support IIOP as their native protocol.

3.10   TypeCode, Any, and DynAny

This section gives details about the interfaces to the generic container type Any and its supporting type, the TypeCode, which it uses to identify its contents. The ORB Portability Specification adopted by the OMG in 1997 extends the functionality available from Anys by adding a new interface called DynAny, which allows programmers to navigate the contents of Anys and access constituent parts without requiring compiled stub code with which to extract the entire contents of an Any.

3.10.1   Any

The Any type is a basic type in IDL. It designates a container that can contain a value of any IDL type and identifies the type of its contents for type-safe extraction of the value. The pseudo-IDL type TypeCode is used to identify the type of a value in an Any and can be used outside of the context of Anys to identify IDL types in general. TypeCodes are not IDL basic types, but they may be declared as parameters to operations and members of structured types.

Since the keyword any in IDL is a basic type, and it does not have a signature represented in PIDL, it is left to each language mapping to define the mechanism for inserting and extracting values from Anys and defining the TypeCodes that identify the values they contain.

3.10.2   Language Mapping for Anys

The mapping for Anys in Java is given in Chapter 6, and provides methods on an Any class that allow the insertion and extraction of all basic types, as well as additional methods on Helper classes for IDL-defined types that produce Anys. To provide a very basic notion of what an Any is, let's look at the C mapping

```
typedef struct CORBA_any {
     CORBA_TypeCode _type;
     void * _value;
} CORBA_any;
```

There are no helper functions defined in the mapping, and programmers are responsible (as is usual in C) for ensuring that the _value structure member is cast in a type-safe manner. To do this the programmer must compare the _type member against TypeCode constants that correspond to known IDL types and then cast the _value member to the mapped C type for that IDL.

3.10.3 *TypeCode*

The ORB specification defines a PIDL interface to a type called TypeCode, which is used to describe any IDL type. TypeCodes are one of only two PIDL types that can be used in IDL definitions as components of structured types or as parameter and return types of operations or attribute values. The other is Principal which is used for Security. The PIDL for TypeCodes is given in the Interface Repository section of the CORBA 2.1 document. However, they are implemented as a combination of library and IDL compiler-generated code and are available to CORBA programmers independent of the Interface Repository.

In concept a TypeCode consists of a *kind* field and a set of parameters that provide more information about that kind of TypeCode. For example, a TypeCode for a struct will give the name of the struct and the names and types (using recursive TypeCodes) of the members of that struct. The PIDL for TypeCode provides operations to allow the programmer access to the parameters, as well as an operation to compare TypeCodes for equality. All of the following PIDL is situated in the CORBA module.

TypeCode kinds. The kinds of types in IDL are given as an enumeration. The kinds have been extended by the IDL Type Extensions Specification (OMG document ptc/97-01-01) to include wide characters and strings, fixed-point decimal numbers, and 64-bit integers and floating-point numbers. The extensions are given in italics below:

```
enum TCKind {
    tk_null, tk_void,
    tk_short, tk_long, tk_ushort, tk_ulong,
    tk_float, tk_double, tk_boolean, tk_char,
    tk_octet, tk_any, tk_TypeCode, tk_Principal, tk_objref,
    tk_struct, tk_union, tk_enum, tk_string,
    tk_sequence, tk_array, tk_alias, tk_except,
    tk_longlong, tk_ulonglong, tk_longdouble,
    tk_wchar, tk_wstring, tk_fixed
};
```

Internationalization is also supported implicitly by the character and string types, whose semantics now include the possible use of two-byte characters.

TypeCode operations. The TypeCode interface provides an equality operator whose semantics are not well defined—interface TypeCode { // PIDL:

```
boolean    equal (in TypeCode tc);
```

Most ORB implementations perform a simple comparison that returns TRUE only when the types compared have the same repository ID. That means that no structural comparisons are performed and no typedef aliasing is taken into account.

Making an analysis of a TypeCode begins with determining its kind with the kind() operation, so that other appropriate operations may then be chosen to learn more about the type:

```
TCKind          kind();
```

Most types also have definitions stored in the Interface Repository, which can be used as an alternative source of type information. The id() operation returns the RepositoryId for any nonbasic type. Basic types are not stored in the Interface Repository, and if the TypeCode's kind is inappropriate, a BadKind exception is raised. This exception is raised whenever an operation inappropriate to a TypeCode's kind is invoked:

```
exception       BadKind {};
RepositoryId    id() raises (BadKind);
```

Object references and structured types, except for sequences, always have an interface or tag name. These are returned using the name() operation:

```
Identifier      name() raises (BadKind);
```

Structs, unions, enums, and exceptions contain named member fields. The number and names of these members are discovered using the following operations. The exception Bounds is raised by indexed operations when the index parameter exceeds the number of elements:

```
exception       Bounds {};
unsigned long   member_count () raises (BadKind);
Identifier      member_name (in unsigned long index)
                    raises (BadKind, Bounds);
```

The members of structs, unions, and exceptions (but not enums) each have a type as well. These are returned as nested TypeCodes, which can be interpreted in the same way as their parent TypeCode:

```
TypeCode        member_type(in unsigned long index)
                    raises (BadKind, Bounds);
```

Unions also have a discriminator type and label values of that type for each member, as well as an optional default case. The member_label() operation will return the value for each case. It returns an Any containing a zero octet for the default case, if it exists. The discriminator_type() operation returns the TypeCode of the ordinal type in the switch clause of the union, and the default_index() operation returns the index of the member that corresponds to the default case or zero if it does not exist.

```
any             member_label (in unsigned long index)
                    raises (BadKind, Bounds);
TypeCode        discriminator_type() raises (BadKind);
long            default_index () raises (BadKind);
```

Sequences and strings may be bounded to a certain length, and arrays are always of a fixed length. The return value from the length() operation is zero for unbounded sequences and strings:

```
unsigned long   length () raises (BadKind);
```

Arrays and sequences contain elements of a particular type, and type-def aliases also refer to a previously declared type. The content_type() operation returns a TypeCode which can be interrogated to find out what type they contain:

```
TypeCode        content_type () raises (BadKind);
```

Standard TypeCode Instances. The CORBA module defines TypeCode constants for all basic IDL types. For example, the constant _tc_long represents the TypeCode for longs.

IDL compilers usually generate TypeCode instances to correspond to all types in an IDL definition. They are named according to the language mapping. However, if no stubs are available for a particular type the ORB interface defines operations to create TypeCodes from relevant parameters and a RepositoryId to nominate the IDL in which the type belongs. These are seldom used, and we will only give an example here:

```
TypeCode create_union_tc (
    in RepositoryId id,
    in Identifier name,
    in UnionMemberSeq members
);
```

The UnionMemberSeq type is defined in the Interface Repository specification.

3.10.4   DynAny

The ability to access the contents of an arbitrary Any had not been specified in CORBA until the adoption of the ORB Portability specification, and very few ORB implementations provided the ability to do so without access to compiled stub code. The implementation of Object Services and other interfaces that use the type Any to pass arbitrary values for storage or transmission often requires some access to these values in order to perform their specified semantics. DynAny provides an interface to do this in a standard way. It is part of the CORBA module.

An Any must first be inserted into a DynAny before its values can be accessed. A DynAny cannot be used as an operation parameter directly, and so a conversion back to an Any is also required. This functionality is provided as follows:

```
Interface DynAny {
    exception Invalid {};
    void from_any (in any value) raises (Invalid);
    any to_any () raises (Invalid);
```

Assignment of one DynAny to another, production of a new copy of an existing DynAny, and the destruction of DynAnys are achieved using the following operations:

◆ void assign (in DynAny dyn_any) raises (Invalid);
◆ DynAny copy();
◆ void destroy();

The DynAny interface also supports operations for the insertion and extraction of all the IDL basic types. These take the form of a pair of operations per basic type:

```
exception InvalidValue {};
exception TypeMismatch {};

void insert_basic_type (in basic_type) raises (InvalidValue);
basic_type get_basic_type() raises (TypeMismatch);
```

However, it is easy enough to insert and extract basic types from Anys, so DynAny extends this functionality by adding operations to traverse structured types. These return new DynAnys that refer to individual components of a structured type, which can be recursively traversed. The model is that of a cursor pointing to a current element.

```
DynAny current_component ();
boolean next ();
boolean seek (in long index);
void rewind ();
//...
};//interface DynAny
```

The boolean return values are set to TRUE if there is a component at the index that they move the cursor to. The components of structured types depend on the type. For example, the components of structures are their members and the components of arrays and sequences are their elements. The specification then defines a number of interfaces that inherit from DynAny to provide more specific access to the components of particular structured types. We will look at a number of significant examples.

Accessing Structs. The interface DynStruct provides a way of getting the names of structure members, and getting and setting their values:

```
typedef string FieldName;
struct NameValuePair {
    FieldName id;
    any value;
};
typedef sequence<NameValuePair> NameValuePairSeq;

interface DynStruct : DynAny {
    FieldName current_member_name ();
    TCKind current_member_kind ();
    NameValuePairSeq get_members ();
    Void set_members (in NameValuePairSeq value)
        Raises (InvalidSeq);
};
```

The operations inherited from DynAny are used to move the current cursor, and the new operations access the value at the cursor.

Accessing Enums. The type DynEnum provides attributes that allow access to and change the value of an enum as either a string tag name or a long integer value:

```
interface DynEnum : DynAny {
    attribute string value_as_string;
    attribute unsigned long value_as_ulong;
};
```

3.11 Dynamic Invocation and Dynamic Skeleton Interfaces

This section describes the interfaces to the symmetrical pair of ORB components, the Dynamic Invocation Interface (DII) on the client side and the Dynamic Skeleton Interface (DSI) on the server side. The DII enables a client to invoke operations on an interface for which it has no compiled stub code. It also allows a client to invoke an operation in deferred synchronous mode. That is, it can send the request, do some further processing, and then check for a response. This is useful regardless of whether or not the interface type is known at compile time, since it is not available via a static, or stub-based, invocation.

The DSI is used to accept a request for any operation, regardless of whether it has been defined in IDL or not. The mechanism allows servers to implement a class of generic operations of which it knows the form but not the exact syntax. It helps in writing client code that uses compiled IDL stubs based on an abstract IDL template. The client can then invoke operations on a compiled proxy stub in a type-safe manner.

3.11.1   Requests (DII)

The heart of the DII is the Request interface. A request has an object reference and a target operation name associated with it, as well as operations to add arguments. Once the request has the correct arguments it is invoked using the invoke() operation, and this blocks in the same way as a stub invocation until the response (or an exception) is returned.

3.11.2   Deferred Synchronous Invocation

The send() operation provides the means for a deferred synchronous invocation. This returns to the caller immediately and allows the client to perform some processing while the request is being transmitted and executed. The get_response() operation, when called in this situation, will either block until the request has returned its response or, if a flag is set, it will return a status value indicating whether or not the request has completed. Operations are also provided, but not specified in PIDL, for sending the requests to multiple objects and getting the responses from these invocations.

The PIDL in the CORBA document does not specify the types of all the parameters and return values of the operations on a Request, and so we provide the details of these operations in Chapter 7. The use of the DII in Java is demonstrated in Chapter 10.

3.11.3   ServerRequests (DSI)

In a particular object adapter implementation, an object reference is usually associated with an object implementation of the equivalent type in a particular language binding. However, an implementation that can deal with requests of several object types, called a Dynamic Implementation Routine (DIR), could be associated with an object reference instead. In this case, the object adapter does not look up a particular method and make an up-call by passing it the arguments in a request. Instead it creates a ServerRequest pseudo-object and passes this to the DIR. This is the definition of the ServerRequest interface:

```
module CORBA {

  pseudo interface ServerRequest {
    Identifier op_name();
    Context  ctx();
    void     params(inout NVList params);
    Any      result();
  };
};
```

The DIR can check the interface on which the request was made and look up its details using the Interface Repository. It could also be expecting requests of a known form and not require any IDL details. It can use the interface above to check the operation name, unpack the arguments, and find a location in which to place the result. The Java language mapping for the DSI is explained in Chapter 7.

3.11.4 Named Value Lists and Contexts

The PIDL for the Request and ServerRequest interfaces uses the PIDL type NVList to represent the values in an argument list. It is a type that is defined in each individual language mapping for the best implementation. However, it is logically equivalent to the following PIDL definition:

```
struct NamedValue {
  Identifier  name;
  any         argument;
  long        len; //length/count of argument value
  Flags       arg_modes; //in, out, or inout
};

typedef sequence <NamedValue> NVList;
```

The other type that is used in requests is the Context. This is another construct that is more concretely defined in particular language bindings. Its PIDL may not be directly translated using the language mapping. The PIDL is not given here but is explained in full in Chapter 7.

3.12 Interface Repository

The Interface Repository is a fundamental service in CORBA that provides information about the interface types of objects supported in a particular ORB installation. It can be thought of as a set of objects that encapsulate the IDL definitions of all CORBA types available in a particular domain.

The Interface Repository specification defines a set of interfaces that correspond to each construct in IDL: module, interface, operation, sequence, constant, etc. It also uses the idea of a containment hierarchy to relate objects of these types to one another. The Container interface is inherited by all

IDL construct description interfaces that contain other constructs, and the Contained interface is inherited by all the interfaces that describe IDL constructs contained in others. For example, an interface can be contained in a module and can contain an attribute.

The term *abstract interface* is used to indicate that an interface is only meant to be inherited into other interfaces. No objects of an abstract interface type will ever be instantiated. The term *concrete interface* is used to indicate that objects of this interface type will be instantiated.

All of the interfaces shown here are defined in the CORBA module. There are two mechanisms for finding out the properties of virtually all IDL constructs:

> The interfaces named *idl-construct*Def provide attributes and operations that explain the construct's properties and relationship to other IDL constructs. For example, SequenceDef is an interface definition with an attribute, bound, that gives the upper bound of a bounded sequence, or zero for an unbounded sequence. It has another attribute to return the type of the elements of the sequence it is describing.

> The Contained interface has a describe() operation that returns an enumerate value to identify the kind of IDL construct and a value of type Any which contains a structure dependent on that kind. The CORBA module defines a structure corresponding to each IDL construct named *idl-construct*Description. The structure contains the name, the repository identifier, the container where this construct is defined, its version, and some other members depending on the kind. For example, InterfaceDescription contains a list of base interfaces of the interface it describes.

This design has received a good deal of criticism. Some of the problems that have been observed with the current specification are

♦ It contains a large amount of redundancy.
♦ Often operations return RepositoryIds, which then need to be resolved at the Repository interface rather than object references to the *idl-construct*Def objects denoted by the Ids.
♦ Values are returned in a generic manner by base interfaces (e.g., in an Any) and then need to be interpreted based on an enumerated type. This functionality should have been pushed down to well-typed operations in the derived interfaces.

We recommend that you use Figure 2.14 as a basis for understanding the relationships between interfaces, since the Interface Repository specification can get rather confusing.

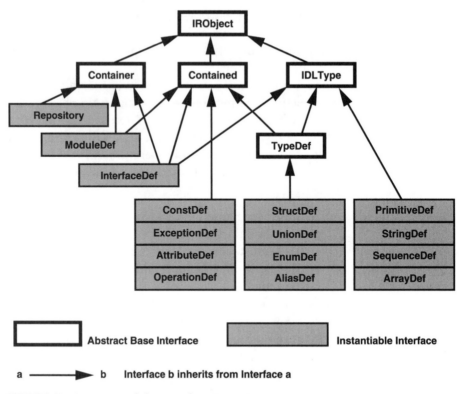

FIGURE 2.14 Structure of the Interface Repository.

3.12.1 *The Abstract Base Interfaces*

The interfaces to various syntactic constructs in IDL share common properties inherited from a number of abstract base interfaces which provide the common properties of these groups.

> The IRObject interface provides an attribute returning a value from an enumerated type that distinguishes between all IDL syntactic constructs. This attribute is available on all object references in the Interface Repository and allows the user to determine what kind of IDL construct description object they have a reference to.

> The Contained interface is inherited by all interfaces representing user-defined IDL constructs and offers attributes to discover the name of the construct and to obtain a structure that describes it.

> The Container interface is inherited by the Repository, ModuleDef, and InterfaceDef interfaces of the Interface Repository and contains operations to look up and describe the contents of these containers. It also contains operations to create all the objects that

inherit from Contained. These creation operations establish a containment relationship between the Container and the object that its operations create.

The IDLType interface is inherited by all the interfaces that represent datatypes, including all the basic type interfaces and user-defined datatype interfaces. It is also inherited by InterfaceDef because interface types can be used wherever datatypes are used in IDL. IDLType offers a single attribute that returns the TypeCode of the construct it describes.

The TypedefDef interface is inherited by all the user-defined type interfaces that are given a type name: structs, unions, enums, and typedef aliases. It offers a single operation which describes the type.

3.12.2 Nondatatype Interfaces

There is an interface for each IDL construct that forms part of an interface:

Repository—top level naming scope; can contain constants, typedefs, exceptions, interface definitions, and modules

ModuleDef—a logical grouping of interfaces; can contain constants, typedefs, exceptions, interface definitions, and other modules

InterfaceDef—can contain constants, typedefs, exceptions, operations, and attributes

AttributeDef

OperationDef—consists of a list of parameters and raised exceptions

ExceptionDef

3.12.3 Datatype Interfaces

The following objects are used to represent the datatypes that IDL offers:

ConstantDef

StructDef

UnionDef

EnumDef

AliasDef—typedefs that rename a defined type

PrimitiveDef—CORBA-defined types that cannot be changed by users

StringDef

SequenceDef

ArrayDef

3.12.4   IDL Definitions of the Interface Repository Interfaces

The IDL for the Interface Repository separates the functionality of the operations and attributes into read and write sections. The implementations of the Interface Repository that we have seen only implement the read part of the specification. The repository is usually populated by the IDL compiler using proprietary means. The purpose of this section is to allow users to investigate the functionality of an interface at runtime, so we will ignore the write interface.

The IRObject Interface. This base interface offers only a read-only attribute which indicates what kind of IDL object you have.

```
enum DefinitionKind {
  dk_none, dk_all,
  dk_Attribute, dk_Constant, dk_Exception, dk_interface,
  dk_Module, dk_Operation, dk_Typedef,
  dk_Alias, dk_Struct, dk_Union, dk_Enum,
  dk_Primitive, dk_String, dk_Sequence, dk_Array,
  dk_Repository
};

interface IRObject {
  readonly attribute DefinitionKind def_kind;
};
```

The Contained Interface.

```
typedef string VersionSpec;

interface Contained: IRObject {

  attribute RepositoryId id;
  attribute Identifier name;
  attribute VersionSpec version;
```

The read/write attributes are a global ID, a simple name, and a version (default set to 1.0).

```
  readonly attribute Container defined_in;
  readonly attribute ScopedName absolute_name;
  readonly attribute Repository containing_repository;
```

The read-only attributes are the module, interface, or repository where the text of this construct is defined; the scoped name of this instance of the construct; and the repository object where this construct definition object is kept.

```
  struct Description {
    DefinitionKind kind;
```

```
   any value;
};
Description describe ();
```

The describe() operation returns a Description structure containing a kind and a value. The value returned depends on the kind. We will see what values correspond to each kind when we reach the concrete interfaces. The type name for the value will be of the form *idl-construct*Description, for example, InterfaceDescription for interfaces.

The Container Interface.

```
typedef sequence <Contained> ContainedSeq;

interface Container: IRObject {
    Contained lookup (in ScopedName search_name);
```

The lookup() operation finds an object with a scoped name relative to this container. If the scoped name begins with "::" then the name is found from the enclosing repository.

```
ContainedSeq contents (
  in DefinitionKind limit_type
  in boolean exclude_inherited
);
```

The contents() operation returns a sequence of the objects in this container. The list may be limited to a certain type and may exclude inherited objects.

```
ContainedSeq lookup_name (
  in Identifier search_name
  in long levels_to_search
  in DefinitionKind limit_type
  in boolean exclude_inherited
);
```

The lookup_name() operation performs a recursive search down the containment hierarchy for a simple name. Restrictions can be placed on the number of levels to search, the types searched for, and whether or not to look at inherited objects.

The IDLType Interface.

```
interface IDLType:IRObject {
  readonly attribute TypeCode type;
};
```

This interface is inherited by built-in types like sequences and arrays, and offers only the TypeCode of the object.

The TypedefDef Interface.

```
interface TypedefDef: Contained, IDLType {};

struct TypeDescription {
    Identifier name;
    RepositoryId id;
    RepositoryId defined_in;
    VersionSpec version;
    TypeCode type;
};
```

This interface combines the functions of the Contained and IDLType interfaces. Since it is the base class for all user-defined datatype description objects and a derived interface of Contained, it has a description structure that is returned by the describe() operation which it inherits. The TypeDescription structure has a similar form to the other *idl-construct*Description structures. It serves for all interfaces derived from TypedefDef, because its type member can describe any CORBA type.

The Repository Interface. This interface is the outer shell of the containment hierarchy and it is where all the definitions for the base or primitive types are contained. It is also the starting point for browsing and allows users to find definitions using their repository IDs.

```
enum PrimitiveKind {
    pk_null, pk_void, pk_short, pk_long, pk_ushort, pk_ulong,
    pk_float, pk_double, pk_boolean, pk_char, pk_octet,
    pk_any, pk_TypeCode, pk_Principal, pk_string, pk_objref
};

interface Repository: Container {
    Contained lookup_id (in RepositoryId search_id);
    PrimitiveDef get_primitive (in PrimitiveKind kind);
};
```

The lookup_id() operation finds an object with a certain identifier in this repository. The get_primitive() operation returns a primitive definition object contained in this repository.

3.12.5   *The Multiply Derived Interfaces*

Figure 2.14 shows that ModuleDef and InterfaceDef are the only concrete interfaces in this specification that inherit directly from more than one abstract interface.

The ModuleDef Interface.

```
interface ModuleDef: Container, Contained {};

struct ModuleDescription {
    Identifier name;
```

```
        RepositoryId Id;
        RepositoryId defined_In;
        VersionSpec version;
    };
```

ModuleDef offers the operations from Container and Contained and a structure that allows them to be described in terms of name, ID, and version. This will be the value in the Any returned from Contained::describe() for modules.

The InterfaceDef Interface. The InterfaceDef interface inherits operations from all three of the second-level base interfaces.

```
    interface InterfaceDef: Container, Contained, IDLType {
        attribute InterfaceDefSeq base_interfaces;
        boolean Is_a (in RepositoryId interface_id);
```

The base_interfaces attribute allows us to find all the interfaces that this interface directly inherits. Is_a() returns TRUE if this interface has the identifier passed as an argument and FALSE otherwise.

```
    struct FullInterfaceDescription {
        Identifier name;
        RepositoryId Id;
        RepositoryId defined_in;
        VersionSpec version;
        OpDescriptionSeq operations;
        AttrDescriptionSeq attributes;
        RepositoryIdSeq base_interfaces;
        TypeCode type;
    };

    }; //InterfaceDef

    FullInterfaceDescription describe_interface();

    struct InterfaceDescription {
        Identifier name;
        RepositoryId Id;
        RepositoryId defined_in;
        VersionSpec version;
        RepositoryIdSeq base_interfaces;
    };
```

The describe_interface() operation returns a FullInterfaceDescription structure that contains all the information about an interface's contents in a number of sequences that contain other *idl-construct*Description structures. A FullInterfaceDescription contains all the information needed to construct a request to invoke an operation on an object of this interface type using the DII. See the DII section in Chapter 10 for an example of its use.

InterfaceDescription is the structure contained in the Any returned by the describe() operation inherited from Contained.

3.12.6 Interfaces Derived from TypedefDef

The TypedefDef abstract interface is derived from Contained and IDLType. TypedefDef adds a TypeCode attribute. All the interfaces derived from it are structured types that must be user defined.

StructDef.

```
struct StructMember {
  Identifier name;
  TypeCode type;
  IDLType type_def;
};

typedef sequence < StructMember > StructMemberSeq;

interface StructDef: TypedefDef {
  attribute StructMemberSeq members;
};
```

A StructDef describes its members by name and type, giving both a TypeCode and a reference to the object that describes that type.

UnionDef.

```
struct UnionMember {
    Identifier name;
  any label;
  TypeCode type;
  IDLType type_def;
};

typedef sequence < UnionMember > UnionMemberSeq;

interface UnionDef: TypedefDef {
  readonly attribute TypeCode discriminator_type;
  attribute IDLType discriminator_type_def;
  attribute UnionMemberSeq members;
};
```

A UnionDef describes its discriminator type with a TypeCode and by reference to the object describing that type with discriminator_type and discriminator_type_def, respectively. Its members are accessed in a similar manner to those of a structure, but contain a label value in addition to the name and type.

EnumDef.

```
typedef sequence < identifier > EnumMemberSeq;

interface EnumDef: TypedefDef {
   attribute EnumMemberSeq members;
};
```

The only information an enumerated type definition requires over that inherited from TypedefDef is the list of names used for its values.

AliasDef.

```
interface AliasDef: TypedefDef {
   attribute IDLType original_type_def;
};
```

Aliases are typedefs that simply provide a new name for an existing type. The AliasDef interface has an attribute that refers to the object that describes the original type.

3.12.7   Interfaces Derived from IDLType

These objects represent the primitives and system-defined types.

PrimitiveDef.

```
interface PrimitiveDef: IDLType {
   readonly attribute PrimitiveKind kind;
};
```

The kind attribute returns an enumerated value identifying the basic type that this object represents.

StringDef.

```
interface StringDef: IDLType {
   attribute unsigned long bound;
};
```

A bound value of zero means that the string is unbounded.

SequenceDef.

```
interface SequenceDef: IDLType {
   attribute unsigned long bound;
   readonly attribute TypeCode element_type;
   attribute IDLType element_type_def;
};
```

A bound of zero means that the sequence is unbounded. The other two attributes identify the type contained in the sequence by TypeCode and object reference.

ArrayDef.

```
interface ArrayDef: IDLType {
  attribute unsigned long length;
  readonly attribute TypeCode element_type;
  attribute IDLType element_type_def;
};
```

Multidimensional arrays are created by having another array as the element, described by element_type and identified by element_type_def.

3.12.8   Interfaces Derived Directly from Contained

ConstantDef.

```
interface ConstantDef: Contained {
  readonly attribute TypeCode type;
  attribute IDLType type_def;
  attribute any value;
};

struct ConstantDescription {
  Identifier name;
  RepositoryId id;
  RepositoryId defined_in;
  VersionSpec version;
  TypeCode type;
  any value;
};
```

A constant has a type described by type and referenced as another Interface Repository object in type_def. It also has a value. The ConstantDescription structure is returned as the value of the Any returned by the describe() operation inherited from Contained.

ExceptionDef.

```
interface ExceptionDef: Contained {
  readonly attribute TypeCode type;
  attribute StructMemberSeq members;
};

struct ExceptionDescription {
  Identifier name;
  RepositoryId id;
  RepositoryId defined_in;
  VersionSpec version;
  TypeCode type;
};
```

An exception, like a structure, has a list of members that return more specific information about the exception. The inherited describe() operation returns an ExceptionDescription structure in an Any.

AttributeDef.

```
enum AttributeMode {ATTR_NORMAL, ATTR_READONLY};

interface AttributeDef: Contained {
  readonly attribute TypeCode type;
  attribute IDLType type_def;
  attribute AttributeMode mode;
};

struct AttributeDescription {
  Identifier name;
  RepositoryId id;
  RepositoryId defined_in;
  VersionSpec version;
  TypeCode type;
  AttributeMode mode;
};
```

AttributeDef supplies information about an attribute's type, as well as a reference to the object in which that type is defined. The mode attribute indicates whether this is a read-only attribute or not. The inherited describe() operation returns an AttributeDescription structure in an Any.

OperationDef. Operations are perhaps the most complex entities that the Interface Repository describes. They contain parameters and return types and may also raise exceptions and carry context. Parameters are represented by structures, whereas definitions of exceptions are objects.

Here are the types required for the OperationDef interface and the OperationDescription structure:

```
enum OperationMode {OP_NORMAL, OP_ONEWAY};

enum ParameterMode {PARAM_IN, PARAM_OUT, PARAM_INOUT};

struct ParameterDescription {
  Identifier name;
  TypeCode type;
  IDLType type_def;
  ParameterMode mode;
};
typedef sequence < ParameterDescription > ParDescriptionSeq;

typedef Identifier ContextIdentifier;
typedef sequence < ContextIdentifier > ContextIdSeq;

typedef sequence < ExceptionDef > ExceptionDefSeq;
typedef sequence < ExceptionDescription > ExcDescriptionSeq;
```

This is the IDL for the interface which describes operations and the structure returned by the describe() operation inherited from Contained.

```
interface OperationDef: Contained {
    readonly attribute TypeCode result;
    attribute IDLType result_def;
    attribute ParDescriptionSeq params;
    attribute OperationMode mode;
    attribute ContextIdSeq contexts;
    attribute ExceptionDefSeq exceptions;
};

struct OperationDescription {
    Identifier name;
    RepositoryId id;
    RepositoryId defined_in;
    VersionSpec version;
    TypeCode result;
    OperationMode mode;
    ContextIdSeq contexts;
    ParDescriptionSeq parameters;
    ExcDescriptionSeq exceptions;
};
```

The params attribute of OperationDef is a list of ParameterDescription structures. The contexts attribute gives a list of scoped names of context objects that apply to the operation.

3.12.9 RepositoryIds

There are three forms of repository identifiers:

IDL format. The string starts with "IDL:" and then uses the scoped name followed by a major and minor version number to globally identify an object. Objects with the same major number are assumed to be derived from one another. The identifier with the larger minor number is assumed to be a subtype of the one with the smaller minor number.

DCE UUID format. The string starts with "DCE:" and is followed by a UUID, a colon, and then a minor version number.

LOCAL format. The string starts with "LOCAL:" and is followed by an arbitrary string. This format is for use with a single repository that does not communicate with ORBs outside its domain.

OMG IDL to C++ Mapping

This chapter provides a detailed explanation of the mapping from OMG IDL to C++ as defined by the corresponding OMG standard (OMG document PTC-97-02-25). The mapping begins with modules and the basic IDL types, then we continue with the structured types. Finally, we explain the mappings for operations and attributes, interfaces and their inheritance relationships, and modules.

The mapping, as defined by the OMG standard, assumes that the C++ environment supports the features described in *The C++ Annotated Reference Manual* by Ellis and Stroustrup, including the namespace construct and exception handling.

1 *Mapping Modules*

An IDL module is mapped to a C++ namespace. Since, at the time of this writing, few C++ compilers currently support namespaces, the specification also allows a module to be mapped to a C++ class:

```
// IDL
  module ABC { . . . };
```

is mapped to

```
// C++ - mapping to a namespace
namespace ABC{. . .};
```

or

```
  // C++ - mapping to a class
class ABC{. . .};
```

Nested module definitions are mapped to nested namespaces or class definitions.

2 Mapping Basic Datatypes

The mapping of IDL basic types to C++ is straightforward and mapped to a CORBA typedef. Because of hardware implementations, some of the mappings are defined differently depending on support for 32-bit and 64-bit implementations. These are defined in Table 3.1 as "platform dependent."

A CORBA type layer masks the different representations on different platforms. For example, a CORBA::Long would be represented as a 32-bit integer whether on a 32-bit machine or a 64-bit machine. For the sake of portability, a programmer would benefit from using the CORBA types.

The boolean type is defined to take only the values 0 or 1. Since many C++ environments provide their own preprocessor macro definitions of TRUE and FALSE, the OMG mapping does not require that an implementation provide

TABLE 3.1 Primitive Type Mappings

OMG IDL	C++
short	CORBA::Short
long	CORBA::Long (platform dependent)
long long	CORBA::LongLong (platform dependent)
unsigned short	CORBA::Ushort
unsigned long	CORBA::Ulong
unsigned long long	CORBA::ULongLong (platform dependent)
float	CORBA::Float
double	CORBA::Double
long double	CORBA::LongDouble (platform dependent)
char	CORBA::Char
wchar	CORBA::Wchar (platform dependent)
wstring	CORBA::Wstring (platform dependent)
boolean	CORBA::Boolean
octet	CORBA::Octet

this mapping, and instead recommends that compliant applications use the values 0 or 1 directly to avoid compilation problems for CORBA applications.

3   *Mapping Strings*

IDL string types can be bounded or unbounded. Both are mapped to the C++ type char* which is null terminated. In addition to the char* mapping, CORBA defines the class String_var (pronounced "string underscore var") that contains a pointer to the memory of the allocated string. This mapping provides simplified memory management for strings. Memory allocated to the string is automatically freed when the String_var object goes out of scope or is destroyed. When a String_var is created from a char* by construction or assignment, the char* is consumed in this process and can no longer be accessed by the caller. Alternatively, assignment from a const char* or another String_var creates a copy of the char* for the caller. The following code illustrates how the String_var class is implemented. It has constructors that allow creation of a String_var object from a char*, and overloaded operators to allow operations such as comparison of String_var types, assignment from char*, type casting from a char* to a String_var, and the ability to access array elements in an intuitive manner.

The String_var class is written as:

```
//C++
    class CORBA {
        class String_var {
        protected:
        char*_p;
        ...
        public:
        String_var();
        String_var(char *p);
        ~String_var();
        String_var& operator=(const char *p);
        String_var& operator=(char *p);
        String_var& operator=(const String_var& s);
        operator const char *() const;
        operator char *();
        char &operator[] (CORBA::ULong index);
        char operator[] (CORBA::ULong index) const;
        friend ostream& operator<<(ostream&, const,
            String_var&);
        inline friend Boolean operator==(const String_var&
            s1,const String_var& s2);
        ...
        };
    ...
    };
```

The following functions are provided for dynamic allocation and deallocation of strings. The `String_var` expects that the string it points to was allocated using these functions.

```C++
//C++
namespace CORBA
{
    ...
    static char *string_alloc(CORBA::ULong len);
    static char *string_dup(const char *str);
    static void string_free(char *data);
    ...
};
```

As declared in the preceding code, the `string_alloc()` operation will return a null pointer if it cannot perform the dynamic allocation. Otherwise it allocates space for the string of length `len` plus a trailing null character. The `string_dup()` operation allocates enough space for a copy of its string argument, copies the contents, and returns a pointer to the allocated memory. If the operation fails, a null pointer is returned. The `string_free()` operation deallocates the memory associated with strings created by these operations.

The examples below illustrate the proper usage of the `String_var` class. The following is correct and `string_ex` is consumed:

```
string_ex = CORBA::string_alloc(10);
string_ex = "char string";
CORBA::String_var String_var1 = string_ex;
```

The next example is in error because the `char*` should point to data allocated with `CORBA::string_alloc()`, so it cannot be consumed:

```
String_var1 = "static string example";
```

The following is correct since a `const char*` is copied, not consumed:

```
String_var1 = (const char *)"another string";
```

Strings can also be constructed using a `CORBA::String_var` constructor:

```
String_var1 = CORBA::String_var(string_ex);
```

The comparison operators let you compare `String_var` to `char*`:

```
if (String_var1 == string_ex)
    cout << "Strings are different "<< endl;
else
    cout <<"Strings are the same" << endl;
```

For wide string types, **CORBA** defines the class `WString_var` which provides similar operations for bounded and unbounded wide strings.

```
class CORBA {
    class WString_var
    {
        public:
        WString_var();
        WString_var(WChar *p);
        WString_var(const WString_var &w);
        ~WString_var();
        WString_var &operator=(WChar *p);
        WString_var &operator=(const WString_var &w);
        operator WChar*();
        operator const WChar*() const;
        WChar &operator[] (ULong index);
        WChar operator[] (ULong index) const;
        ...
    };
    ...
};
```

Likewise dynamic allocation and deallocation of wide strings must be performed via the following functions:

```
// C++

WChar *wstring_alloc(ULong len);
void wstring_free(WChar*);
```

4 Mapping Constants

IDL constants are mapped directly to a C++ constant declaration. The following is a simple IDL declaration and a sample of the generated C++ code. The C++ code shown here is only a snippet of the actual compiler output. For this example only the relevant parts are shown.

```
//IDL
const long Long_Ex=1966;
interface Interface_Ex
{
  const string String_Ex="Your Name Here";
  const boolean Boolean_Ex=TRUE;
};
```

```
//C++
const CORBA::Long Long_Ex = 1966;

class Interface_Ex : public virtual CORBA_Object {
...
public:
 static const char* String_Ex; // "Your Name Here"
 static const CORBA::Boolean Boolean_Ex; // 1
```

```
...
};
```

Under certain conditions an IDL to C++ compiler will generate the value of the constant rather than the constant's name in the resultant C++ code. If a constant is declared and then that constant is used as part of a declaration of an array or other constructed type, the compiler will replace the use of the constant name with the actual value of the constant. Below we show an example:

```
//IDL
interface Interface_Ex
{
  const long Array_Index=10;
  typedef long Long_Array[Array_Index];
};
```

will produce

```
//C++
class Interface_Ex {
public:
 static const CORBA::Long Array_Index; // 10
 typedef CORBA::Long Long_Array[10];

};
```

5 Mapping Enumerations

Enumerations defined in IDL are mapped directly to C++ enumerations, for example,

```
//IDL
enum Enum_Ex{fire, earth, water, air};
```

maps to

```
//C++
enum Enum_Ex {fire, earth, water, air};
```

6 Mapping for Structured Types

The IDL structured types are `struct`, `union`, `sequence`, and `array`. All but the array are mapped to a C++ struct or class with a default constructor, a copy constructor, an assignment operator, and a destructor. The array is mapped to a C++ array.

The default constructor for structured types initializes object reference members to nil and initializes string members to null. All other members are initialized with default constructors. The copy constructor performs a deep copy, duplicating all object reference members and allocating the heap for string members. The assignment operator releases all object reference members, frees the string members, and performs a deep copy. The destructor releases all object references and frees all string members. The mapping for each structured type varies slightly depending on whether it is fixed length or variable length. The following types are variable length:

◆ An unbounded or bounded sequence
◆ A struct or union with a variable length member
◆ An array with a variable length element type

The variation in mapping fixed and variable length types allows more flexibility in allocation of out parameters and return values of an operation. The mapping of a variable length type as an out parameter or return value is a pointer to the associated class or array. For managing this pointer, the IDL/C++ specification defines a mapping to an additional class that automatically deletes the pointer when an instance is destroyed or reassigned. This type is named by adding the suffix _var (pronounced "underscore var") to the original type name. It behaves similarly to the original, only the members are accessed indirectly. We have already seen an example for such a mapping for the simplest variable type, IDL string. For reasons of consistency the fixed length struct is also mapped to an _var type. The form of the _var type is

```
// C++
class T_var
{
    public:
    T_var();
    T_var(T *);
    T_var(const T_var &);
    ~T_var();
    T_var &operator=(T *);
    T_var &operator=(const T_var &);
    T *operator-> const ();
// other conversion operators to support
// parameter passing will be covered later
};
```

The default constructor creates a T_var containing a null T*. Before it can be converted to a T*, or its operator -> can be used, it must be assigned a valid T* value or another T_var. The copy constructor performs a deep copy of the T_var parameter, calling _duplicate() on all object reference members. The normal assignment operator deep copies the data pointed to by T_var.

The `T*` assignment operator deallocates any old storage pointed to by the `T_var` before assuming ownership of the `T*` parameter.

The `T*` constructor creates a `T_var` that will delete the storage pointed to by the `T*` when the `T_var` is destroyed. `T_var` types do not work with a `const T*` as a parameter. Instead, the copy constructor for `T` can be used for explicit copying of `const T*` objects into `T_var` types:

```
//C++
const T *t = ...;
T_var tv = new T(*t);
```

When the `T_var` is destroyed, or assigned a new value, the storage is also destroyed.

6.1   Mapping for Struct Types

IDL struct types are mapped to C++ `structs` and also to an `_var` class. The fixed length member types are mapped to their corresponding C++ types with exception to strings and object references which have mappings to corresponding `_var` types. In order to allow for simple field access and aggregate initialization, C++ structs cannot have user-defined constructors, destructors, or assignment operators.

Assignment of strings or object reference members to corresponding `_var` types is performed by copying the data, whereas assignment of these members to pointers does not result in copying the data, but rather the pointer to the data. The exception to this is the `const char*`, where, when assigned to a member, the storage is copied. Next is an example of an IDL-defined fixed struct and its mapping to C++.

```
//IDL
struct Struct_Ex{
   long param1;
   float param2;
};
```

```
//C++
struct Struct_Ex {
 CORBA::Long param1;
 CORBA::Float param2;
};
```

Following is an example of how the members are accessed and the memory management that occurs when using variable length structs. Note that the string member and the interface member both map to an `_var` class.

```
//IDL
interface Interface_Ex;
```

```
      struct Struct_Ex{
        string name;
        Interface_Ex Interface_Member;
      };
```

```
//C++
struct Struct_Ex {
 CORBA::String_var name;
 Interface_Ex_var Interface_Member;
};
...
class Struct_Ex_var {
 ...
};
```

The following example uses the above defined structures in different ways to illustrate the memory management that occurs. Note the different ways of accessing the struct members depending on whether the struct or the struct_var is used. We illustrate that assignment from a const char* results in old memory being freed and data copied. Similarly assignment between a string or object reference member and the corresponding _var types results in data being freed from the _var and the new data being deep copied. We show that when assignments are made to the struct member name from a pointer, the memory will be freed, but data will not be copied if the pointer is not declared as const.

```
//C++

Struct_Ex struct1;
Struct_Ex_var struct2 = new Struct_Ex;
char *non_const;
String_var string_var;
const char *const_a;
const char *const_b = ìstring 1î;
const char *const_c = ìstring 2î;
```

Because const_b and const_c are const data, the storage in the field name in the structure is freed and the new value is copied:

```
struct1.name = const_b;
struct2->name = const_c;
```

When dealing with pointers, the pointers are assigned and no storage is freed/copied:

```
non_const = struct1.name;
const_a = struct2->name;
```

In the first line below, the storage area of struct1.name is freed but the data is not copied. A pointer is just assigned since the assigned value is a non_const char*. In the second line the old storage is also freed. The assigned value is copied as it is a const char*.

```
struct1.name = non_const;
struct1.name = const_b;
```

In the following lines, the storage is freed and copied. In the first line, a member is assigned to another member. In the other two lines we make assignments to and from a String_var.

```
struct2->name = struct1.name;
struct1.name = string_var;
string_var = struct2->name;
```

Direct assignments to the _ptr member of a struct do not free storage and do not copy data. Such assignments should be avoided.

6.2   Mapping Union Types

IDL unions map to a C++ class. Accessor functions are defined for setting and retrieving the value of the data members. When accessor functions are used to initialize the data, a deep copy is performed and any memory previously associated with that member is freed.

Accessor functions for array union members return a pointer to the array slice. The slice is defined as the original array, but less the first dimension. Slices are covered in section 6.4 on arrays. A discriminant type, having the name _d, is set by the application or may be automatically set by the ORB when any of the data members are set.

```
//IDL
interface Ex_Obj;
struct Struct_Ex{
    long Long_member;
};
typedef string StringArray[10]
union Union_Ex switch (long){
    case 1: long x;
    case 2: string y;
    case 3: Struct_Ex z;
    case 4: StringArray list99;
    default: Ex_Obj obj;
};
```

The above defined IDL union, Union_Ex, is mapped to the C++ class Union_Ex below.

```
//C++
class Union_Ex {
```

```
private:
 CORBA::Long _disc;
 CORBA::Long __x;
 CORBA::String_var __y;
 Struct_Ex __z;
 StringArray __list99;
 Ex_Obj_var __obj;
...

public:
 Union_Ex() : _disc((CORBA::Long)0) {}
 ~Union_Ex() {}
 Union_Ex(const Union_Ex& _obj);
 Union_Ex& operator=(const Union_Ex& _obj);

 void _d(CORBA::Long _val) { _disc = _val; }
 CORBA::Long _d() const { return _disc; }

 void _default() { _disc = ...; }//orb implementation dependent

 void x(CORBA::Long _val) {
  __x = _val;
  _disc = 1;
 }

 CORBA::Long x() const { return __x; }
 void y(char * _val) {
  __y = _val;
  _disc = 2;
 }

 void y(const char * _val) {
  __y = _val;
  _disc = 2;
 }

 const char *y() const { return __y; }

 void z(Struct_Ex _val) {
  __z = _val;
  _disc = 3;
 }

 const Struct_Ex& z() const { return __z; }

 Struct_Ex& z() { return __z; }

 void obj(Ex_Obj_ptr _val) {
  __obj = _val;
  _disc = 4;//implementation dependant
 }

 void list99(StringArray_slice *_val) {
  StringArray_forany _t_list99(__list99);
  StringArray_forany __t_list99((StringArray_slice *)_val);
```

```
     _t_list99 = __t_list99;
     _disc = 5;
   }

   const StringArray& list99() const { return __list99; }

   StringArray& list99() { return __list99; }
   Ex_Obj_ptr obj() const { return __obj; }
   ...
};
```

The generated code above shows the union constructors and the accessor functions for the union members. The default union constructor does not initialize any of the union members, and the discriminator must be set before accessing a member of the union. The copy constructor and the assignment operator both perform deep copies of their parameters and the assignment operator releases the old storage where necessary. If a default value is not explicitly defined in the union, then the compiler sets the discriminant to a legal value. The destructor releases the storage assigned to the union. Unlike accessors for simple datatypes and strings, accessors for struct, union, sequence, and any will reference to a non-const object for read-write access. Also, the array slice returned from an array accessor allows read-write access via subscript referencing to the array. The following illustrates usage of accessor functions and the discriminator _d.

```
//C++
Struct_Ex struct_A = {10};
Union_Ex union_A ;

union_A.z(struct_A) ; //member z is selected
union_A._d(3); //member z is selected

union_A._d(1);// member x is selected
union_A.x(99);//modifies member x

cout << union_A.z(); // Error ! Member x is currently selected
```

6.3   Mapping Sequence Types

An IDL sequence is a one-dimensional array with two characteristics: a maximum size and a length. It is mapped to a class for the sequence as well as a sequence _var class. The maximum size of a bounded sequence is explicitly defined in the IDL specification and cannot be changed by the application. Doing so will produce undefined behavior. On the other hand, the maximum length of an unbounded sequence can be specified as a parameter to the constructor to control initial buffer allocation and can be manipulated by the programmer. The current length of either sequence is modifiable by the application.

Memory management of the data vector of the sequence is determined by the release flag. When TRUE, the flag indicates that the sequence owns the storage of the data array. The contents of the vector will have to be allocated with the sequence allocbuf() function and deallocated using the sequence freebuf() function. The default constructor of a bounded sequence automatically sets the release flag to TRUE.

Set to FALSE, the caller owns the storage of the data vector and is responsible for freeing each of the elements of the data array, and the contents buffer, whenever assignment occurs or the sequence goes out of scope. When FALSE, users should avoid accessing the elements of the data array with the [] operator because memory management errors may occur.

In the following example we will examine the results of compiling IDL that defines a bounded and an unbounded sequence. Both are sequences of type Data_Type.

```
// IDL
typedef sequence<Data_Type> UnB_Seq; // unbounded sequence
typedef sequence<Data_Type, 2> B_Seq; // bounded sequence
```

```
// C++
class UnB_Seq // unbounded sequence
{
public:
static CORBA::Long *allocbuf(ULong _nelems);
static void freebuf(Long *_data);
UnB_Seq();
UnB_Seq(ULong max);
UnB_Seq(ULong max, ULong length,Data_Type* data,
Boolean release = FALSE);
UnB_Seq(const UnB_Seq&);
~ UnB_Seq();
UnB_Seq &operator=(const UnB_Seq&);
ULong maximum() const;
void length(ULong);
ULong length() const;
Data_Type &operator[] (ULong index);
const Data_Type &operator[] (ULong index) const;
static void _release(UnB_Seq *_ptr)
...
};

class B_Seq // bounded sequence
{
public:
static CORBA::Long *allocbuf(ULong _nelems);
static void freebuf(Long *_data);
B_Seq();
B_Seq(ULong length, Data_Type *data, Boolean release = FALSE);
B_Seq(const B_Seq&);
```

```
~B_Seq();
B_Seq &operator=(const B_Seq&);
ULong maximum() const;
void length(ULong);
ULong length() const;
Data_Type &operator[] (ULong index);
const Data_Type &operator[] (ULong index) const;
static void _release(B_Seq *_ptr)
...
};
```

Table 3.2 describes the operations generated for sequence types:

An example of memory management and the release constructor parameter will help illustrate the functionality provided by the ORB with relation to the release flag. Below is a declaration of an unbounded sequence that, by default, has the release flag set to FALSE. Also declared is an unbounded sequence which passes TRUE in the constructor, setting the release flag and thereby bestowing ownership of the data array upon the sequence. When this sequence goes out of scope it will call string_free() for each of its elements and freebuf() on the buffer passed into the constructor.

```
//IDL
typedef sequence<string, 3> String_seq;
```

TABLE 3.2 Sequence Operations

Function	*Description*
allocbuf(ULong _nelems)	Allocates memory for the sequence to be passed to the constructor and initializes each member.
Freebuf(Long *_data)	Free storage allocated for the data buffer.
UnB_Seq(ULong max)	Constructor for the unbounded sequence.
UnB_Seq(ULong max, ULong length, Data_Type* data, Boolean release =	Release flag !=0. ORB manages memory of *data when data buffer is increased. Differs from bounded sequence constructor in that maximumlength is specified.
FALSE); UnB_Seq(const UnB_Seq&)	Copy constructor. Copies data storage of parameter.
~ UnB_Seq()	If release flag !=0, destructor frees data storage.
UnB_Seq &operator=(const UnB_Seq&)	Deep copy.
ULong maximum()	Returns the size of the sequence.
ULong length()	Two length functions. One sets, one gets.
&operator[] (ULong index)	Two index operations. One sets, one only gets.
_release(UnB_Seq *_ptr)	Releases the sequence. If the release flag of the sequence is non-zero, then the ORB releases each element of the sequence before releasing the contents buffer.

```
//C++ app
char *static_array[] = {ìAî, ìBî, ìCî};
char **dynamic_array = StringSeq::allocbuf(3);

String_Seq static_seq(3, static_array); //Release flag
//defaults to FALSE
String_Seq dynamic_seq(3, dynamic_array, 1); //Flag set to TRUE

static_seq[1] = ìAî; //old memory not freed, no copying of data
char *str = string_dup(ìDî);
dynamic_seq[1] = str; //old memory freed, no copying
```

6.4   Mapping for Arrays

IDL arrays are mapped to C++ arrays. IDL arrays can be statically initialized. If the array element is a string or an object reference it will be mapped,
like a structure member, to its _var type. This mapping to _var types lets the
ORB manage the data storage of the elements so that an assignment of an
element will automatically release the storage of the previous value. The
_var type also provides an overloaded [] operator for intuitive access to
array elements.

The mapping also provides a type definition for an array slice, specified by the original array name followed by the suffix _slice. An array slice
is an array that has all the dimensions of the original array specified, except
the first. Slices are provided as a convenience for passing multidimensional
out and return arrays and will be discussed more in the section on parameter passing.

```
//IDL
interface Interface_Ex{
   ...
};
typedef long Long_Array[10];
typedef string String_Array[10][20][30];
typedef Interface_Ex Interface_Array[10];
```

The following is a snippet of what is generated by the compiler:

```
//C++
...
typedef CORBA::Long Long_Array[10];

typedef CORBA::Long Long_Array_slice;
class Long_Array_var {
   ...
};
```

```
typedef CORBA::String_var String_Array[10] [20] [30];
typedef CORBA::String_var String_Array_slice[20] [30];
class String_Array_var {
      ...
};

typedef Interface_Ex_var Interface_Array[10];
typedef Interface_Ex_var Interface_Array_slice;
class Interface_Array_var {
      ...
};
   ...
```

In addition to the above mappings, an IDL compiler is required to generate a special mapping for each array to accommodate the type-safe `any`. The name of this C++ type is the name of the array followed by the suffix `_forany`. `Array_forany` types allow access to underlying array elements, similar to the `array_var` types. The reason for the special array type is that when the `array_var` type is destroyed, it systematically deletes the underlying storage, but because an `any` type retains ownership of its storage, the `array_forany` does not delete the storage of the underlying array upon its own destruction. This ownership is retained by the `any` type, and memory management will be discussed shortly when we undertake the discussion of the `any` type. The `_forany` classes generated by the compiler for the previous example is presented next.

```
    //C++

class Long_Array_forany {
...
public:
 Long_Array_forany(Long_Array_slice *slice) :_ptr(slice) {}
...
};

class String_Array_forany {
...
public:
 String_Array_forany(String_Array_slice *slice) :_ptr(slice) {}
...
};

class Interface_Array_forany {
...
public:
 Interface_Array_forany(Interface_Array_slice *slice)
:_ptr(slice) {}
...
};
```

Finally, for dynamic allocation and deallocation of arrays, special functions are provided at the same scope of each array type. These functions allow the ORB to implement its memory management of the array.

```
//C++
Long_Array_slice *Long_Array_alloc() {
 return new CORBA::Long[10];
}

Long_Array_free(Long_Array_slice *_data) {
 if (_data) delete[] _data;
}

String_Array_slice *String_Array_alloc() {
 return new CORBA::String_var[10] [20] [30];
}

String_Array_free(String_Array_slice *_data) {
 if (_data) delete[] _data;
}

Interface_Array_slice *Interface_Array_alloc() {
 return new Interface_Ex_var[10];
}

Interface_Array_free(Interface_Array_slice *_data) {

 if (_data) delete[] _data;

}
```

6.5   Mapping Typedefs

A typedef declares an alias for a type. Since the IDL to C++ mapping may create several C++ types for an IDL type, the compiler will create corresponding aliases for each type. For example, an IDL array will map to an array_slice, so a typedef for an array will also map to the corresponding array_slice.

```
//IDL
typedef long Long_Ex;
interface Interface_Ex;
typedef Interface_Ex Interface_Ex2;
typedef sequence<long>Sequence_Ex;
typedef Sequence_Ex Sequence_Ex2;
typedef long Long_Array_Ex[10];
typedef Long_Array_Ex Long_Array_Ex2;
```

```
//C++
typedef CORBA::Long Long_Ex;
```

```
class Interface_Ex_var {
...
};
typedef Interface_Ex Interface_Ex2;
typedef Interface_Ex_var Interface_Ex2_var;

class Sequence_Ex_var {
...
};
typedef Sequence_Ex Sequence_Ex2;
typedef Sequence_Ex_var Sequence_Ex2_var;

class Long_Array_Ex_var{
...
};
typedef CORBA::Long Long_Array_Ex[10];

typedef Long_Array_Ex Long_Array_Ex2;
typedef Long_Array_Ex_var Long_Array_Ex2_var;
```

6.6   Mapping the Type Any

The any type is a self-describing type, which can hold values of an arbitrary IDL type (including an any type). The IDL to C++ mapping of the type any fulfills two requirements:

   ♦ Handling C++ types in a type-safe manner
   ♦ Handling values whose type is unknown prior to implementation compile time

In other words, it must handle the conversions required to insert into and extract from an any, and it must accommodate requests or responses containing an any that holds data of a type that was unknown to the caller at compile time.

Handling C++ types in a type-safe manner requires the C++ mapping to provide overloaded functions for each distinct IDL type. For those IDL types that do not produce distinct C++ types (boolean, octet, char, and wchar) separate functions are provided to distinguish them from one another.

6.6.1   Insertion into an Any

Insertion into an any is accomplished with the overloaded "left-shift-assign" operator. For smaller datatypes, including bounded strings (passed as char*), enumerations, and object references (passed as _ptr), the operator copies the data, and uses the following form:

```
//C++
void operator<<=(Any&, Data_Type); // copies the data
```

These last two functions are created to handle more complex types:

```
void operator<<=(Any&, const Data_Type &);//copies the data
void operator<<=(Any&, Data_Type*); //non-copying form
```

Note that with the noncopying form of the operator, the inserted data is consumed and cannot be accessed by an application once it has been inserted into the any. For insertion of IDL types without a distinct C++ mapping, such as octet, char, wchar, and bounded string; special "helper types" are provided and will be covered shortly in a section devoted to these types.

The following function signature is generated for the IDL defined below:

```
//IDL

struct Struct_Ex{
  long param1;
  float param2;
};
```

```
//C++
void operator<<=(CORBA::Any& _a, const Struct_Ex& _val)
```

so that an application could insert values into an any in the following manner:

```
//C++
...
struct_1 = {10, 20.0};
long long_val = 30;
char *string_val = "Forty";
Any a,b,c;

a <<= struct_1;
b <<= long_val
c <<= string_val;
```

6.6.2 *Inserting an Array into an Any*

Insertion of arrays into an any is accomplished with the Array_forany types generated for each array defined in IDL. A copying insertion is the default. Depending upon the implementation provided by the ORB vendor, the user may be able to set a nocopy flag in the Array_forany constructor. With the nocopy flag set to TRUE, the inserted value will be consumed by the any.

```
//IDL
typedef long Long_Array[10][20];
```

```
//C++
typedef CORBA::Long Long_Array[10] [20];
class Long_Array_forany {
...
};
...
operator<<=(CORBA::Any& _a, const Long_Array_forany& _val)...;
```

The above generated types can be used in an application as shown below:

```
//C++ app
Long_Array array1;

//...initialize array...

Any any_data;
any_data <<= Long_Array_forany(array1);
```

6.6.3 *Retrieving from an Any*

To retrieve a value from an any, the mapping overloads the "right-shift-assign" operator for each IDL type. The function returns a boolean, indicating whether or not the type being extracted is indeed the same type to which it is being assigned. If successful, the value will be copied, or its pointer assigned (depending on the type). For primitive types, the following function signature will suffice:

```
//C++
Boolean operator>>=(const CORBA::Any&, Data_Type&);
```

for nonprimitive datatypes:

```
//C++
CORBA::Boolean operator>>=(const CORBA::Any&, Data_Type*&);
```

and for arrays:

```
//C++
CORBA::Boolean operator>>=(const CORBA::Any& , _forany& )
```

The following illustrates the use of the extraction operator for the various types:

```
// C++
Any any_value;
// ... any_value is assigned a value ...

if (any_value >>= Long_value) {
    // ... use the value ...
```

```
else if (any_value >>= struct_ptr) {
    // ... use the value ...

else if (any_value >>= Array_forany_ref) {
    // ... use the value ...
```

6.6.4 *Inserting boolean, octet, char, wchar, and bounded string*

Helper types are provided to distinguish these datatypes because as mentioned previously in the basic datatypes section, the IDL to C++ mapping does not require them to map to distinct C++ types. A means of distinguishing them from each other is necessary so that they can be inserted and extracted from the type any. These are functions which, when passed a variable of the specific type, are inserted to a type any. Also included, of course, are functions for extracting the specified type from the any.

```
//C++
    from_boolean {
        from_boolean(CORBA::Boolean b) : val(b) {}
        CORBA::Boolean val;
    };

    from_octet {
        from_octet (CORBA::Octet b) : val (b) {}
        CORBA::Octet val;
    };

    from_char {
        from_char(CORBA::Char b) : val(b) {}
        CORBA::Char val;
    };

    from_string {
        from_string(char *s, CORBA::ULong b,
            CORBA::Boolean no_copy=0)
            : val(s), bound(b), nocopy(no_copy) {}
        char *val;
        CORBA::ULong bound;
        CORBA::Boolean nocopy;
    };

    from_wchar {
        from_wchar(CORBA::WChar b) : val(b) {}
        CORBA::WChar val;
    };

    from_wstring {
        from_wstring(CORBA::WChar *s, CORBA::ULong b,
                CORBA::Boolean no_copy=0)
            : val(s), bound(b), nocopy(no_copy) {}
```

```
            CORBA::WChar *val;
            CORBA::ULong bound;
            CORBA::Boolean nocopy;
    };

    void operator<<=(from_boolean);
    void operator<<=(from_octet);
    void operator<<=(from_char);
    void operator<<=(from_string);
    void operator<<=(from_wchar);
    void operator<<=(from_wstring);

    to_boolean {
        to_boolean(CORBA::Boolean& b) : ref(b) {}
        CORBA::Boolean& ref;
    };

    to_octet {
        to_octet(CORBA::Octet& b) : ref(b) {}
        CORBA::Octet& ref;
    };

    to_char {
        to_char(CORBA::Char& b) : ref(b) {}
        CORBA::Char& ref;
    };

    to_object {
        to_object(CORBA::Object_ptr &obj) : ref(obj) {}
        CORBA::Object_ptr &ref;
    };

    to_string {
        to_string(char *&s, CORBA::ULong b)
            : val(s), bound(b) {}
        char *&val;
        CORBA::ULong bound;
    };

    to_wchar {
        to_wchar(CORBA::WChar& b) : ref(b) {}
        CORBA::WChar& ref;
    };

    to_wstring {
        to_wstring(CORBA::WChar *&s, CORBA::ULong b)
            : val(s), bound(b) {}
        CORBA::WChar *&val;
        CORBA::ULong bound;
    };
```

```
CORBA::Boolean operator>>=(to_boolean) const;
CORBA::Boolean operator>>=(to_char) const;
CORBA::Boolean operator>>=(to_octet) const;
CORBA::Boolean operator>>=(to_object) const;
CORBA::Boolean operator>>=(to_string) const;
CORBA::Boolean operator>>=(to_wchar) const;
CORBA::Boolean operator>>=(to_wstring) const;
```

These operators are defined in the vendor's any class interface. Insertions would be similar to the following, depending on the vendor's Any_Class name:

```
//C++
any_value <<=Any_Class::from_Boolean(boolean_val);

any_value<<=Any_Class::from_Octet(octet_val);

any_value<<=Any_Class::from_string(char_ptr_val,str_len,1);
//nocopy flag set to FALSE, and the any consumes the string
//and bound value > 0 indicates a bounded string

if (any_value>>=Any_Class::to_string(char_ptr_val,str_len)){
 //then any contained a string of length 8
};
```

6.6.5 *The Any Class*

The default constructor creates an any with its TypeCode set to type tk_null, which means that the type of the value which the any can contain is undefined. The copy constructor creates a deep copy of the any passed as a parameter. The final constructor duplicates the pseudo-object reference and assumes ownership of the storage of the value parameter if the release flag is set to TRUE. Otherwise, if the flag is set to FALSE the caller owns the storage.

```
//C++
CORBA_Any();
CORBA_Any(const CORBA_Any&);
CORBA_Any(CORBA_TypeCode_ptr tc, void *value,
          CORBA::Boolean release=0);
...
```

Also defined is an Any_var class similar to the _var class encountered earlier, which is useful for the convenience of the memory management provided by the ORB.

```
//C++
{
Any_var();
Any_var(CORBA_Any *a);
Any_var(const Any_var &a);
~Any_var();
```

```
Any_var &operator=(CORBA_Any *a);
Any_var &operator=(const Any_var &a);

CORBA_Any *operator->();

};
```

The any class is a useful construct for handling values of generic types that may be unknown at compile time. Creating an any is as simple as declaring a standard datatype, and may also be constructed by duplicating another any as seen in the any and any_var constructors. Following is a simple example of creating an any:

```
//C++
Struct_Ex struct_1 = {10, 20.0};
Struct_Ex * struct_2

//create an any and shuffle structure into it
any_struct = new CORBA::Any();
*any_struct <<= struct_1;

// Now to extract the struct from the any.
if ( *any_struct >>= struct_2) {
...//use the value
}
```

To this point we have covered all the basic datatypes, constructed types, and types that handle all these, even if they are undetermined at implementation time. The last type we have to cover is the exception type.

7 Mapping for the Exception Types

The IDL to C++ mapping of exceptions is similar to that of variable length structs in that each exception member must self-manage its storage. An IDL exception mapping derives from the UserException class, which in turn derives from the base Exception class. Following is an example of a user-defined exception:

```
//IDL
exception SomethingWrong{
        string reason;
        long id;
};
```

```
//C++
class SomethingWrong : public CORBA_UserException {
public:
```

```
static const CORBA_Exception::Description _description;
CORBA::String_var reason;
CORBA::Long id;

SomethingWrong() {}
SomethingWrong(
  const char * _reason,
  CORBA::Long _id) {
 reason = _reason;
 id = _id;
}
...
```

The default constructor creates the object, leaving the fields to be filled in. The second constructor initializes the object with the parameter values.

The standard exceptions are derived from the SystemException class, which, like the UserException class, also derives from the base Exception class. An exception is caught in a try block, thrown as a value, and caught as a reference to the Exception type. UserException and SystemException, derived from the base Exception class, narrow the scope of the exception.

```
// C++
try {
...
} catch (const UserException &ue) {
...
} catch (const SystemException &se) {
...
```

All CORBA system exceptions include a completion_status code which will be one of the following three values: COMPLETED_YES, COMPLETED_NO, COMPLETED_MAYBE. Table 3.3 is a list of CORBA system exceptions:

8 *Mapping Operations and Attributes*

IDL-defined operations and attributes are mapped to C++ functions. IDL operations map to C++ functions of the same name. Attributes map to a pair of functions of the same name, one to set the value and one to get the value. By default, all attributes are read-write, but if the attribute has been defined as read-only, then only the "set" function is available. IDL allows specification of operations that have no return value. A return type must not be specified for oneway operations. The following example illustrates the mapping of the IDL for attributes and functions:

```
//IDL
interface A
```

TABLE 3.3 Standard Exception Types

Exception	Explanation
BAD_PARAM	An invalid parameter was passed
NO_MEMORY	Dynamic mem allocation failure
IMP_LIMIT	Violated implementation limit
COMM_FAILURE	Communication failure
INV_OBJREF	Invalid object reference
NO_PERMISSION	No permission for attempted operation
INTERNAL	ORB internal error
MARSHAL	Error marshalling parameter result
INITIALIZE	ORB initialization failure
NO_IMPLEMENT	Operation implementation unavailable
BAD_TYPECODE	Bad typecode
BAD_OPERATION	Invalid operation
NO_RESOURCES	Insufficient resources for request
NO_RESPONSE	Response to request not yet available
PERSIST_STORE	Persistent storage failure
BAD_INV_ORDER	Routine invocations out of order
TRANSIENT	Transient failure, reissue request
FREE_MEM	Cannot free memory
INV_IDENT	Invalid identifier syntax
INV_FLAG	Invalid flag was specified
INTF_REPOS	Error accessing interface repository
BAD_CONTEXT	Error processing context object
OBJ_ADAPTER	Failure detected by object adapter
DATA_CONVERSION	Data conversion error
OBJECT_NOT_EXIST	Nonexistent object, delete reference
TRANSACTION_REQUIRED	Transaction required
TRANSACTION_ROLLEDBACK	Transaction rolled back
INVALID_TRANSACTION	Invalid transaction
UNKNOWN	An unknown exception

```
    {
        string f();
        oneway void g();
        attribute long x;
        readonly attribute string y;
    };

//C++
A_var() : _ptr(A::_nil()) {}
A_var(A_ptr _p) : _ptr(_p) {}


. . .


char* A::y() { . . .} //get function only

CORBA::Long A::x() {. . .} // get function for x
```

```
void A::x(CORBA::Long _val) {. . .}// set function for x

void A::g() {. . .} //oneway operation

char* A::f() {. . .}

}
```

The following code could be implemented by a client:

```
//C++
A_var a;
a = ... // initialize the object reference
a->f();
a->g();
Long n = a->x();//get
a->x(n + 1);//set
```

9 *Argument Passing*

Primitive types and enumerations are passed by their defined type. For object references, the `ptr` type is used. Passing structured types requires greater attention to the details of memory management. In-parameter storage is simplest because the caller has allocated and owns the storage of the parameter. Out and inout parameters are more complicated.

If the out parameter is a fixed length aggregate, then the mapping is by reference, `T&`. If the out parameter is a variable length aggregate then both `T` and `T*&` can be used. Using the aggregate's `_var` class frees the user from this consideration in that the mapping is `T_var&` for both in and out (see Tables 3.4 and 3.5).

The cases described in Table 3.5 are the following:

1. Caller allocates all necessary storage, except that which is encapsulated and managed within the parameter itself. For inout parameters, the caller provides the initial value and the callee may change that value. For out parameters, the caller allocates the storage but need not initialize it, and the callee sets the value. Function returns are by value.

2. Caller allocates storage for the object reference. For inout parameters, the caller provides an initial value; if the callee wants to reassign the inout parameter, it first calls `CORBA::release` on the original input value. To continue to use an object reference passed in as an inout, the caller must first duplicate the reference. The caller is responsible for the release of all out and return object references. Release of all object references embedded in other structures is performed automatically by the structures themselves.

TABLE 3.4 Basic Argument and Result Passing

Datatype	In	Inout	Out	Return
short	Short	Short&	Short&	Short
long	Long	Long&	Long&	Long
long long	LongLong	LongLong&	LongLong&	LongLong
unsigned	UShort	UShort&	UShort&	Ushort
short unsigned	ULong	ULong&	ULong&	Ulong
long unsigned	ULongLong	ULongLong&	ULongLong&	ULongLong
long long float	Float	Float&	Float&	Float
double	Double	Double&	Double&	Double
long double	LongDouble	LongDouble&	LongDouble&	LongDouble
boolean	Boolean	Boolean&	Boolean&	Boolean
char	Char	Char&	Char&	Char
wchar	Wchar	WChar&	WChar&	Wchar
octet	Octet	Octet&	Octet&	Octet
enum	enum	enum&	enum&	enum
object reference ptr	objref_ptr	objref_ptr&	objref_ptr&	objref_ptr
struct, fixed	const struct&	struct&	struct&	struct
struct, variable	const struct&	struct&	struct*&	struct*
union, fixed	const union&	union&	union&	union
union, variable	const union&	union&	union*&	union*
string	const char*	char*&	char*&	char*
wstring	const wchar*	wchar*&	wchar*&	wchar*
sequence	const sequence&	sequence&	sequence*&	sequence*
array	fixed const array	array	Array	array slice*2
array	variable const array	array	array slice*&2	array slice*2
any	const any&	any&	any*&	any*
fixed const	Fixed&	Fixed&	Fixed&	Fixed&

3. For out parameters, the caller allocates a pointer and passes it by reference to the callee. The callee sets the pointer to point to a valid instance of the parameter's type. For returns, the callee returns a similar pointer. The callee is not allowed to return a null pointer in either case. In both cases the caller is responsible for releasing the returned storage. To maintain local/remote transparency, the caller must always release the returned storage, regardless of whether the callee is located in the same address space as the caller or located in a different address space. Following the completion of a request, the caller is not allowed to modify any values in the returned storage—to do so the caller must first copy the returned instance into a new instance, then modify the new instance.

4. For inout strings, the caller provides storage for both the input string and the char* or wchar* pointing to it. Since the callee may deallocate

TABLE 3.5 Memory Management Rules for Parameter Passing

Datatype	Inout parameter	Out parameter	Return result
short	1	1	1
long	1	1	1
long long	1	1	1
unsigned short	1	1	1
unsigned long	1	1	1
unsigned long long	1	1	1
float	1	1	1
double	1	1	1
long double	1	1	1
boolean	1	1	1
char	1	1	1
wchar	1	1	1
octet	1	1	1
enum	1	1	1
object reference ptr	2	2	2
struct, fixed	1	1	1
struct, variable	1	3	3
union, fixed	1	1	1
union, variable	1	3	3
string	4	3	3
wstring	4	3	3
sequence	5	3	3
array, fixed	1	1	6
array, variable	1	6	6
any	5	3	3
fixed	1	1	1

the input string and reassign the char* or wchar* to point to new storage to hold the output value, the caller should allocate the input string using string_alloc() or wstring_alloc(). The size of the out string is therefore not limited by the size of the in string. The caller is responsible for deleting the storage for the out using string_free() or wstring_free(). The callee is not allowed to return a null pointer for an inout, out, or return value.

5. For inout sequences and anys, assignment or modification of the sequence or any may cause deallocation of owned storage before any reallocation occurs, depending upon the state of the boolean release parameter with which the sequence or any was constructed.

6. For out parameters, the caller allocates a pointer to an array slice, which has all the same dimensions of the original array except the first, and passes the pointer by reference to the callee. The callee sets the pointer to point to a valid instance of the array. For returns, the callee returns a similar pointer. The callee is not allowed to return a

null pointer in either case. In both cases, the caller is responsible for releasing the returned storage. To maintain local/remote transparency, the caller must always release the returned storage, regardless of whether the callee is located in the same address space as the caller or located in a different address space. Following completion of a request, the caller is not allowed to modify any values in the returned storage—to do so the caller must first copy the returned array instance into a new array instance, then modify the new instance.

9.1 Examples

This section contains examples, which illustrate the passing of various IDL types as arguments to CORBA method invocations. In particular, we see how the following IDL types, whose IDL-to-C++ mappings were discussed in the previous sections, can be passed as arguments:

- ◆ fixed and variable struct type
- ◆ fixed and variable length union type
- ◆ fixed and variable length array
- ◆ fixed and variable length sequences
- ◆ octet
- ◆ object reference

9.1.1 Fixed Length Struct

Consider the following IDL with a fixed length struct Time:

```
//HelloWorld.idl
module HelloWorld{
    struct Time{
      short hour;
      short minute;
    };
    interface GoodDay{
      Time hello( in Time in_time,
                inout Time inout_time,
                out Time out_time );
    };
};
```

In the above IDL, we have declared a struct Time with two short members, hour and minute. Since the sizes of hour and minute are fixed, Time is a fixed length struct. We have also declared an interface GoodDay that supports one operation, hello(). The hello() operation takes an in argument in_time, of type Time, an inout argument inout_time, of type Time, and an out argument out_time, also of type Time. In addition, the hello() operation has a return value of type Time.

If the above IDL is passed through the IDL compiler (the actual compiler used in these examples was `idl2cpp` from Inprise VisiBroker), the following signature is generated in `HelloWorld_c.hh` corresponding to the method invocation:

```
HelloWorld::Time hello(
    const HelloWorld::Time& _in_time,
    HelloWorld::Time& _inout_time,
    HelloWorld::Time& _out_time
);
```

The code generated above adheres to the mapping rules specified by the CORBA specification. A typical client program that uses the above generated stub code simply needs to understand the memory management rules for parameter passing, allocate storage for the parameters (or not allocate storage and depend on the callee to do it), and initialize the values for the parameters. A typical client program could look like the following:

```
HelloWorld::Time in_time, inout_time, out_time;
HelloWorld::Time return_time;

in_time.hour = 15; in_time.minute = 30;
inout_time.hour = 20; inout_time.minute = 35;

return_time = goodDay->hello(
            in_time, inout_time, out_time );
```

In the above code we declare three variables, each of type `Hello-World::Time`, which is the `struct` generated from the corresponding IDL type. We then assign values to the variables that are to be the in and inout arguments to the hello() operation. To do this we simply set values to the two `short` members, `hour` and `minute` of the `struct`. We also declare another variable `return_time`, to hold the return value from the operation. However, we do not initialize the `out_time` and the `return_time` parameters. The values for these are set by the hello() operation. We then invoke the hello() method in accordance with its signature generated by the IDL compiler (shown above).

It is important to note that in the above code, we have adhered to the memory management rules for parameter passing listed earlier in Table 3.5. As an example, for a fixed length `struct` used as an in parameter, we see that in the generated code such a parameter is passed as a `const` reference, `const HelloWorld::Time&`. In accordance with case 1, we have allocated storage for this parameter on the stack (by declaring it as a local variable) and have passed it by reference to the callee. Similarly, for passing a fixed length `struct` as an inout parameter to a method, we have used case 1, which calls for caller allocated storage. We have allocated storage on the stack for the `struct` passed as an inout parameter and have initialized it with a value. We do realize that the callee could change this value upon returning from the method invocation. As for the out parameter, the table indicates that we use case 1. Therefore we allocate storage but do not initialize it with a value. The callee is supposed to set a value to it. So also, for the return type, the callee initializes the struct returned with the correct value and returns it by value to the caller.

In the skeleton code (in the files HelloWorld_s.hh, HelloWorld_s.cpp) generated from HelloWorld.idl, the signature of the hello() operation is as follows:

```
virtual HelloWorld::Time hello(
            const HelloWorld::Time& in_time,
            HelloWorld::Time& inout_time,
            HelloWorld::Time& out_time) = 0;
```

The IDL compiler generates a pure virtual function that needs to be implemented by a servant.

A typical implementation of the hello() method by a servant named GoodDayImpl that implements the HelloWorld::GoodDay object is as follows:

```
HelloWorld::Time GoodDayImpl::hello(
            const HelloWorld::Time& in_time,
            HelloWorld::Time& inout_time,
            HelloWorld::Time& out_time ) {

    out_time.hour = 18; out_time.minute = 31;

    // Replace the values received as an
    // inout argument
    inout_time.hour = 19; inout_time.minute = 32;

    // Create a return value
    HelloWorld::Time ret_time:
    ret_time.hour = 17; ret_time.minute = 30;

    return ret_time;
}
```

In the above implementation, the signature of the method matches that of what was generated by the IDL compiler in the skeleton code. We set values to the out_time argument, replace the values in the inout_time argument, create a return_time, set a value to it, and return it to the client.

In terms of memory management associated with the example above, all storage allocation was done on the stack. We could modify the above example to use the _var types generated by the IDL compiler for the struct Time. It enables storage allocation on the heap. In such a case, the client code would look like

```
HelloWorld::Time_var in_time,
                     inout_time, out_time;
HelloWorld::Time_var ret_time;

in_time = new HelloWorld::Time();
in_time->hour = 15; in_time->minute = 30;
inout_time = new HelloWorld::Time();
inout_time->hour = 20; inout_time->minute = 35;

return_time = goodDay->hello(
                     in_time,
                     inout_time.inout(),
                     out_time.out() );
```

In the above code segment, we declare three variables, each of type `HelloWorld::Time_var`, namely, `in_time`, `inout_time`, and `out_time`. Here we use the _var convenience class generated by the IDL compiler. The constructor for the _var class allocates memory on the heap. The destructor for the _var class gets invoked when the _var class goes out of scope and frees the allocated memory. Had we not used the `HelloWorld::Time_var` class but instead used `HelloWorld::Time_ptr`, we would have had to keep track of the storage allocated (when we call new) and remember to free it appropriately before the method returns. The _var class takes care of this problem by managing memory associated with the _ptr. So we allocate storage for the `in_time` and `inout_time` variables by invoking the _var class constructor. Like before, we assign values to `in_time` and `inout_time`. We do not allocate any memory for `out_time` and for `return_time`. The memory for these is allocated by the ORB and is freed when these variables go out of scope. As a general rule, we always try to use the _var convenience class generated for us by the IDL compiler whenever possible.

Also note that in the method invocation above, we pass `inout_time.inout()` and `out_time.out()` as the second and third arguments, respectively. Invoking the `inout()` on a `HelloWorld::Time_var` returns a `HelloWorld::Time&`. So also, invoking the `out()` on a `HelloWorld::Time_var` returns a `HelloWorld::Time&`. The `inout()` and `out()` methods of the _var class return the appropriate types expected by the `hello()` method. We could have used `inout_time` and `out_time` directly instead of using the `inout_time.inout ()` and `out_time.out()` as arguments to the `hello()` method, since these variables are of the _var type and the _var class has implicit conversion operators to return the appropriate types expected by the `hello()` method. However, some compilers have problems with this approach and hence it is better to use the `inout()` and `out()` explicitly.

Similarly, the servant implementation would look as follows if we use `HelloWorld::Time_var` instead of using stack based storage allocation:

```
HelloWorld::Time GoodDayImpl::hello(
                const HelloWorld::Time& in_time,
                HelloWorld::Time& inout_time,
                HelloWorld::Time& out_time ) {

    out_time.hour = 18; out_time.minute = 31;

    // Replace the values received as
    // an inout argument
    inout_time.hour = 19; inout_time.minute = 32;

    // Create a return value
    HelloWorld::Time_var return_time =
                    new HelloWorld::Time();
    return_time->hour = 17; return_time->minute = 30;
    return return_time._retn();
}
```

We only use the _var class while allocating memory for the return_time parameter. The in_time and inout_time parameters are passed by const reference and reference, respectively. Storage for these parameters has been allocated already. Similarly, for the out parameter out_time, storage has already been allocated by the caller of the method. We just have to assign values to its members.

One special thing to note is the use of the _retn() method while returning return_time to the method. The _retn() method is generated as part of the _var class and returns the appropriate type that matches the return type of the method, which is HelloWorld::Time. Use of the _retn() method is similar to the use of the inout() and out() methods on the _var class in the client code above.

9.1.2 *Variable Length Struct*

The variable length struct example is interesting because of the memory management rules that apply to the out parameter and the return type. We follow case 3 for the out parameter and the return type. Consider the following IDL:

```
//HelloWorld.idl
module HelloWorld{
    struct Time{
        short hour;
        short minute;
        string location;
    };
    interface GoodDay{
        Time hello( in Time in_time,
                    inout Time inout_time,
                    out Time out_time );
    };
};
```

In the above IDL, we have declared a struct Time with two short members, hour and minute, and a string member, location. Since the sizes of hour and minute are fixed but the size of string is variable, Time is a variable length struct. We have also declared an interface GoodDay that supports one operation hello(). The hello() operation takes an in argument in_time, of type Time, an inout argument inout_time, of type Time, and an out argument out_time, also of type Time. In addition, the hello() operation has a return value of type Time.

If the above IDL is passed through the IDL compiler (the actual compiler used in these examples was idl2cpp from Inprise VisiBroker), the following signature is generated in HelloWorld_c.hh corresponding to the method invocation:

```
HelloWorld::Time *hello(
    const HelloWorld::Time& _in_time,
    HelloWorld::Time& _inout_time,
    HelloWorld::Time_ptr& _out_time
);
```

Following is a typical client program that uses the above generated stub code:

```
HelloWorld::Time_var in_time,
                     inout_time, out_time;
HelloWorld::Time_var return_time;

in_time = new HelloWorld::Time;
in_time->hour = 15; in_time->minute = 30;
in_time->location = CORBA::string_dup ("San Mateo");
inout_time = new HelloWorld::Time;
inout_time->hour = 20; inout_time->minute = 35;
inout_time->location = CORBA::string_dup("San Bruno");

return_time = goodDay->hello(
            in_time,
            inout_time.inout(),
            out_time.out() );
```

In this code we declare three variables, each of type HelloWorld::Time _var, which is the _var class corresponding to the struct generated from the corresponding IDL type. We then allocate storage (on the heap, by invoking new) and assign values to the variables that are going to be the in and inout arguments to the hello() operation. We set values to the two short members, hour and minute, and the string member location of the struct contained in the HelloWorld::Time_var.

We also declare another variable return_time, to hold the return value from the operation. However, we do not initialize the out_time and the return_time parameters. In accordance with case 3, which should be used for the out parameter, we only allocate storage for the pointer, which in this case is just the declaration of the _var. Note that the _var class contains the _ptr as a member, and just declaration of the _var class constitutes allocation of storage for the pointer, _ptr. The callee is supposed to set the pointer contained in the _var to a valid instance of the parameter's type, which in this case is HelloWorld::Time*. The same rule also applies to the return type. We then invoke the hello() method in accordance with its signature generated by the IDL compiler (shown above). In terms of freeing storage, case 3 makes the caller responsible for releasing storage allocated for the out and return parameters. Since we use the _var class for all the variables, storage is released automatically. In addition, use of the _var class also takes care of releasing the storage allocated for the in and inout parameters, storage for which was allocated on the heap.

In the skeleton code (in the files HelloWorld_s.hh, HelloWorld_s.cpp) generated from HelloWorld.idl, the signature of the hello() operation is as follows:

```
virtual HelloWorld::Time_ptr hello(
            const HelloWorld::Time& in_time,
            HelloWorld::Time& inout_time,
            HelloWorld::Time_ptr& out_time) = 0;
```

The IDL compiler generates a pure virtual function that must be implemented by a servant.

A typical implementation of the hello() method by a servant named GoodDayImpl that implements the HelloWorld::GoodDay object is as follows:

```
HelloWorld::Time_ptr GoodDayImpl::hello(
            const HelloWorld::Time& in_time,
            HelloWorld::Time& inout_time,
            HelloWorld::Time_ptr& out_time ) {

    out_time = new HelloWorld::Time;
    out_time->hour = 18; out_time->minute = 31;

    // Replace the values received as an
    // inout argument
    inout_time.hour = 19; inout_time.minute = 32;

    // Create a return value
    HelloWorld::Time_var return_time =
                new HelloWorld::Time;
    return_time->hour = 17; return_time->minute = 30;
    return return_time._retn();
}
```

In the above implementation, notice that the signature of the method matches that of what was generated by the IDL compiler in the skeleton code. We set values to the `out_time` argument, replace the values in the `inout_time` argument, and create a `return_time`, set value to it, and return it to the client. We use the `_var` class whenever possible to ensure proper memory management.

9.1.3 Fixed Length Union

With regard to memory management, a fixed length union is treated identically to a fixed length struct. We follow case 1 when a fixed length union is passed as an in, inout, or out parameter or if used as a return type. The caller allocates storage and passes by reference or const reference to the callee. The caller is responsible for releasing allocated storage. Consider the following IDL:

```
// HelloWorld.idl
module HelloWorld{
    struct Time{
        short hour;
        short minute;
    };

    union TimeUnion switch( long ){
        case 1:
            Time time;
        case 2:
        default:
            long value;
    };

    interface GoodDay {
        TimeUnion hello( in TimeUnion in_union,
                    inout TimeUnion inout_union,
                    out TimeUnion out_union );

    };
};
```

In the above IDL, we have declared a struct Time with two short members, hour and minute. We have also declared a union TimeUnion, which has a discriminator of type long, and two members: time, of type Time and a long value. Since Time is a fixed struct and long is of a fixed size, the length of the union is fixed. We have also declared an interface GoodDay that supports one operation hello(). The hello() operation takes an in argument in_union, of type TimeUnion, an inout argument inout_union, of type TimeUnion, and an out argument out_union, also of type TimeUnion. In addition, the hello() operation has a return value of type TimeUnion.

If the above IDL is passed through the IDL compiler (the actual compiler used in these examples was `idl2cpp` from Inprise VisiBroker), the following signature is generated in `HelloWorld_c.hh` corresponding to the method invocation:

```
HelloWorld::TimeUnion hello(
    const HelloWorld::TimeUnion& _in_union,
    HelloWorld::TimeUnion& _inout_union,
    HelloWorld::TimeUnion& _out_union
);
```

Following is a typical client program that uses the above generated stub code:

```
HelloWorld::TimeUnion_var in_union,
                    inout_union, out_union;
HelloWorld::TimeUnion_var return_union;

in_union = new HelloWorld::TimeUnion;
inout_union = new HelloWorld::TimeUnion;

HelloWorld::Time_var time =
                    new HelloWorld::Time;
time->hour = 15; time->minute = 10;

// Set in_union's time member
in_union->time = time;

// Set inout_union's value member
inout_union->value = (CORBA::Long)20;

return_union = goodDay->hello(
            in_union,
            inout_union.inout(),
            out_union.out() );
```

In the above code, we declare three variables, each of type `HelloWorld::TimeUnion_var`, which is the `_var` class corresponding to the union generated from the corresponding IDL type. We also declare another variable `return_union` to hold the return value from the operation. To set value to the union, set the `time` member of the union, `in_union`, which is the in parameter, and the location member of the union, `inout_union`, which is the inout parameter and set values to these. To set value to the `time` member, declare a variable `time`, of type `HelloWorld::Time_var`. We use the `_var` class in the declaration for the `in_union` as well as for its contained element `time`. This is necessary for proper memory management. Wherever possible we use the memory managed `_var` class so that we do not have to keep track of freeing memory. We do not initialize the out_union **and the** return_union **parameters. The values for these will be set by the** hello() **operation. We then invoke the** hello() **method in accordance with its signature generated by the IDL compiler, which is shown above.**

In the skeleton code (in the files HelloWorld_s.hh, HelloWorld_s.cpp) generated from HelloWorld.idl, the signature of the hello() operation is as follows:

```
virtual HelloWorld::TimeUnion hello(
        const HelloWorld::TimeUnion& in_union,
        HelloWorld::TimeUnion& inout_union,
        HelloWorld::TimeUnion& out_union) = 0;
```

The IDL compiler generates a pure virtual function, as shown above, that must be implemented by a servant.

Following is an implementation of the hello() method by a servant named GoodDayImpl that implements the HelloWorld::GoodDay object:

```
HelloWorld::TimeUnion GoodDayImpl::hello(
            const HelloWorld::TimeUnion& in_union,
            HelloWorld::TimeUnion& inout_union,
            HelloWorld::TimeUnion& out_union ) {

    // declare and set a time variable
    HelloWorld::Time_var time = new HelloWorld::Time;
    time->hour = 18; time->minute = 30;
    // set the time member in out_union
    out_union.time(time);

    // Replace the values received as an

    // inout argument
    time->hour = 19; time->minute = 32;
    inout_union.time(time);

    // Create a return value
    HelloWorld::TimeUnion return_union;

    // Set the time member in return_union
    time->hour = 17; time->minute = 30;
    return_union.time(time);

    return return_union;
}
```

In the above implementation, notice that the signature of the method matches that of what was generated by the IDL compiler in the skeleton code. We set values to the `out_union` argument, replace the values in the `inout _union` argument, and create a `return_union`, set value to it, and return it to the client. We use the `_var` class whenever possible to ensure proper memory management. We could have used stack-based allocation for `time` in the above code instead of using the `_var` class because the size of the `struct` is very small.

9.1.4 *Variable Length Union*

With regard to memory management, a variable length union is treated identically to a variable length struct. We follow case 3 in terms of allocating and freeing storage for out and return parameters. Consider the following IDL:

```
// HelloWorld.idl
module HelloWorld{
    struct Time{
        short hour;
        short minute;
    };

    union TimeUnion switch( long ){
        case 1:
            Time time;
        case 2:
            string location;
        case 3:
        default:
            short value;
    };

    interface GoodDay{
        TimeUnion hello( in TimeUnion in_union,
                    inout TimeUnion inout_union,
                    out TimeUnion out_union );
    };
};
```

In the above IDL, we have declared a struct Time with two short members, hour and minute, and a string member, location. Since the size of struct Time is fixed but the size of string is variable, TimeUnion is a variable length union. We have also declared an interface GoodDay that supports one operation hello(). The hello() operation takes an in argument in_union, of type TimeUnion, an inout argument inout_time, of type TimeUnion, and an out argument out_time, also of type TimeUnion. In addition, the hello() operation has a return value of type TimeUnion.

If the above IDL is passed through the IDL compiler (the actual compiler used in these examples was `idl2cpp` from Inprise VisiBroker), the following signature is generated in `HelloWorld_c.hh` corresponding to the method invocation:

```
HelloWorld::TimeUnion *hello(
    const HelloWorld::TimeUnion& _in_union,
    HelloWorld::TimeUnion& _inout_union,
    HelloWorld::TimeUnion_ptr& _out_union
);
```

Notice the difference in the signature of the `hello()` method in contrast to the signature generated when a fixed length union is used as an argument to the `hello()` operation. A typical client program that uses the above generated stub code could look like the following:

```
HelloWorld::TimeUnion_var in_union,
                  inout_union, out_union;

HelloWorld::TimeUnion_var return_union;

in_union = new HelloWorld::TimeUnion;

HelloWorld::Time_var time =
            new HelloWorld::Time;
time->hour = 15; time->minute = 30;
in_union->time(time);

inout_union = new HelloWorld::TimeUnion;
inout_union->location =
        CORBA::string_dup("San Bruno");

return_union = goodDay->hello(
            in_union,
            inout_union.inout(),
            out_union.out() );
```

In the above code, we declare three variables, each of type `Hello-World::TimeUnion_var`, which is the `_var` class corresponding to the `union` generated from the corresponding IDL type. We then assign values to the variable that are going to be the in and inout arguments to the hello() operation. To do this, we set values to the two `short` members, `hour` and `minute`, and the `string` member `location` of the `struct` contained in the `HelloWorld::Time_var`. We also declare another variable `return_union`, to hold the return value from the operation. However, we do not initialize the `out_union` and the `return_union` parameters. The values for these are set by the hello() operation. We then invoke the `hello()` method in accordance with its signature generated by the IDL compiler, which is shown above.

In the skeleton code (in the files `HelloWorld_s.hh`, `HelloWorld_s.cpp`) generated from `HelloWorld.idl`, the signature of the `hello()` operation is as follows:

```
virtual HelloWorld::TimeUnion *hello(
        const HelloWorld::TimeUnion& in_union,
        HelloWorld::TimeUnion& inout_union,
        HelloWorld::TimeUnion_ptr& out_union) = 0;
```

Note that the IDL compiler generates a pure virtual function that needs to be implemented by a servant.

Following is an implementation of the `hello()` method by a servant named GoodDayImpl that implements the HelloWorld::GoodDay object:

```
HelloWorld::TimeUnion *GoodDayImpl::hello(
        const HelloWorld::TimeUnion& in_union,
        HelloWorld::TimeUnion& inout_union,
        HelloWorld::TimeUnion_ptr& out_union ) {

    out_union = new HelloWorld::TimeUnion;

    HelloWorld::Time_var time =
                        new HelloWorld::Time;
    time->hour = 18; time->minute = 31;
    out_union->time = time;

    // Replace the values received as an
    // inout argument
    inout_union->location =
                CORBA::string_dup("San Mateo");

    // Create a return value
    HelloWorld::TimeUnion_var return_union =
                    new HelloWorld::TimeUnion;
    return_union->value = (CORBA::Long)30;

    return return_union._retn();
}
```

In the above implementation, the signature of the method matches the signature generated by the IDL compiler in the skeleton code. We set values to the out_union argument, replace the values in the inout_union argument, and create a return_union, set value to it, and return it to the client. We use the _var class whenever possible to ensure proper memory management.

9.1.5   Fixed Length Array

The rule to be used for a fixed length array when used as in, inout, or out parameter is case 1, and when used as a return parameter is case 6. Consider the following IDL:

```
// HelloWorld.idl
module HelloWorld{
    struct Time{
      short hour;
      short minute;
    };
    typedef Time TimeArray[10];
    interface GoodDay{
      TimeArray hello( in TimeArray in_arr,
              inout TimeArray inout_arr,
              out TimeArray out_arr );
    };
};
```

In the above IDL, we have declared an array, TimeArray, which contains ten elements each of type struct Time with two short members, hour and minute. Since the sizes of hour and minute are fixed, the array is of fixed length. We have also declared an interface GoodDay that supports one operation hello(). The hello() operation takes an in argument in_arr, of type TimeArray, an inout argument inout_arr, of type TimeArray, and an out argument out_arr, also of type TimeArray. In addition, the hello() operation has a return value of type TimeArray.

If the above IDL is passed through the IDL compiler, the following signature is generated in HelloWorld_c.hh corresponding to the method invocation:

```
HelloWorld::TimeArray_slice *hello(
 const HelloWorld::TimeArray _in_arr,
 HelloWorld::TimeArray _inout_arr,
 HelloWorld::TimeArray _out_arr
);
```

Notice the peculiar return parameter HelloWorld::TimeArray_slice *. This type represents a pointer to a slice of the array, which has all the same dimensions of the original array except the first. A typical client program that uses the above generated stub code could look like the following:

```
HelloWorld::TimeArray_var in_arr,
                    inout_arr, out_arr;
HelloWorld::TimeArray_var return_arr;

HelloWorld::Time_var time=
          new HelloWorld::Time;

in_arr = HelloWorld::TimeArray_alloc();
for( CORBA::ULong i = 0; i < 10; i++ ) {
  time->hour = i; time->minute = i + 10;
  in_arr[i] = time;
}
```

```
inout_arr = HelloWorld::TimeArray_alloc();
for( CORBA::ULong j = 0; j < 10; j++ ) {
  time->hour = j; time->minute = (j*2) + 20;
  inout_arr[j] = time;
}

return_arr = goodDay->hello(
        in_arr,
        inout_arr.inout(),
        out_arr.out() );
```

In the above code, we declare three variables, each of type `HelloWorld`
`::TimeArray_var` which is the `_var` class generated from the corresponding
IDL type `TimeArray`. To dynamically allocate storage to `in_array`, we invoke
the `HelloWorld::TimeArray_alloc()` method found in the generated code. This
method is generated by the IDL compiler when an array is used in IDL. The
implementation of this method is as follows:

```
HelloWorld::TimeArray_slice
      *HelloWorld::TimeArray_alloc() {
          return new HelloWorld::Time[10];
}
```

To assign a value to each element of `in_array`, we do the following. We
declare time, of type `HelloWorld::Time_var`, and, in a for loop, assign arbitrary
values (just to illustrate) to the hour and minute members of time and then
assign this time to an element of `in_array`. Similarly, we allocate storage and
assign values to `inout_array`. We also declare another variable `return_time`, to
hold the return value from the operation. However, we do not initialize the
`out_arr` and the `return_arr` parameters. We only allocate storage sufficient
enough for the pointer `_ptr` contained in the `_var` associated with the `out_arr`
and `return_arr` types. The values for these will be set by the callee. We then
invoke the `hello()` method in accordance with its signature generated by the
IDL compiler (shown above). The caller is responsible for releasing storage. In
this case we use the `_var` class for all variables possible, so releasing storage
happens automatically when the `_var` class goes out of scope.

In the skeleton code (in the files `HelloWorld_s.hh`, `HelloWorld_s.cpp`) generated from `HelloWorld.idl`, the signature of the `hello()` operation is as follows:

```
virtual HelloWorld::TimeArray_slice *hello(
        const HelloWorld::TimeArray in_arr,
        HelloWorld::TimeArray inout_arr,
        HelloWorld::TimeArray out_arr) = 0;
```

The IDL compiler generates a pure virtual function, as shown above, which
must be implemented by a servant.

Following is an implementation of the `hello()` method by a servant named `GoodDayImpl` that implements the `HelloWorld::GoodDay` object:

```
HelloWorld::TimeArray_slice *GoodDayImpl::hello(
        const HelloWorld::TimeArray in_arr,
        HelloWorld::TimeArray inout_arr,
        HelloWorld::TimeArray out_arr ) {

    // Set values to out_arr
    HelloWorld::Time_var time=
                new HelloWorld::Time;
    for( CORBA::ULong i = 0; i < 10; i++ ) {
      time->hour = i; time->minute = (i*2) + 20;
      out_arr[i] = time;
    }

    // Replace the values received as an
    // inout argument
    for( CORBA::ULong j = 0; j < 10; j++ ) {
      time->hour = j; time->minute = (j*3) + 30;
      inout_arr[j] = time;
    }

    // Create a return value
    HelloWorld::TimeArray_var return_arr =
                    HelloWorld::TimeArray_alloc();
    for( CORBA::ULong k = 0; k < 10; k++ ) {
      time->hour = k; time->minute = (k*4) + 40;
      return_arr[k] = time;
    }

    return return_arr._retn();
}
```

In the above implementation, the types in the signature of the method match the signature types generated by the IDL compiler in the skeleton code. We assign values to the `out_arr` argument, replace the values in the `inout_arr` argument, and create a `return_arr`, set value to it, and return it to the client. We use the `_var` class whenever possible so that memory management is taken care of. In particular, we do use the `_var` class for each element of the array, which is of type `struct Time`.

9.1.6 *Variable Length Array*

The only difference between fixed length arrays and variable length arrays in terms of memory management is when passing them as out parameters. We apply case 1 while passing a fixed length array as an out parameter, whereas we apply case 6 while passing a variable length array as an out parameter. Consider the following IDL:

```
// HelloWorld.idl
module HelloWorld{
    struct Time{
      short hour;
      short minute;
      string location;
    };
    typedef Time TimeArray[10];
    interface GoodDay{
      TimeArray hello( in TimeArray in_arr,
                inout TimeArray inout_arr,
                out TimeArray out_arr);
    };
};
```

In the above IDL, we have declared a struct Time with two short members, hour and minute, and a string member, location. Since the sizes of hour and minute are fixed but the size of string is variable, Time is a variable length struct. Hence the size of the array TimeArray is also variable. Like before, we have also declared an interface GoodDay which supports one operation hello(). The hello() operation takes an in argument in_arr, of type TimeArray, an inout argument inout_arr, of type TimeArray, and an out argument out_arr, also of type TimeArray. In addition, the hello() operation has a return value of type TimeArray. If the above IDL is passed through the IDL compiler (the actual compiler used in these examples was idl2cpp from Inprise VisiBroker), the following signature is generated in HelloWorld_c.hh corresponding to the method invocation:

```
HelloWorld::TimeArray_slice *hello(
 const HelloWorld::TimeArray _in_arr,
 HelloWorld::TimeArray _inout_arr,
 HelloWorld::TimeArray_slice_ptr& _out_arr
);
```

Following is a client program that uses the above generated stub code:

```
HelloWorld::TimeArray_var in_arr,
                    inout_arr, out_arr;
HelloWorld::TimeArray_var return_arr;

in_arr = HelloWorld::TimeArray_alloc();
HelloWorld::Time_var time =
            new HelloWorld::Time;
for( CORBA::ULong i = 0; i < 10; i++ ) {
  time->hour = i; time->minute = i + 20;
  time->location =
        CORBA::string_dup("San Mateo");
  in_arr[i] = time;
}
```

```
inout_arr = HelloWorld::TimeArray_alloc();
for( CORBA::ULong j = 0; j < 10; j++ ) {
  time->hour = j; time->minute = (j*2) + 30;
  time->location =
          CORBA::string_dup("San Francisco");
  inout_arr[j] = time;
}


return_arr = goodDay->hello(
          in_arr,
          inout_arr.inout(),
          out_arr.out() );
```

The client code above is almost identical to the client code written for the fixed length array example in the previous section. The only difference is the setting of the location member of the struct Time. Since the generated code declares the location member of struct Time as a CORBA::String_var, we must set value to the _var. The only point to note here is that we use the _var class for each element of TimeArray in addition to using the _var class for the TimeArray itself.

In the skeleton code (in the files HelloWorld_s.hh, HelloWorld_s.cpp) generated from HelloWorld.idl, the signature of the hello() operation would look like

```
virtual HelloWorld::TimeArray_slice *hello(
      const HelloWorld::TimeArray in_arr,
      HelloWorld::TimeArray inout_arr,
      HelloWorld::TimeArray_slice_ptr& out_arr) = 0;
```

The IDL compiler generates a pure virtual function, as shown above, which must be implemented by a servant.

Following is an implementation of the hello() method by a servant named GoodDayImpl that implements the HelloWorld::GoodDay object:

```
HelloWorld::TimeArray_slice *GoodDayImpl::hello(
      const HelloWorld::TimeArray in_arr,
      HelloWorld::TimeArray inout_arr,
      HelloWorld::TimeArray_slice_ptr& out_arr ) {

  HelloWorld::Time_var time =
                   new HelloWorld::Time;
  out_arr = HelloWorld::TimeArray_alloc();
  for( CORBA::ULong i = 0; i < 10; i++ ) {
    time->hour = i; time->minute = (i*2) + 20;
    time->location =
            CORBA::string_dup( "Scotts Valley" );
    out_arr[i] = time;
  }
```

```
// Replace the values received as an
// inout argument
for( CORBA::ULong j = 0; j < 10; j++ ) {
  time->hour = j; time->minute = (j*3) + 30;
  time->location =
          CORBA::string_dup( "Santa Cruz" );
  inout_arr[j] = time;
}

// Create a return value
HelloWorld::TimeArray_var return_arr =
                  HelloWorld::TimeArray_alloc();
for( CORBA::ULong k = 0; k < 10; k++ ) {
  time->hour = k; time->minute = (k*4) + 40;
  time->location =
          CORBA::string_dup( "Monterey" );
  return_arr[k] = time;
}
return return_arr._retn();
}
```

In the above implementation, the types in the signature of the method matches the signature types by the IDL compiler in the skeleton code. We set values to the out_arr argument, replace the values in the inout_arr argument and create a return_arr, set value to it and return it to the client. We use the generated method TimeArray_alloc() to allocate memory and the _var class whenever possible to ensure proper memory management.

9.1.7 Sequences

The memory management rules for both fixed length and variable length sequences are the same. Hence we only consider a variable length sequence in this section. Consider the following IDL:

```
// HelloWorld.idl
module HelloWorld{
    struct Time{
      short hour;
      short minute;
      string location;
    };
    typedef sequence<Time> TimeSeq
    interface GoodDay{
      TimeSeq hello( in TimeSeq in_seq,
                inout TimeSeq inout_seq,
                out TimeSeq out_seq );
    };
};
```

In the above IDL we have declared a struct Time with two short members, hour and minute, and a string member, location. We have then declared a sequence TimeSeq, whose elements are of type struct Time. We have also declared an interface GoodDay which supports one operation hello(). The hello() operation takes an in argument in_seq, of type TimeSeq, an inout argument inout_seq, of type TimeSeq, and an out argument out_seq, also of type TimeSeq. In addition, the hello() operation has a return value of type TimeSeq. If the above IDL is passed through the IDL compiler (the actual compiler used in these examples was idl2cpp from Inprise VisiBroker), the following signature is generated in HelloWorld_c.hh corresponding to the method invocation:

```
HelloWorld::TimeSeq_ptr hello(
 const HelloWorld::TimeSeq& _in_seq,
 HelloWorld::TimeSeq& _inout_seq,
 HelloWorld::TimeSeq_ptr& _out_seq
);
```

Following is a typical client program that uses the above generated stub code:

```
HelloWorld::TimeSeq_var in_seq,
                        inout_seq, out_seq;
HelloWorld::TimeSeq_var return_seq;

in_seq = new HelloWorld::TimeSeq;
CORBA::ULong in_seq_len = 10;
in_seq->length( in_seq_len );
for( CORBA::ULong i = 0; i < in_seq_len; i++ ) {
  time->hour = i; time->minute = i + 10;
  time->location =
        CORBA::string_dup( "San Mateo" );
  in_seq[i] = time;
}

inout_seq = new HelloWorld::TimeSeq;
CORBA::ULong inout_seq_len = 20;
inout_seq->length( inout_seq_len );
for( CORBA::ULong j = 0;
                 j < inout_seq_len; j++ ) {
  time->hour = j; time->minute = (j*2) + 20;
  time->location=
        CORBA::string_dup( "San Francisco" );
  in_out_seq->time = time;
}

return_seq = goodDay->hello(
            in_seq,
            inout_seq.inout(),
             out_seq.out() );
```

In the above code, we declare three variables, each of type HelloWorld ::TimeSeq_var, which is the _var class corresponding to the sequence generated from the corresponding IDL type. We then assign values to the variables that are going to be the in and inout arguments to the hello() operation. To do this we simply set values to each member of the sequence in a loop. We arbitrarily set values to each member just for illustrative purpose. Note that the _var class provides an overloaded operator[], thus making it convenient to assign values to the elements, like we would do with an array. We also declare another variable return_time, to hold the return value from the operation. However, we do not initialize the out_seq and the return_seq parameters. The values for these will be set by the hello() operation. We then invoke the hello() method in accordance with its signature generated by the IDL compiler, which is shown above.

In the skeleton code (in the files HelloWorld_s.hh, HelloWorld_s.cpp) generated from HelloWorld.idl, the signature of the hello() operation is as follows:

```
virtual HelloWorld::TimeSeq_ptr hello(
        const HelloWorld::TimeSeq& in_seq,
        HelloWorld::TimeSeq_& inout_seq,
        HelloWorld::TimeSeq_ptr& out_seq) = 0;
```

Note that the IDL compiler generates a pure virtual function that needs to be implemented by a servant.

Following is a typical implementation of the hello() method by a servant named GoodDayImpl that implements the HelloWorld::GoodDay object:

```
HelloWorld::TimeSeq_ptr GoodDayImpl::hello(
        const HelloWorld::TimeSeq& in_seq,
        HelloWorld::TimeSeq_& inout_seq,
        HelloWorld::TimeSeq_ptr& out_seq ) {

    HelloWorld::Time_var time =
                new HelloWorld::Time;

    out_seq = new HelloWorld::TimeSeq;
    CORBA::ULong out_seq_len = 20;
    out_seq->length( out_seq_len );
    for( CORBA::ULong i = 0; i < out_seq_len; i++ ) {
      time->hour = i; time->minute = (i*2) + 20;
      time->location =
            CORBA::string_dup ( "Scotts Valley" );
      out_seq[i] = time;
    }

    // Case 5. Release inout parameter
    // inout_seq is passed in as _ptr
    // assigning it to an _var ensures automatic
```

```
// release
Seq_var release_seq( inout_seq );

// Create a new sequence
HelloWorld::TimeSeq_var new_seq =
  new HelloWorld::TimeSeq;

// Replace the values received as an
// inout argument
for( CORBA::ULong j = 0;
                  j < inout_seq->length(); j++ ) {
  time->hour = j; time->minute = (j*3)+30;
  time->location =
          CORBA::string_dup( "Santa Cruz" );
  new_seq[j] = time;
}
inout_seq = new_seq._retn();
```

Here, we must use case 5, which applies to inout parameters. Case 5 implies that we release the storage contained in the _ptr passed as an inout parameter. To do this we declare a variable release_seq of type HelloWorld::TimeSeq_var and assign inout_seq to it. This forces a release of the storage that was allocated to inout_seq. (Look at the implementation of the assignment operator, copy constructor for the HelloWorld::TimeSeq_var class in HelloWorld_c.hh). Following this, we create a new sequence, assign values to it, and use its _retn() value to assign it to the inout argument that is then returned to the client.

```
// Create a return value
HelloWorld::TimeSeq_var return_seq =
                  new HelloWorld::TimeSeq;
CORBA::ULong return_seq_len = 20;
return_seq->length( return_seq_len );
for( CORBA::ULong k = 0;
                  k < return_seq_len; k++ ) {
  time->hour = k; time->minute = (k*4) + 40;
  time->location =
          CORBA::string_dup( "Monterey" );
  return_seq[k] = time;
};

return return_seq._retn();
}
```

In the above implementation, the types of the signature of the method matches the signature types generated by the IDL compiler in the skeleton code. We set values to the out_seq argument, replace the values in the inout_seq argument, and create a return_seq, set value to it, and return it to the client. We use the _var class whenever possible to ensure proper memory management. We use the _var class for each element contained in the TimeSeq as well.

9.1.8 Octet

Octets are similar to IDL primitive types such as long, or float, with regard to argument passing. We follow case 1 when an octet is passed as an argument to a method. An octet is passed by value if it occurs as an in argument, passed by reference if an out or inout argument, and returned by value from a method. Consider the following IDL:

```
// HelloWorld.idl
module HelloWorld{
    interface GoodDay{
      octet hello( in octet in_octet,
                    inout octet inout_octet,
                    out octet out_octet);
    };
};
```

In the above IDL, we have declared an interface GoodDay which supports one operation hello(). The hello() operation takes an in argument in_octet, of type octet, an inout argument inout_octet, of type octet, and an out argument out_octet, also of type octet. In addition, the hello() operation has a return value of type octet.

If the above IDL is passed through the IDL compiler (the actual compiler used in these examples was idl2cpp from Inprise VisiBroker), the following signature is generated in HelloWorld_c.hh corresponding to the method invocation:

```
CORBA::Octet hello(
 CORBA::Octet _in_octet,
 CORBA::Octet& _inout_octet,
 CORBA::Octet& _out_octet
);
```

Following is a typical client program that uses the above generated stub code:

```
CORBA::Octet in_octet, inout_octet, out_octet;
CORBA::Octet return_octet;

in_octet = 'a';
inout_octet = 'b';

return_octet = goodDay->hello(
            in_octet,
```

```
inout_octet,
out_octet );
```

In the above code, we declare three local variables, `in_octet`, `inout_octet`, and `out_octet`, each of type `CORBA::Octet`, which is the type corresponding to an IDL octet. We then assign values to the variable that are going to be the in and inout arguments to the hello() operation. We also declare another variable `return_octet`, to hold the return value from the operation. However, we do not initialize the `out_octet` and the `return_octet` parameters. The values for these will be set by the hello() operation. We then invoke the `hello()` method in accordance with its signature generated by the IDL compiler (shown above).

In the skeleton code (in the files `HelloWorld_s.hh`, `HelloWorld_s.cpp`) generated from `HelloWorld.idl`, the signature of the `hello()` operation is as follows:

```
virtual CORBA::Octet hello(
CORBA::Octet in_octet,
CORBA::Octet& inout_octet,
CORBA::Octet& out_octet) = 0;
```

The IDL compiler generates a pure virtual function that needs to be implemented by a servant.

Following is an implementation of the `hello()` method by a servant named `GoodDayImpl` that implements the `HelloWorld::GoodDay` object:

```
CORBA::Octet GoodDayImpl::hello(
        CORBA::Octet   in_octet,
        CORBA::Octet&  inout_octet,
        CORBA::Octet&  out_octet ) {

    out_octet = 'c';

    // Replace the value received as an
    // inout argument
    inout_octet = 'd';

    // Create a return value
    CORBA::Octet return_octet = 'e';
    return return_octet;
}
```

In the above implementation, the types of the signature of the method matches the signature types generated by the IDL compiler in the skeleton code. We set values to the `out_octet` argument, replace the values in the `inout_octet` argument, and create a `return_octet`, set value to it, and return it to the client.

9.1.9 Object Reference

We follow case 2 when passing interfaces as arguments to an operation. IDL interfaces are passed as pointers to object references. It is interesting to observe the invocation of duplicate and release on object references. Consider the following IDL:

```
// HelloWorld.idl
module HelloWorld{
    interface MyObject{
      void my_method();
    };
    interface GoodDay{
      MyObject hello( in MyObject in_obj,
                inout MyObject inout_obj,
                out MyObject out_obj);
    };
};
```

In the above IDL, we have declared an interface MyObject that supports one operation, my_method. This operation does not take any arguments and does not return any value, just to keep things simple. We have also declared an interface GoodDay which supports one operation hello(). The hello() operation takes an in argument in_obj, of type MyObject, an inout argument inout_obj, of type MyObject, and an out argument out_obj, also of type MyObject. In addition, the hello() operation has a return value of type MyObject. Note that all the arguments are IDL interfaces. If the above IDL is passed through the IDL compiler (the actual compiler used in these examples was idl2cpp from Inprise VisiBroker), the following signature is generated in HelloWorld_c.hh corresponding to the method invocation:

```
HelloWorld::MyObject_ptr hello(
 HelloWorld::MyObject_ptr _in_obj,
 HelloWorld::MyObject_ptr& _inout_obj,
 HelloWorld::MyObject_ptr& _out_obj
);
```

Following is a client program that uses the above generated stub code:

```
HelloWorld::MyObject_var in_obj,
                    inout_obj, out_obj;
HelloWorld::MyObject_var return_obj;
// somehow obtain a reference to MyObject
// either by calling _bind() or _narrow() or
// from the Naming Service
in_obj =
   HelloWorld::MyObject::_bind( "InObject" );
```

```
// obtain a reference to MyObject
// and initialize inout_obj
inout_obj =
   HelloWorld::MyObject::_bind( "InOutObject" );

return_obj = goodDay->hello(
           in_obj,
           inout_obj.inout(),
           out_obj.out() );
```

In the above code, we declare three variables, each of type `HelloWorld::MyObject_var`, which is the `_var` class corresponding to the `MyObject` class generated from the corresponding IDL type, MyObject. Following case 2, the caller allocates storage for an object reference and passes a pointer to the object reference as an in parameter. In our example we obtain an object reference by invoking `_bind()`, which is used to initialize `in_obj`.

`_bind()` is one way to obtain an object reference. We could also have used `_narrow()` or other means to obtain an object reference. We similarly initialize `inout_obj`. We also declare another variable `return_obj` to hold the return value from the operation. However, we do not initialize the `out_obj` and the `return_obj` parameters. The values for these are set by the hello() operation. We then invoke the `hello()` method in accordance with its signature generated by the IDL compiler (shown above). We pass as the second and the third arguments to the `hello()` method the results of invoking `inout()` and `out()` on the `_var` class corresponding to `HelloWorld::MyObject`. One subtle thing to note is that we have used the `_var` class for all parameters. This ensures the appropriate releasing of the object reference contained in them when the `_var` goes out of scope. Had we used an `_ptr` instead of the `_var`, we would have had to remember to invoke `CORBA::release` on the object reference contained in the inout and out parameters.

In the skeleton code (in the files `HelloWorld_s.hh`, `HelloWorld_s.cpp`) generated from `HelloWorld.idl`, the signature of the `hello()` operation is as follows:

```
virtual HelloWorld::MyObject_ptr hello(
        HelloWorld::MyObject_ptr in_obj,
        HelloWorld::MyObject_ptr& inout_obj,
        HelloWorld::MyObject_ptr& out_obj) = 0;
```

Note that the IDL compiler generates a pure virtual function that needs to be implemented by a servant.

A typical implementation of the `hello()` method by a servant named `GoodDayImpl` that implements the `HelloWorld::GoodDay` object is as follows:

```
HelloWorld::MyObject_ptr GoodDayImpl::hello(
        HelloWorld::MyObject_ptr in_obj,
        HelloWorld::MyObject_ptr& inout_obj,
        HelloWorld::MyObject_ptr& out_obj ) {

    // if we need to hold onto the object
    // reference passed as in parameter, need to
    // duplicate it, ORB would release it otherwise
    HelloWorld::MyObject_ptr save_in_obj =
        HelloWorld::MyObject::_duplicate( in_obj );

    // obtain an object reference
    // either by invoking _bind(), _narrow() or
    // other means to initialize out_obj
    out_obj =
      HelloWorld::MyObject::_bind( "OutObject" );

    // Release incoming inout parameter
    CORBA::release( in_obj );

    // Now initialize the inout argument
    inout_obj =
      HelloWorld::MyObject::_bind( "InOutObject" );

    // Create a return value
    HelloWorld::MyObject_var ret_obj =
      HelloWorld::MyObject::_bind( "RetObject" );

    // if we need to hold onto this object's
    // reference, duplicate it before we return it
    // to the caller, else the ORB would release it
    HelloWorld::MyObject::_duplicate( ret_obj );

    return ret_obj;
}
```

In the above implementation, the types of the signature of the method matches the signature type generated by the IDL compiler in the skeleton code. Again we use _bind() to obtain an object reference, which we then use to initialize out_obj and return_obj. The important points to note here are the memory management rules. If we need to hold onto the object reference passed to us an in parameter, we need to call _duplicate() on the object reference so that it is not released by the ORB. In accordance with case 2, we have to release the object reference stored in the inout parameter before we assign a new one to it. Also, before we return an object reference, if we need to hold onto it for later use, we need to call _duplicate() on it before we return the value. This rule applies not only to object references but all variable types.

Following these principles we set values to the out_obj argument, replace the values in the inout_obj argument, and create a return_obj, initialize it, and return it to the client. We use the _var class whenever possible to ensure proper memory management.

10   *Mapping of Interfaces*

IDL interfaces are mapped to C++ classes that contain datatype definitions and function declarations for the operations of the interfaces. The mapping can be divided into client side (caller) and a server side (called) mapping.

10.1   Client Side Mapping

Given the background information on the mapping types and the rules for passing parameters, we now look at how to use this information to create distributed applications. The IDL compiler is responsible for creating the skeleton from which we can build our applications. The client side pieces of this skeleton, commonly referred to as stubs, are implementations of the C++ classes created by the IDL compiler from the corresponding IDL interface. From an object reference obtained by the client, a client side proxy object is generated from the stubs which allows the client to invoke functions as though the object were local. Upon execution, the proxy object forwards the call to the implementation object and all the data marshaling and low-level communication are transparently handled by the ORB to make remote invocations appear local. In a client program you need only declare an object reference of the C++ class type, such as

```
Tester_var myTester;
```

and assign a value to the variable, for example,

```
CORBA::Object obj = orb->string_to_object(iorString);
myTester = myTester._narrow(obj);
```

The client can now invoke functions on this object in the usual manner. The difference is in the execution of the function. The proxy object forwards the call to the implementation object by calling the ORB library to send the call to the remote object.

10.2   Server Side Mapping

For the server side mapping we have to consider different cases. We have to consider two object adapters, the BOA and the POA. In either case the mapping the IDL compiler generates is a skeleton class for each IDL interface. The implementor's task is to implement the attributes and operations defined in the IDL specification and to glue them together with the skeleton.

The gluing can be done in two ways, using an inheritance approach or a delegation approach. In the inheritance approach you define an implementation class that inherits the skeleton class generated by the IDL compiler. In the delegation approach the IDL compiler generates an additional class, called the tie class. The tie class is a pseudo-implementation class. The tie class inherits the skeleton class and holds a reference to the real implementation class you provide.

The BOA specification is rather vague and it is particular in the area of the interface implementation. Hence the mappings vary. For details on the various BOA details, review the reference manuals of the particular products.

For demonstration purposes we use the Inprise VisiBroker for C++ idl2cpp compiler. For example,

```
// Example.idl
interface Example {
    void f();
};
```

compiles to produce the following C++ files:

```
interface_ex_c.hh
interface_ex_c.cc
interface_ex_s.hh
interface_ex_s.cc
```

Within `interface_ex_s.hh` is the skeleton class of the `interface_ex`, named with the prepended `_sk_`. From this the developer inherits and provides the class implementation and method definitions.

```
// Interface_Ex_Implementation.h

#include Interface_Ex_s.hh

Class Example : public virtual _sk_Example
{
protected:
    _sk_Example(const char *_obj_name = (const char *)NULL);
...

public:
  virtual void f() = 0; //operation stub
```

```
  ...

};

// Interface_Ex_Implementation.cpp

#include Interface_Ex_Implementation.h

//constructor
Example::Example () {
... //initialization(s);
}

void Example::f() {
...//do something
    }
```

The POA takes the same approach as the BOA, but exactly defines the names and conventions of the generated classes. First of all, the mapping defines a virtual C++ class with the same name as the IDL interface, the class is as follows:

```
//C++
class Example : public virtual CORBA::Object {
    public:
        virtual void f();
};
```

There is a choice for ORB implementors of where to apply the virtual keyword, but the signature of the interface is in any case the same. The mapping of the operations follows the rules explained above.

The mapping defines two more classes for use in the inheritance and the delegation approach, respectively. For the inheritance approach, a class POA_interface_name is generated. It inherits a servant base class and has the same signature as the class interface_name. For our example it would look like the following:

```
// C++
class POA_Example :: public virtual PortableServer::ServantBase {
    public:
    // +
        virtual void f();
};
```

An implementation class is as follows:

```
class ExampleImpl : public virtual POA_Example {
    public
        void foo() throw( CORBA::SystemException ) {
```

```
                        cout << ìfoo invokedî << endl;
};
};
```

For the delegation approach, the compiler generates an additional class, the tie class. The tie class is named `POA_interface_name_tie`. The tie class inherits the skeleton class. The tie class for our example is:

```
// C++
template<class T>;
class POA_Example_tie : public POA_Example {
    public:

};
```

It is now the application programmer's responsibility to provide the implementation of the template class. For our example that is:

```
// C++
template<class T>
void POA_Example_tie<T>::foo() throw( CORBA::SystemException ) {
    cout << "foo invoked" << endl;
};
```

In the next chapter we explain the C++ mapping of the POA. More examples using the POA are given throughout the remainder of the book, specifically in chapters 6 and 7.

4

ORB Runtime System

The CORBA specification defines the ORB runtime system in the form of the pseudo-objects ORB, BOA and POA, and Object. They are called pseudo-objects because they provide interfaces like normal objects, but the operations on those interfaces are implemented in libraries and do not usually result in a remote invocation. Interfaces of pseudo-objects are specified in OMG IDL, which are commented as pseudo-IDL (PIDL). In this chapter we explain the implementation of these pseudo-objects for C++ ORBs, that is, their corresponding C++ APIs. Besides the three pseudo-objects, we introduce the C++ mapping for TypeCodes, the DII, the DSI, and the Contexts.

This chapter contains mappings for the following interfaces:

- ♦ CORBA::Object
- ♦ CORBA::ORB
- ♦ CORBA::BOA
- ♦ TypeCode
- ♦ DII
- ♦ DSI
- ♦ CORBA::Context
- ♦ CORBA::POA

1 *Object Interface*

Using the BOA, all CORBA objects, that is, objects that have been specified in OMG IDL and implemented in a CORBA environment, are extensions of CORBA::Object. The interface CORBA::Object defines the operations that are applicable to any object. These operations are implemented by the ORB itself instead of being passed to the implementation of the derived object. POA servants are connected with CORBA::Object by delegation.

In this section we will discuss the mapping of these operations to C++. The mappings will be presented in the following format:

CORBA definition   CORBA::Object

C++ mapping   CORBA::Object

1.1 get_implementation()

The Implementation Repository contains information that allows the ORB to locate and activate object implementations. This information is accessible from an object with a CORBA definition CORBA::ImplementationDef. Note that the specification of CORBA::ImplementationDef is left to the particular ORB implementation since it deals with operating-system-specific information. The operation returns an object that can then be queried about details of the object implementation.

CORBA definition   ImplementationDef get_implementation();

C++ mapping   CORBA_ImplementationDef_ptr::_get_implementation()

1.2 get_interface()

The Interface Repository contains type information of IDL-defined types. Although the Interface Repository can be modified directly through an IDL-defined interface, the type information is usually created and stored by the IDL compiler, with the appropriate options switched on. The type information is kept in objects with the CORBA definition CORBA::InterfaceDef. Operations on this interface allow the query of type information in the Interface Repository. The operation get_interface() returns an ImplementationDef object that represents the interface type of the object it was called on.

CORBA definition   ImplementationDef get_interface();

C++ mapping   CORBA_InterfaceDef_ptr::_get_interface()

1.3   is_nil()

An object reference can be tested for this value by the operation is_nil().
This operation returns TRUE if the value of the reference is nil, otherwise
FALSE. The ORB determines the result; the implementation of the object is
not involved. Its parameter is the object pointer which needs to be checked.

CORBA definition	boolean is_nil()
C++ mapping	static CORBA::Boolean CORBA::is_nil (NVList_ptr obj)

1.4   duplicate() and release()

The operations duplicate() and release() provide memory management for
object references. The operation duplicate() is a public member of the C++
class CORBA::Object. The operation release() is defined in the CORBA namespace.

CORBA definition	Object duplicate();
	void release();
C++ mapping	static Object_ptr_duplicate
	(Object_ptr obj);
	CORBA::release(Object_ptr obj);

The semantics and use of these operations are explained in Chapter 2.

1.5   is_a()

The operation is_a() tests if the object the operation is called on is of the
interface type supplied as an argument. This string argument to is_a() is
interpreted as an Interface Repository identifier (see Chapter 2 for an explanation). It returns TRUE if the object is of the type identified. This means
either that the object's type and the identified type are the same, or that the
identified type is a base type of the object's type. A FALSE return value does
not necessarily mean that the object is not substitutable. The parameter for
the C++ mapping is the repository identifier to check.

CORBA definition	boolean is_a(in string logical_type_id);
C++ mapping	CORBA::Boolean _is_a(const char* logical_type_id);)

1.6   non_existent()

The operation non_existent() can be used to test if an object has been
destroyed. It returns TRUE if the ORB can authoritatively determine that

the referenced object does not exist, otherwise it returns FALSE. Note that the FALSE may not mean that the object still exists.

CORBA definition   boolean non_existent();

C++ mapping   `CORBA::Boolean _non_existent()`

1.7   is_equivalent()

The operation `is_equivalent()` determines if two object references are equivalent, that is, are they identical or do they refer to the same object. The operation returns TRUE if the object reference on which the object was called and the reference `other_object` are known to be equivalent, otherwise it returns FALSE. Note that the FALSE does not mean that the object could not possibly be the same.

CORBA definition   is_equivalent(in Object other_object);

C++ mapping   `CORBA::Boolean _is_equivalent(CORBA::Object_ptr`
                                     `other_object)`

1.8   hash()

The operation `hash()` is used to effectively manage large numbers of object references. It generates a hash value for the object reference on which the operation is called. The hash value relates to an ORB-internal identifier. As usual with hash functions, different object references can result in the same hash value and further operations, such as the operation `is_equivalent()`, need to be called.

CORBA definition   unsigned long hash(in unsigned long maximum);

C++ mapping   `CORBA::ULong hash(CORBA::ULong maximum);`

1.9   create_request()

The operation `create_request()` is used to create a dynamic invocation request when using the DII. It is discussed in this context in Chapter 7.

CORBA definition   Status create_request(

                              in Context ctx,

                              in Identifier operation,

                              in NVList arg_list,

                              inout NamedValue result,

                              out Request request,

                              in Flags req_flags);

C++ mapping

```
CORBA::Status _create_request (
Context_ptr ctx,
Const char *operation,
CORBA::NVList_ptr arg_list,
CORBA::NamedValue_ptr& result,
CORBA::Request_out request,
Flags req_flags )
```

2 ORB Interface

The ORB interface provides operations to bootstrap a CORBA application. This requires the initialization of an object adapter, the conversion of object references into strings and vice versa, and the resolution of initial references.

There are more operations defined on the ORB pseudo-interface that are concerned with TypeCodes, contexts, the DII, and the DSI. The mappings for these operations are explained in the appropriate sections. The ORB interface is mapped as follows:

CORBA definition   CORBA::ORB

C++ mapping   `CORBA::ORB`

2.1 ORB Initialization

Before an application can use the operations on the ORB interfaces it needs a reference to an ORB pseudo-object. The `CORBA::ORB_init()` method initializes the ORB. A pointer to the ORB is returned. The `orb_id` parameter identifies the type of ORB to be used.

CORBA definition   ORB ORB_init(inout arg_list argv, in ORB orb_identifier);

C++ mapping

```
CORBA::ORB_init( int& argc,
        char* const *argv,
        const char* orb_id = NULL);
```

2.2 Converting Object References into Strings and Vice Versa

Object references can be externalized by converting them into strings. A stringified object reference can be conveniently stored in a file or passed around by means other than CORBA, for example, by ftp or email. Of course, a stringified object reference must be reconvertible into a real object reference, which refers to the same object as the original one.

There are two operations of the ORB interface which stringify and destringify object references. The `object_to_string()` operation converts an interoperable object reference (IOR) into a string.

CORBA definition   string object_to_string(in Object obj);

C++ mapping   `char *object_to_string (CORBA::Object_ptr obj)`

The operation `string_to_object()` converts a stringified object reference back into an IOR.

CORBA definition   Object string_to_object(in string obj);

C++ mapping   `CORBA::Object_ptr string_to_object`

            `( const char *str)`

A stringified IOR that has been produced by `object_to_string()` is guaranteed to be reconvertible by `string_to_object()` independent of which ORB the operations have been invoked on. Note that the result of `string_to_object()` is of type CORBA::Object and must be narrowed to the object type expected.

2.3   Obtaining Initial References

Besides initializing an ORB, client and server programs need to access initial objects such as a root naming context, usually to bootstrap themselves. The ORB defines two operations for this purpose.

CORBA definition   typedef string ObjectId;

                  Typedef sequence <ObjectId> ObjectIdList;

                  exception InvalidName{};

                  ObjectIdList list_initial_services();

C++ mapping   `typedef char* ObjectId;`

            `class ObjectIdList { … };`

            `class InvalidName { … };`

            `ObjectIdList * list_initial_services();`

CORBA definition   Object resolve_initial_services(in ObjectId identifier)

                        raises(InvalidName);

C++ mapping   `Object resolve_initial_services(`

                  `const char *identifier );`

2.4   BOA Initialization

A server also needs to initialize an object adapter. The ORB pseudo-interface provides the operation `BOA_init()` to obtain a BOA.

CORBA definition	BOA BOA_init(inout arg_lit argv, in OADid boa_identifier);
C++ mapping	`CORBA::BOA_ptr ORB::BOA_init(int & argc, char`
	`*const *argv,`
	`const char *boa_identifier = (char *) NULL);`

2.5   POA Initialization

A reference to an initial POA can be obtained using the operation resolve_ initial_services(), as defined above. The object identifier for the initial POA is RootPOA. An application program can obtain further, more refined POAs from the root POA, which is explained below.

3   *Basic Object Adapter*

Earlier we introduced the operation `BOA_init()`, which initializes a BOA and provides a server with a pseudo-object reference to a BOA. In this section we introduce the operations specified in BOA pseudo-interface and their mapping to C++. The IDL-specified BOA pseudo-interface CORBA::BOA is mapped to the C++ class CORBA::BOA_ptr.

3.1   Activation and Deactivation

The operation object_is_ready() makes the specified object available for clients.

CORBA definition	void object_is_ready(in Object obj,
	In ImplementationDef impl);
C++ mapping	`void obj_is_ready( CORBA::ImplementationDef_ptr`
	`impl_ptr = NULL);`

Although an object reference can be passed to clients, for example, via a Naming or Trading Service, or externalized with object_to_string() as soon as an object is created, methods can only be invoked after obj_is_ready() has been called for this particular object.

The operation deactivate_object() will deactivate the specified object. Once an object has been deactivated it is no longer accessible to clients. An attempt to invoke a method on a deactivated object will raise the exception CORBA::NO_IMPLEMENT.

CORBA definition   void deactivate_object(in Object obj);

C++ mapping   `void deactivate_object(CORBA::Object_ptr obj);`

The operation `impl_is_ready()` activates objects on a per-server basis, that is, all objects that have been created by a particular server are made accessible to clients.

CORBA definition   void impl_is_ready(in ImplementationDef impl);

C++ mapping   `void impl_is_ready(`

                       `CORBA::ImplementationDef_ptr impl_def = NULL );`

Visibroker for C++, however, implements the method with slightly different semantics. Visibroker requires a call to `obj_is_ready()` for each object. The method `impl_is_ready()` makes a program listen for requests to the objects it has created.

3.2   Other Operations

The BOA interface description provided in the CORBA module contains several additional operations that are seldom used by any ORB implementation. The generation of object references is usually done implicitly when a programming language reference to an implementation object is passed as a parameter. The handling of authentication and access control is done by a higher-level service. The reference data in an object reference may be used for many purposes, among them retrieval of persistent state.

Note that the principal has been deprecated and we only show it for historical reasons. If you want to implement your own access control, use the service context instead of the principal to pass the identity of a caller along with an invocation.

```
//interface CORBA::BOA PIDL cont...

interface Principal;
typedef sequence <octet, 1024> ReferenceData;

Object create(
    In ReferenceData        id,
    In InterfaceDef         intf,
    In ImplementationDef impl);

void dispose(in Object obj);
ReferenceData get_id(in Object obj);
```

```
Void change_implementation(
    In Object            obj,
    In ImplementationDef impl);

Principal get_principal(
    In Object            obj,
    In Environment              env);
}; // interface BOA
}; // module CORBA
```

The get_id() operation will return the reference data of an object reference which is guaranteed to be unique within the server that implements the object. Activation and deactivation of servers requires that object state information be stored persistently, for example, in a database. The reference data can be used as a database key to retrieve this information when a server is reactivated.

4 *TypeCodes*

TypeCodes represent IDL type definitions at runtime. They can be created and examined at runtime. TypeCodes are defined in the CORBA specification by the pseudo-CORBA definition CORBA::TypeCode. They are used in the following contexts:

The Any type—describes the type of the value contained by the Any object.

DII—used to determine the type of the parameters of a Request.

Interface repository—represents type specifications stored in the Interface Repository.

IORs—represents the type of the referenced object.

4.1 Interface TypeCode

The pseudo-CORBA definition is mapped to C++ mappings or classes:

CORBA definition   CORBA::TypeCode

C++ mapping   `CORBA::TypeCode`

The following is a list of the TypeCode constants for IDL datatypes. All of the TypeCode constants have a datatype of `TypeCode_ptr`.

```
_tc_null
_tc_void
_tc_short
```

```
_tc_long
_tc_longlong
_tc_ushort
_tc_ulong
_tc_ulonglong
_tc_float
_tc_double
_tc_longdouble
_tc_boolean
_tc_char
_tc_wchar
_tc_wstring
_tc_octet
_tc_Any
_tc_TypeCode
_tc_Principal
_tc_Object
_tc_string
_tc_NamedValue
```

4.1.1   TCKind

The CORBA module defines a pseudo-IDL definition of an enum, TCKind. This enum defines constants to determine various "kinds" of TypeCodes. Different operations are allowed on different kinds of TypeCodes.

CORBA definition   CORBA::TCKind

C++ mapping   `CORBA::TCKind`

This class is used by the Interface Repository and the IDL compiler to represent the type of arguments or attributes. TypeCode objects are also used in a Request to specify an argument's type, in conjunction with the Any class. TypeCode objects have a `kind` and parameter list property.

```
tk_null
tk_void
tk_short
tk_long
tk_longlong
tk_ushort
tk_ulong
tk_ulonglong
tk_float
tk_double
tk_longdouble
tk_boolean
tk_char
tk_wchar
tk_wstring
tk_octet
```

```
tk_any
tk_TypeCode
tk_Principal
tk_objref
tk_struct
tk_union
tk_enum
tk_string
tk_sequence
tk_array
```

4.1.2 General Methods

The operation `equal()` returns TRUE if the TypeCode is structurally equivalent to a `typecode`, FALSE otherwise. Additionally, if the objects' kind is not `CORBA::tk_union`, a BadKind exception will be raised.

CORBA definition   boolean equal(in TypeCode tc);

C++ mapping   `CORBA::Boolean equal`
                   `( CORBA::TypeCode_ptr tc ) const;`

The operation `kind()` returns the kind of the TypeCode as defined in CORBA::TCKind.

CORBA definition   TCKind kind();

C++ mapping   `CORBA::TCKind kind() const;`

The operation `id()` returns a RepositoryId for a type in the Interface Repository.

CORBA definition   RepositoryID id() raises (BadKind);

C++ mapping   `CORBA::String_var id();`

There are three forms of repository identifiers:

IDL format. The string starts with "IDL:" and then uses the scoped name followed by a major and minor version number to globally identify an object. We assume that objects with the same major number are derived from one another. The identifier with the larger minor number is assumed to be a subtype of the one with the smaller minor number.

DCE UUID format. The string starts with "DCE:" and is followed by a UUID, a colon, and then a minor version number.

LOCAL format. The string starts with "LOCAL:" and is followed by an arbitrary string. This format is for use with a single repository that does not communicate with ORBs outside its naming domain.

The operation `name()` returns the unscoped name of the type as specified in the IDL. This is only valid for `tk_objref`, `tk_struct`, `tk_union`, `tk_enum`, `tk_alias`, `tk_except`.

CORBA definition   Identifier name() raises (BadKind);

C++ mapping   `const char *name() const;`

4.1.3 Methods for Structured Types

The operation `member_count()` returns the number of members in the type description. It is only for the following TypeCode kinds: `tk_struct`, `tk_union`, `tk_enum`, and `tk_except`.

CORBA definition   unsigned long member_count() raises (BadKind);

C++ mapping   `CORBA::ULong member_count() const;`

    `Throws system exception BadKind()`

The operation `member_name()` returns the name of the indexed member. The index is zero-based. It is only valid for the following TypeCode kinds: `tk_struct`, `tk_union`, `tk_enum`, and `t_except`.

CORBA definition   Identifier member_name (in unsigned long index)

    Raises (BadKind, Bounds);

C++ mapping   `const char member_name CORBA::ULong index) const;`

    `Throws system exception BadKind and Bounds`

The operation `member_type()` returns the type of the indexed member only valid for the following Typecode kinds: `tk_union`, `tk_except`.

CORBA definition   TypeCode member_type(in unsigned long index)

    Raises (BadKind);

C++ mapping   `CORBA_TypeCode_ptr::member_type(CORBA::ULong`

    `index) const;`

4.1.4 Methods for Unions

The operation `member_label()` returns the label of member index (of a case statement). It is only valid for the `tk_union` TypeCode kind.

CORBA definition   any member_label(in unsigned long index)

    Raises (BadKind, Bounds);

C++ mapping   `CORBA::Any_ptr CORBA_TypeCode::member_label(`

    `CORBA::ULong index) const;`

    `Throws system exceptions BadKind and Bounds`

The operation `discriminator_type()` returns the type of the union discriminator (only valid for `tk_union`).

CORBA definition   TypeCode discriminator_type() raises (BadKind);

C++ mapping

```
CORBA::TypeCode_ptr
        CORBA_TypeCode::discriminator_type()
        Throws system exception BadKind
```

The operation `default_index()` returns the default index of the union (only valid for `tk_union`).

CORBA definition   long default_index() raises (BadKind);

C++ mapping

```
CORBA::Long default_index() const;
        Throws system exception BadKind
```

4.1.5 *Methods for Template Types*

The operation `length()` returns the number of elements contained by the type; it returns zero for unbounded strings and sequences. It is only valid for the following TypeCode kinds: `tk_string`, `tk_sequence`, `tk_array`.

CORBA definition   unsigned long length() raises (BadKind);

C++ mapping

```
CORBA::Ulong length() const;
        Throws system exception BadKind
```

The operation `content_type()` returns the base type of the template types (`tk_sequence`, `tk_array`) or the aliased type (`tk_alias`).

CORBA definition   TypeCode content_type() raises (BadKind);

C++ mapping

```
CORBA::TypeCode_ptr context_type() const;
        Throws system exception BadKind
```

4.2 Creating TypeCodes

TypeCodes are created using operations in the CORBA::ORB interface. We will provide the method signatures in this section. All the TypeCode creation methods follow a similar pattern. The result of the method is the newly created TypeCode object. These methods must be recursively applied for TypeCodes of recursive types.

4.2.1 *Structured and Flat Types*

The methods to create TypeCodes for structured and flat types, that is, structs, unions, enums, alias, exception, and interface, have the same first two parameters. The first parameter is a Repository Identifier specifying the type in IDL. The second parameter is the unscoped type name of the type. Further parameters determine specific components depending on the kind of TypeCode. This will be explained below.

The method `create_struct_tc()` creates a TypeCode describing an IDL structure. The parameter members determine an array of structures defining the members of the type.

```
static CORBA::TypeCode_ptr create_struct_tc(
                    const char *repository_id,
                    const char *type_name,
                    const CORBA::StructMemberSeq& members);
```

The method `create_union_tc()` creates a TypeCode describing an IDL union. The parameter `discriminator_type` determines the type of the discriminator, for example, the type used in the switch statement. The parameter members determine an array of structures defining the members of the type.

```
static CORBA::TypeCode_ptr create_union_tc(
                    const char *repository_id,
                    const char *type_name,
                    CORBA::TypeCode_ptr discriminator_type,
                    const CORBA::UnionMemberSeq& members);
```

The method `create_enum_tc()` creates a TypeCode describing an IDL enum. The parameter members determine an array of strings defining the members of the type.

```
static CORBA::TypeCode_ptr create_enum_tc(
                    const char *repository_id,
                    const char *type_name,
                    const CORBA::EnumMemberSeq& members);
```

The method `create_alias_tc()` creates a TypeCode describing an IDL typedef alias. The parameter original_type determines the aliased type.

```
static CORBA::TypeCode_ptr create_alias_tc(
                        const char *repository_id,
                        const char *type_name,
                        CORBA::TypeCode_ptr original_type);
```

The method `create_exception_tc()` creates a TypeCode describing an IDL exception. The parameter members determine an array of structures defining the members of the type.

```
static CORBA::TypeCode_ptr create_exception_tc(
                          const char *repository_id,
                          const char *type_name,
                          const CORBA::StructMemberSeq& members);
```

The method `create_interface_tc()` creates a TypeCode describing a CORBA interface.

```
static CORBA::TypeCode_ptr create_interface_tc(
                        const char *repository_id,
                        const char *type_name);
```

4.2.2 Template Types

The methods to create TypeCodes for template types, that is, strings, sequences, and arrays, have the same first parameter, length. These parameters specify the length of bounded types. A zero value determines an unbounded type.

The method `create_string_tc()` creates a TypeCode describing an IDL string.

```
static CORBA::TypeCode_ptr create_string_tc(
                          CORBA::ULong bound);
```

The method `create_sequence_tc()` creates a TypeCode describing an IDL sequence. The parameter element_type determines the type of the elements contained by the sequence.

```
static CORBA::TypeCode_ptr create_sequence_tc(
                          CORBA::ULong bound,
                          CORBA::TypeCode_ptr element_type);
```

The method `create_recursive_sequence_tc()` creates a TypeCode describing an IDL sequence. The parameter offset determines how many levels up in the type hierarchy the TypeCode's definition can be found.

```
static CORBA::TypeCode_ptr create_recursive_sequence_tc(
                          CORBA::ULong bound,
                          CORBA::ULong offset);
```

The method `create_array_tc()` creates a TypeCode describing an IDL array. The parameter element_type determines the type of the elements contained in the array.

```
static CORBA::TypeCode_ptr create_array_tc(
                          CORBA::ULong length,
                          CORBA::TypeCode_ptr element_type);
```

5 Dynamic Invocation Interface

The DII enables clients to invoke operations on objects without compile-time knowledge of their IDL type, that is, without the stub code generated by the IDL compiler. A client creates a request, which is the dynamic equivalent of an operation. A request contains an object reference, an operation name, type information, and the values of the arguments which are supplied by the client. Eventually a request can be invoked that has the same semantics as invoking the operation using stub code.

In this section we will explain common data structures, the request interface, and the NVList interface. The use of the DII is explained by an example in Chapter 7.

5.1 Common Data Structures

There are a number of common data structures to be used in the context of the DII and elsewhere in the ORB. In this section we introduce NamedValue and NamedValueList and their respective mapping to C++.

Named values usually describe results and parameters of operations. A named value list is used to describe a parameter list of an operation.

5.1.1 Named Values

A named value is specified in PIDL as

```
pseudo interface NamedValue {
  readonly attribute Identifier name;
  readonly attribute any argument;
  readonly attribute Flags flags;
};
```

where name determines the name of the parameter. The argument carries the value of the parameter encapsulated in an Any. Note that the argument not only carries the value but also the type (in the form of a TypeCode) of a value. The len parameter determines the length of the value (argument) in bytes. The arg_modes can have the value CORBA::ARG_IN, CORBA::ARG_INOUT, or CORBA::ARG_OUT to determine if the parameter is in, inout, or out.

The type NamedValue is mapped as follows:

CORBA definition   CORBA::NamedValue

C++ mapping   `CORBA::NamedValue`

Its members are mapped to the following methods:

C++ mapping	`const char *name() const;`
C++ mapping	`CORBA::Any *value() const;`
C++ mapping	`CORBA::Flags flags() const;`

Note that objects implementing the NameValue interface cannot be created directly. Instead, they must be obtained via the NVList interface as shown below.

5.2   Creating an NVList

An NVList can be created by using the operation `create_list()` provided on the ORB pseudo-interface.

CORBA definition	Status create_list(in long count,
	out NVList new_list);
C++ mapping	`CORBA::Status create_list(CORBA::Long count,`
	`                  CORBA::NVList_ptr& nvlist);`

The operation `create_list()` creates a pseudo-object of type NVList where count determines the length of the list. The return type `Status` can be defined as either `typedef unsigned long Status` (intended to describe a status code rather than raising an exception) or `typedef void Status`.

5.3   NVList Interface

The interface NVList is defined in pseudo-IDL in the CORBA module. It provides the operations in the following subsections.

5.3.1   Adding Elements to NVLists

There are three operations defined in pseudo-IDL to add arguments to an NVList.

CORBA definition	Status add (in Flags flags);
C++ mapping	`NamedValue_ptr add(CORBA::Flags flags);`
CORBA definition	Status add_item (in Identifier item_name, in Flags flags);
C++ mapping	`NamedValue_ptr add_item(const char *,`
	`                  CORBA::Flags flags);`
CORBA definition	Status add_value (in Identifier item_name, in any value in Flags flags);

C++ mapping   `NamedValue_ptr add_value(`

                   `const char *,`

                   `const Any&,`

                   `CORBA::Flags flags);`

The flags parameter can take the values ARG_IN, ARG_OUT, or ARG_INOUT, which correspond to the parameter tags in, out, and inout. The C++ language defines values for these flags in the **CORBA** class.

The TypeCode and the value pointer parameters in the IDL are replaced by the Any in the methods. There is also no need for the length parameter because the `void *` is replaced by a reference to a C++ Any object, and hence is of known length.

5.3.2   *Freeing Lists*

The CORBA definition provides two operations to handle garbage collection.

5.3.3   *List Management*

The pseudo-CORBA definition provides the operation `get_count()` which returns the total number of items in the list.

CORBA definition   Status get_count(out long count);

C++ mapping   `CORBA::Long count() const;`

A number of other useful operations are provided. The `item()` method returns the indexed element from the list.

C++ mapping   `CORBA_NamedValue_ptr item(CORBA::Long index )`

The `remove()` method removes the indexed element from the list. The exception BAD_PARAM is thrown if the index is out of range.

C++ mapping   `CORBA_NamedValue_ptr remove(CORBA::Long index )`

5.4   DII Request

Request is a pseudo-CORBA definition that provides the mechanism to dynamically invoke operations on objects. Requests are created by the ORB.

5.5   Creating a Request

The pseudo-interface CORBA::ORB provides an operation to create Request objects. The operation `create_request()` returns a new Request pseudo-object.

CORBA definition	Status create_request(
	in Context ctx,
	in Identifier operation,
	in NVList arg_list,
	inout NamedValue result,
	out Request request,
	in Flags req_flags);

C++ mapping

```
CORBA::Status _create_request(
    CORBA::Context_ptr ctx,
    const char *operation,
    CORBA::NVList_ptr arg_list,
    CORBA::NamedValue_ptr result,
    CORBA::Request_ptr& request,
    Flags req_flags);
```

The ctx parameter specifies the context of the request. The operation parameter determines the name of the operation to be invoked. The arg_list parameter provides the arguments to that operation. The result parameter provides a type expected as the result of the operation. The req_flags and flags parameters indicate the memory management required for the out parameters. If they are set to CORBA::OUT_LIST_MEMORY, all memory associated with out parameters can be freed by the ORB when freeing the arg_list, otherwise it has to be freed explicitly. The newly created Request object is returned as the result of the method. There is an additional operation to create partially initialized Request objects:

C++ mapping   `CORBA::Request_ptr _request(const char* operation)`

All other parameters of the Request object must be set through the object's interface as described below.

5.6   Request Interface

The pseudo-interface Request is defined in the module CORBA. It is mapped to the C++ mapping CORBA::Request. The pseudo-interface defines the following operations. The add_arg() operation incrementally adds arguments of type NamedValue to the Request's parameter list (of type NVList).

CORBA definition	Status add_arg(
	in Identifier name,
	in TypeCode arg_type,

    in void *value,

    in long len,

    in Flags   arg_flags

    );

C++ mapping   `CORBA::Any& _add_in_arg(const char *name);`

When the Request is correctly initialized it can be invoked by calling the `invoke()` operation:

CORBA definition   Status invoke(in Flags arg_flags);

C++ mapping   `CORBA::Status invoke();`

If the operation returns successfully, the result is set in the result field of the Request and the inout and out parameters have been modified in the Request's parameter list by the object implementation.

The operation `destroy()` deletes the Request object.

CORBA definition   void destroy();

C++ mapping   `void destroy();`

The operation `send()` allows an asynchronous Request to be made. The semantics are that the operation returns without waiting for the target object to invoke the operation. It is paired with the operation `get_response()` which allows the caller to check for results at a later time. The invoke_flags parameter may contain the flag CORBA::INV_NO_RESPONSE to indicate that the operation is one way, or that the caller expects no results in any case.

The `send()` operation is mapped to a pair of methods. The method `send_oneway()` is mapping for `send()` with the flag CORBA::INV_NO_RESPONSE. It does not block and does not result in a response being sent from the object implementation to the client application. The method `send_deferred()` is the mapping for `send()` without this flag set. It will not block waiting for a response. The client application can retrieve the response using the `get_response()` method.

CORBA definition   Status send(in Flags invoke_flags);

C++ mapping   `CORBA::Status send_oneway();`

                     `CORBA::Status send_deferred()`

The operation result and any inout or out parameters won't be valid until the operation `get_response()` has been invoked and has returned. The operation `get_response()` receives the result as well as inout and out parameters from an operation invocation initiated by the send() operation.

CORBA definition   Status get_response(in Flags arg_flags);

C++ mapping   `CORBA::Status get_response();`

The methods block until the operation invocation initiated by the Request is complete.

There is an additional method, `poll_response()`, which returns a boolean value indicating whether or not the operation invocation is complete.

C++ mapping   `CORBA::Boolean poll_response();`

It returns TRUE if the response to the asynchronous invocation is available, FALSE otherwise. Note that `get_response()` must be called even if `poll_response()` returns TRUE, since only `get_response()` reads in the result values.

The CORBA specification provides an operation for making multiple requests, `send_multiple_requests()`, and a corresponding response operation `get_next_response()`. These operations are defined in C syntax.

The operations are mapped to the following C++ methods provided in the **CORBA::ORB** class. The method `send_multiple_requests_oneway()` sends all the requests in its argument array, and the method `send_multiple_requests_deferred()` sends all of the requests provided to it and returns.

C++ mapping   `CORBA::Status send_multiple_requests_oneway(`

`const CORBA::RequestSeq& seq);`

The method `get_next_response()` blocks until a response to a deferred Request is available. The method `poll_next_response()` informs the caller if any invocations have completed.

C++ mapping   `CORBA::Status get_next_response(`

`CORBA::Request*& request)`

C++ mapping   `CORBA:Boolean poll_next_response();`

6 Dynamic Skeleton Interface

The DII provides a mechanism to invoke operations from a client without compile-time knowledge about the interface. The DSI provides a similar mechanism for the other side; that is, the ORB can invoke an object implementation without compile knowledge about the interface, that is, without the skeleton. For an object implementation, a call via a compiler-generated skeleton and the DSI are indistinguishable.

The idea behind the DSI is to invoke all object implementations via the same general operation. This operation is provided by an interface of the pseudo-object, called ServerRequest, which is similar to the Request pseudo-object of the DII. We illustrate the use of the DSI in Chapter 7.

6.1 ServerRequest Interface

The pseudo-IDL specification of ServerRequest provides the following operations. The operation op_name() returns the name of the operation that was invoked.

CORBA definition   Identifier op_name();

C++ mapping   `const char* op_name() const;`

The ctx() operation provides the invocation Context of the operation.

CORBA definition   Context ctx();

C++ mapping   `CORBA::Context_ptr ctx() const;`

The params() operation returns the list of parameters passed to the invocation.

CORBA definition   void params(inout NVList params);

C++ mapping   `void params(CORBA::NVList_ptr params);`

The result() operation returns the Any in which the result is to be placed.

CORBA definition   Any result();

C++ mapping   `void result(CORBA::Any_ptr result)`

7 *Context Interface*

A context object contains a list of properties, pairs of names, and values. CORBA restricts values to type string. The intended role of context objects is similar to that of environment variables in various operating systems, which can determine a user's or an application's preferences. They could be defined for a system, for a user, or for an application. Context objects can be manipulated by concatenating their property lists or by arranging them into context trees. We demonstrate the use of contexts in Chapter 7.

Operations can be declared with a context by adding a context clause after the raises expression. A context is made available to the server by an additional argument to the stub and skeleton interfaces. When an operation with a context is invoked through either the stub or the DII, the ORB will insert the values of the properties of the specified context.

7.1   Creating a Context Object

Contexts are organized in trees. Each context has an internal reference to its parent context. The root context is the global default context. The pseudo-interface Context is mapped to C++ mappings and classes.

CORBA definition   CORBA::Context

C++ mapping   `CORBA::Context`

The ORB pseudo-interface provides the operation `get_default_context()` to obtain the root context. The equivalent method is provided by the C++ class CORBA::ORB.

CORBA definition   Status get_default_context(out Context ctx);

C++ mapping   `CORBA::Status`
`get_default_context(CORBA::Context_ptr&);`

7.2   Manipulating a Context Object

The pseudo-CORBA definition CORBA::Context provides operations to manipulate a context object. The operation `set_one_value()` sets the value of the named property.

CORBA definition   Status set_one_value(
in Identifier proper_name,
in string value
);

C++ mapping   `CORBA::Status set_one_value(const char *name,`
`const CORBA_Any&);`

The value is supplied as an Any rather than a String. Note that NamedValue also has values of type Any.

The operation `set_values()` sets the values of those properties that are named in the values parameter.

CORBA definition   Status set_values(in NVList values);

C++ mapping   `CORBA::Status set_values(CORBA::NVList_ptr);`

Note that the flags of the items of the NVList must be zero and that the TypeCode field of the values of the items must be TC_String.

Values can be read with the operation `get_values()`.

CORBA definition   Status get_values(
in Identifier start_scope,

```
                         in Flags op_flags,

                         in Identifier prop_Name,

                         out NVList value

                         );
```

C++ mapping
```
CORBA::Status get_values(const char *start_scope,
        CORBA::Flags, const char *name,
        CORBA::NVList_ptr&);
```

The prop_name parameter specifies the name of the returned properties. A string can specify multiple property names by using a naming convention with a wildcard "*" similar to the notations used in various operating system shells. The parameter start_scope determines the scope of this query within the context hierarchy. The naming of scopes is implementation dependent. The op_flags parameter can have the value CORBA::CTX_RESTRICT_ SCOPE, which limits the scope to the specified start_scope. An empty flag uses the whole context tree. The value parameter carries the named properties, including their values contained in Anys.

The operation delete_values() deletes the named properties from the context object.

CORBA definition   Status delete_values(in Identifier prop_name);

C++ mapping   `CORBA::Status delete_values(const char *name)`

Finally, there is a method that returns the name of the context object.

C++ mapping   `const char *context_name() const;`

7.3   Manipulating the Context Object Tree

There are additional operations on the context object to manipulate the context tree. The operation create_child() creates a new context object that is a child of the object on which the operation is invoked.

CORBA definition   Status create_child(

                    in Identifier ctx_name,

                    out Context child_ctx

                    );

C++ mapping
```
CORBA::Status create_child(
const char *name,
        CORBA::Context_ptr&)
```

The methods mapping this operation assign a parent context to an existing context which is obtained through the get_default_context() operation.

C++ mapping   `CORBA::Status get_default_context(CORBA::Context_ptr&)`

The operation `delete()` deletes the context object on which it is invoked. The del_flags parameter can take the value CORBA::CTX_DELETE_ DESCENTS. If this flag is specified it causes the deletion of all descendent objects. If the flag is not specified and the object has children, an exception is raised.

CORBA definition   Status delete(in Flags del_flags);

C++ mapping   `void operator delete(void *p)`

There is an additional C++ function that returns the parent context of the object. It returns null if the context is the global default context.

C++ mapping   `CORBA::Context_ptr parent();`

8   *Portable Object Adapter*

This section describes the C++ mapping of the portable object adapter (POA). The POA has recently been added to the CORBA specification and supercedes the BOA. Basically the POA plays the same role as the BOA, being an object adapter, but in contrast to the BOA, the POA is fully specified.

The POA-related interfaces are defined in a separate module from the CORBA module. It is called the PortableServer module.

8.1   POA Policies

The POA::create_POA operations are derived interfaces from CORBA::Policy. Policy objects are created using factory operations on any preexisting POA. Policy objects are specified when a POA is created. Policies may not be changed on an existing POA. Policies are not inherited from the parent POA.

We will discuss the various policies that are defined for the POA. Each of the policies may have several values which influence the mechanisms of the policy.

- ♦ Thread policy
- ♦ Lifespan policy
- ♦ Object ID uniqueness policy
- ♦ ID assignment policy
- ♦ Request processing policy
- ♦ Implicit activation policy

8.1.1 *Thread Policy*

The POA::create_thread_policy() operation creates ThreadPolicy objects. These are passed to the POA::create_POA() operation to indicate which threading model to use for the POA that was created.

CORBA definition   ThreadPolicy create_thread_policy(in ThreadPolicyValue value);

C++ mapping
```
ThreadPolicy_ptr create_thread_policy(
            ThreadPolicyValue value);
```

The values that can be passed to the value parameter are

ORB_CTRL_MODEL. Assigning requests for an ORB-controlled POA to threads is the responsibility of the ORB.

SINGLE_THREAD_MODEL. Single-threaded POA requests are processed sequentially.

The default value for the parameter is ORB_CTRL_MODEL.

8.1.2 *Lifespan Policy*

The POA::create_lifespan_policy() operation creates LifespanPolicy objects. These are passed to the POA::create_POA operation to specify the lifespan of the objects implemented for the POA that was created.

CORBA definition   LifespanPolicy create_lifespan_policy(in LifespanPolicyValue value);

C++ mapping
```
LifespanPolicy_ptr create_lifespan_policy(
            LifespanPolicyValue value);
```

The values that can be passed to the value parameter are

TRANSIENT. The POA-implemented objects cannot outlive the process that created them. An **OBJECT_NOT_EXIST** exception will be raised for any object references that use the deactivated POA.

PERSISTENT. The POA-implemented objects are allowed to outlive the process that created them.

The default value for the parameter is TRANSIENT.

8.1.3 *Object ID Uniqueness Policy*

The POA::create_id_uniqueness_policy operation creates IdUniquenessPolicy objects. These are passed to the POA::create_POA operation to indicate whether the servants activated in the created POA must have unique object identities.

CORBA definition   IdUniquenessPolicy create_id_uniqueness_policy(in
                              IdUniquenessPolicy value);

C++ mapping   `IdUniquenessPolicy_ptr create_id_uniqueness_policy`
                              `(IdUniquenessPolicyValue value);`

The values that can be passed to the value parameter are

UNIQUE_ID. Servants activated with that POA support exactly one object ID.

MULTIPLE_ID. Servants activated with that POA may support one or more object IDs.

The default value for the parameter is UNIQUE_ID.

8.1.4 *ID Assignment Policy*

The POA::create_id_assignment_policy operation creates IdAssignmentPolicy objects. These are passed to the POA::create_POA operation to indicate whether object IDs in the created POA are generated by the application or by the ORB.

CORBA definition   IdAssignmentPolicy create_id_assignment_policy(in
                              IdAssignmentPolicy value);

C++ mapping   `IdAssignmentPolicy_ptr create_id_assignment_policy`
                              `(IdAssignmentPolicyValue value);`

The values that can be passed to the value parameter are

USER_ID. The application can only assign object IDs to the created POA.

SYSTEM_ID. The POA can only assign object IDs to the created POA. If the POA also has the PERSISTENT policy, assigned object IDs must be unique across all instantiations of the same POA.

The default value for the parameter is SYSTEM_ID.

8.1.5 *Servant Retention Policy*

The POA::create_servant_retention_policy operation creates ServantRetentionPolicy objects. These are passed to the POA::create_POA() operation to indicate whether the created POA retains active servants in an active object map.

CORBA definition   ServantRetentionPolicy create_servant_retention_policy
                                   (in ServantRetentionPolicy value);

C++ mapping   `ServantRetentionPolicy_ptr`
                              `create_servant_retention_policy`
                              `(ServantRetentionPolicyValue value);`

The values that can be passed to the value parameter are

RETAIN. Active servants will be retained by the POA in its active
object map.

NON_RETAIN. Servants are not retained by the POA.

The default value for the parameter is RETAIN.

8.1.6 *Request Processing Policy*

The POA::create_request_processing_policy() operation creates RequestProcessing-
Policy objects. These are passed to the POA::create_POA() operation to indicate
how requests are processed by the created POA.

CORBA definition   RequestProcessingPolicy create_id_assignment_policy

(in RequestProcessingPolicy value);

C++ mapping   `RequestProcessingPolicy_ptr request_processing`

`_policy`

`(RequestProcessingPolicyValue value);`

The values that can be passed to the value parameter are

USE_ACTIVE_OBJECT_MAP_ONLY. The RETAIN policy is also required for this parameter. If the object ID is not found in the
active object map, an OBJECT_NOT_EXIST exception is returned to the client. The POA does no automatic object activation. The server must activate all objects served by the POA
explicitly.

USE_DEFAULT_SERVANT. With the RETAIN policy, there is a default
servant defined for all requests involving unknown objects. The
POA first tries to find a servant in the active object map for a
given object. If it does not find such a servant, it uses the default
servant. With the NON_RETAIN policy, the request is dispatched
to the default servant, if the default servant was registered with
the POA. An OBJ_ADAPTER exception is returned to the client
since no default servant has been registered. The MULTIPLE_ID
policy is also required.

USE_SERVANT_MANAGER. This value, along with the RETAIN policy, will make the object try to determine the servant by means of
invoking the incarnate() method in the ServantManager, if the POA
doesn't find a servant in the active object map. With the
NON_RETAIN policy, one servant is used per method call. The
POA does not try to find a servant in the active object map
because the active object map doesn't exist. In every request, the

POA will invoke the appropriate operation on the default servant registered with the POA. If no default servant is available, the POA will raise the OBJECT_ADAPTER system exception.

The default value for the parameter is USE_ACTIVE_MAP_ONLY.

8.1.7 *Implicit Activation Policy*

The POA::create_implicit_activation_policy() operation creates ImplicitActivationPolicy objects. These are passed to the POA::create_POA() operation to indicate whether implicit activation of servants is supported in the created POA.

> CORBA definition   ImplicitActivationPolicy create_implicit_activation_policy
>
> (in ImplicitActivationPolicy value);
>
> C++ mapping   `ImplicitActivationPolicy_ptr`
>
> `create_implicit_activation_policy`
>
> `(ImplicitActivationPolicyValue value);`

The values that can be passed to the value parameter are

IMPLICIT_ACTIVATION. Implicit activation of servants is supported by the POA. This also requires the SYSTEM_ID and RETAIN policies.

NO_IMPLICIT_ACTIVATION. Implicit activation of servants is not supported by the POA.

The default value for the parameter is NO_IMPLICIT_ACTIVATION.

8.2 POAManager Interface

Each POA object has an associated POAManager object. There are four methods within the POAManager object construct. These operations correspond directly to four of the possible processing states: active, inactive, holding, and discarding.

8.2.1 *activate()*

The `activate()` operation changes the state of the POA manager to an active state. The operation will raise an AdapterInactive exception if `activate()` is issued while the POA manager is in the inactive state. The POAs can process requests while in the active state.

> CORBA definition   void activate()
>
> raises (AdapterInactive);
>
> C++ mapping   `void activate();`

8.2.2   hold_requests()

The state of the POA manager is changed to holding when this operation is used. An AdapterInactive exception is raised if `hold_requests()` is issued while the POA manager is in the inactive state. POAs can queue incoming requests while in the holding state. Requests will continue to be queued while in the holding state for any requests that have been queued and have not started executing.

The operation returns immediately after changing the state for a FALSE value of the `wait_for_completion` parameter. For a TRUE value of the parameter, the operation does not return until either there are no actively executing requests in any of the POAs associated with this manager or the state of the POA manager is changed to a state other than holding.

CORBA definition
```
void hold_requests( in boolean wait_for_completion )
raises (AdapterInactive);
```

C++ mapping
```
void hold_requests(
        CORBA::Boolean wait_for_completion )
```

8.2.3   discard_requests()

The state of the POA manager is changed to discarding when this operation is used. An AdapterInactive exception is raised while the POA manager is in the inactive state. The POAs discard incoming requests when entering the discarding state. Also, any requests that have been queued and are not executing are discarded. A TRANSIENT system exception is raised to the client when a request is discarded.

The operation returns immediately after changing the state for a FALSE value of the `wait_for_completion` parameter. For a TRUE value of the parameter, the operation does not return until either there are no actively executing requests in any of the POAs associated with this manager or the state of the POA manager is changed to a state other than discarding.

CORBA definition
```
void discard_requests( in boolean wait_for_completion )
raises (AdapterInactive);
```

C++ mapping
```
void discard_requests(CORBA::Boolean
        wait_for_completion )
```

8.2.4   deactivate()

The state of the POA manager is changed to inactive when this method is used. An AdapterInactive exception is raised if the `deactivate()` method is issued while the POA manager is in the inactive state. The associated POAs reject requests that have not begun to be executed, as well as any new requests upon entering the inactive state.

If the `etherealize_objects` parameter is TRUE, the POA manager will cause all associated POAs that have the RETAIN and USE_SERVANT_MANAGER policies to perform the `etherealize()` operation on the associated servant manager for all active objects. If the `etherealize_objects` parameter is FALSE, the `etherealize()` method is not called. This is so that developers can be provided with a means to shut down POAs in some unrecoverable error situation or in a crisis.

The method will return immediately after changing the state, if the `wait_for_operation` parameter is FALSE. In the case of a TRUE value for the `wait_for_completion` parameter, the method will not return until there are no actively executing requests in any of the POAs associated with this POA manager. In addition, if the `etherealize_objects` parameter is TRUE, then all invocations of `etherealize()` have completed for POAs having the RETAIN and USE_SERVANT_MANAGER policies.

CORBA definition   void deactivate(in boolean etherealize_objects,

in boolean wait_for_completion)

raises (AdapterInactive);

C++ mapping   void deactivate(

CORBA::Boolean etherealize_objects,

CORBA::Boolean wait_for_completion)

8.3   AdapterActivator Interface

Adapter activators are associated with POAs. The ability to create child POAs on demand is the domain of the adapter activator. Note that an application server that creates all its needed POAs at the beginning of execution does not need to use or provide an adapter activator. We only need the adapter activators in the case of POAs that need to be created during request processing. An AdapterActivator object must be local to the process containing the POA objects it is registered with.

8.3.1   *unknown_adapter()*

When the ORB receives a request for an object reference that identifies a target POA that does not exist, then this operation is invoked. For each POA that must be created in order for the target POA to exist, the ORB must invoke this operation. The method is invoked in the adapter activator associated with the POA that is the parent of the POA that needs to be created.

The parent parameter represents the parent POA that is passed. The name parameter represents the name of the POA to be created.

When the method returns TRUE, the ORB will process the request. If the method returns FALSE, the ORB will process the request and it will return OBJECT_NOT_EXIST to the client. If multiple POAs need to be created, the ORB will invoke unknown_adapter once for each POA that needs to be created. The OBJECT_NOT_EXIST exception will be raised if the parent of a nonexistent POA does not have an associated adapter activator. The ORB will report an OBJ_ADAPTER exception if the method raises a system exception.

CORBA definition
```
boolean unknown_adapter(in POA parent,
                            in string name);
```

C++mapping
```
CORBA::Boolean unknown_adapter(
    PortableServer::POA_ptr parent,
    const char *name);
```

8.4 ServantActivator Interface

Servant managers are associated with POAs. When the POA has the RETAIN policy, it uses servant managers that are ServantActivators. There are a couple of methods that help in the management of this concept.

8.4.1 incarnate()

Whenever the POA receives a request for an object that is not currently active, this operation is invoked by the POA. We are assuming that the POA has the USE_SERVANT_MANAGER and RETAIN policies.

The oid parameter contains the object ID value associated with the incoming request. The adapter parameter is an object reference for the POA in which the object is being activated.

If the incarnate() operation returns a servant that is already active for a different object ID and if the POA also has the UNIQUE_ID policy, the incarnate() has violated the POA policy and is considered to be in error. The POA will raise an OBJ_ADAPTER system exception for the request.

CORBA definition
```
Servant incarnate(in ObjectId oid,
                      in POA adapter)
raises (ForwardRequest);
```

C++ mapping
```
PortableServer::Servant_ptr incarnate(
    const ObjectId& oid,
    POA_ptr adapter);
```

8.4.2 etherealize()

Whenever a servant for an object is deactivated, this operation is invoked. The POA must have the USE_SERVANT_MANAGER and RETAIN policies. An active servant may be deactivated by the servant manager via etherealize(), even if it was not incarnated by the servant manager.

The oid parameter contains the object ID value of the object being deactivated. The adapter parameter is an object reference for the POA in whose scope the object was active. The serv parameter contains a reference to the servant that is associated with the object being deactivated. The serv parameter has a value of TRUE if the denoted servant is associated with other active objects in the POA's active map at the time that etherealize() is called, otherwise it is FALSE. If the cleanup_in_progress parameter is TRUE, the reason for the etherealize() operation is that either the deactivate or destroy operation was called with an etherealize_objects parameter of TRUE. For a FALSE parameter, the etherealize() operation is called for other reasons.

CORBA definition
```
void etherealize (in ObjectId oid,
                  in POA adapter,
                  in Servant serv,
                  in boolean cleanup_in_progress,
                  in boolean remaining_activations);
```

C++ mapping
```
void etherealize (const ObjectId& oid,
                  POA_ptr adapter,
                  Servant_ptr serv,
                  CORBA::Boolean cleanup_in_progress,
                  CORBA::Boolean remaining_activations);
```

8.5   ServantLocator Interface

When the POA has the NON_RETAIN policy, it uses servant managers that are ServantLocators.

8.5.1   preinvoke()

This method is invoked by the POA whenever the POA receives a request for an object that is not currently active, assuming the POA has the USE_SERVANT_MANAGER and NON_RETAIN policies. The oid parameter contains the object ID value associated with the incoming request. The adapter parameter is an object reference for the POA in which the object is being activated. The Cookie parameter is a type that is opaque to the POA which can be set by the servant manager for use later by the `postinvoke` method. The operation is the name of the operation that will be called by the POA when the servant is returned.

CORBA definition
```
Servant preinvoke( in ObjectID oid,
                   in POA adapter,
                   in CORBA::Identifier operation,
                   out Cookie the_cookie)
raises (ForwardRequest);
```

C++ mapping
```
PortableServer::Servant_ptr preinvoke(
        ObjectId& oid,
        POA_ptr adapter,
        CORBA::Identifier_ptr operation,
        Cookie_ptr& the_cookie);
```

8.5.2 *postinvoke()*

This method is invoked whenever a servant completes a request, assuming the POA has the USE_SERVANT_MANAGER and NON_RETAIN policies. The `oid` parameter contains the object ID value associated with the incoming request. The `adapter` parameter is an object reference for the POA in which the object is being activated. The `Cookie` parameter is a type that is opaque to the POA which can be set by the servant manager for use later by the `postinvoke` method. The `operation` is the name of the operation that will be called by the POA when the servant is returned. The `in_servant` parameter contains a reference to the servant that is associated with the object. Please note that destroying a servant that is known to the POA can lead to undefined results.

CORBA definition
```
Servant postinvoke( in ObjectId oid,
                    in POA adapter,
                    in CORBA::Identifier operation,
                    in Cookie the_cookie,
                    in Servant the_servant)
raises (ForwardRequest);
```

C++ mapping
```
PortableServer::Servant_ptr preinvoke(
        ObjectId& oid,
        POA_ptr adapter,
        CORBA::Identifier_ptr operation,
        Cookie_ptr the_cookie,
        Servant_ptr the_servant);
```

8.6   POA Interface

A POA object manages the implementation of a collection of objects. There is support for a namespace for the objects that are identified by object IDs. In addition, a POA also provides a namespace for POAs. A POA is created as a child of an existing POA, which forms a hierarchy starting with the root POA.

8.6.1   *create_POA()*

This method creates a new POA as a child of the target POA. The `adapter _name` parameter identifies the new POA with respect to other POAs with the same parent POA. A new POAManager object is created and associated with the new POA if the `a_POAManager` parameter is null. Otherwise the specified POAManager object is associated with the new POA. The POAManager object can be obtained using the attribute name `the_POAManager`. The `policies` parameter indicates which specified policy objects are associated with the POA. It is used to control the POA behavior. Policies are not inherited from the parent POA.

   The method will raise the AdapterAlreadyExists exception if the target POA already has a child POA with the specified name. An InvalidPolicy exception is raised if conflicting policy objects are specified, or if any of the specified policy objects require prior administrative action that has not been performed. The exception contains the index in the policies parameter value of the first offending policy object.

CORBA definition   POA create_POA(in string adapter_name,

in POAManager a_POAManager,

in CORBA::PolicyList policies)

raises (AdapterAlreadyExists, InvalidPolicy);

C++ mapping

```
PortableServer::POA_ptr create_POA(
    const char *adapter_name,
    POAManager_ptr a_POAManager,
    CORBA::PolicyList_ptr policies);
```

8.6.2   *find_POA()*

This method will return the child POA if the target POA is the parent of a child POA with the specified name. If the value of the `activate_it` parameter is TRUE and if a child POA with the specified name does not exist, then the target POA's adapter activator is invoked, if it exists. If it successfully activates the child POA, then that child POA is returned. An AdapterNonExistent exception is raised otherwise.

CORBA definition   POA find_POA(in string adapter_name,

in boolean activate_it);

raises (AdapterNonExistent)

C++ mapping

```
PortableServer::POA_ptr find_POA (
                    const char *adapter_name,
                    CORBA::Boolean activate_it);
```

8.6.3   destroy()

This method destroys the POA and all descendant POAs. The destroyed POA may be re-created later in the same process. When a POA is destroyed, any requests that have started execution continue to completion. Any requests that have not started execution are processed as if they were newly arrived, that is, the POA will attempt to cause re-creation of the POA by invoking one or more adapter activators.

The parameters to this method have boolean values. If the `etherealize_objects` parameters is TRUE, the POA has the RETAIN policy, and a servant manager is registered with the POA, then the `etherealize` operation on the servant manager will be called for each active object in the active object map. If an `etherealize()` method attempts to invoke the operations on a destroyed POA, then it will receive an OBJECT_NOT_EXIST exception.

If the `wait_for_completion` parameter is TRUE, the `destroy()` operation will return only after all requests in process have completed and all invocations of `etherealize` have completed. Otherwise the `destroy()` operation returns after destroying the POAs.

CORBA definition   void destroy(in boolean etherealize_objects,

in boolean wait_for_completion);

C++ mapping

```
void destroy(CORBA::Boolean etherealize_objects,
                    CORBA::Boolean wait_for_completion);
```

8.6.4   get_servant_manager()

The USE_SERVANT_MANAGER policy is required for this method. Otherwise a WrongPolicy exception is raised. This method returns the servant manager associated with the POA. If no servant manager has been associated with the POA, it returns a null reference. It is system dependent whether the root POA initially has a servant manager; the application is free to assign its own servant manager to the root POA.

CORBA definition   ServantManager get_servant_manager()

raises (WrongPolicy);

C++ mapping

```
ServantManager_ptr get_servant_manager();
```

8.6.5 *set_servant_manager()*

This method sets the default servant manager associated with the POA. The USE_SERVANT_MANAGER policy is required for this method. If not present, the WrongPolicy exception is raised.

CORBA definition   void set_servant_manager(in ServantManager imgr)

raises (WrongPolicy);

C++ mapping   `void set_servant_manager(ServantManager_ptr imgr);`

8.6.6 *get_servant()*

This method returns the default servant associated with the POA. A NoServant exception is raised if no servant has been associated with the POA. The USE_DEFAULT_SERVANT policy is required for this method. If not present, the WrongPolicy exception is raised.

CORBA definition   Servant get_servant()

raises (NoServant, WrongPolicy);

C++mapping   `Servant_ptr get_servant();`

8.6.7 *set_servant()*

The specified servant (with the POA as the default servant) is registered with this method. This method will be used for all requests for which no servant is found in the active object map. The USE_DEFAULT_SERVANT policy is required for this method. If not present, the WrongPolicy exception is raised.

CORBA definition   void set_servant(in Servant p_servant)

raises (WrongPolicy);

C++mapping   `void set_servant(Servant_ptr p_servant);`

8.6.8 *activate_object()*

This method generates an object ID and enters the object ID and the specified servant in the active object map. The object ID is returned. The SYSTEM_ID and RETAIN policies are required for this method, otherwise a WrongPolicy exception is raised. Also, a ServantAlreadyActive exception is raised if the POA has a UNIQUE_ID policy and the specified servant is already in the active object map.

CORBA definition   ObjectId activate_object(in Servant p_servant)

raises (ServantAlreadyActive, WrongPolicy);

C++ mapping   `ObjectId* activate_object(`

`Servant_ptr servant);`

8.6.9   activate_object_with_id()

This method enters an association between the specified object ID and the specified servant in the active object map. However, an ObjectAlreadyActive exception is raised if the CORBA object denoted by the object ID value is already active in this POA. A ServantAlreadyActive exception is raised if the POA has the UNIQUE_ID policy and the servant is already in the active object map. A WrongPolicy exception is raised if the RETAIN policy is not present. In addition, a BAD_PARAM system exception is raised if the POA has the SYSTEM_ID policy and it detects that the object ID value was not generated by the system or for this POA.

CORBA definition   void activate_object_with_id(in ObjectId oid,

in Servant p_servant)

raises (ObjectAlreadyActive, ServantAlreadyActive, WrongPolicy);

C++ mapping   `void activate_object_with_id(ObjectId_ptr oid, Servant_ptr p_servant);`

8.6.10   deactivate_object()

The removal from the active object map of the association of the object ID map specified by the `oid` parameter and its servant is performed by this method. An ObjectNotActive exception is raised if there is no active object associated with the specified object ID. The method ServantLocator::etherealize will be invoked with the `oid` and the servant if a servant manager is associated with the POA.

CORBA definition   void deactivate_object(in ObjectId oid)

raises (ObjectNotActive, WrongPolicy);

C++ mapping   `void deactivate_object(ObjectId_ptr oid);`

8.6.11   create_reference()

An object reference that encapsulates a POA-generated object ID value and the specified Interface Repository ID is created by this method. This method does not cause an activation to take place. The resulting reference may be passed to clients. This means that subsequent requests on those references will cause the appropriate servant manager to be invoked, if one is available. The generated object ID value may be obtained by invoking POA::reference _to_id with the created reference. A WrongPolicy exception is raised if the method does not use the SYSTEM_ID policy.

CORBA definition   Object create_reference(in CORBA::RepositoryID intf)

raises (WrongPolicy);

C++ mapping `Object_ptr create_reference(CORBA::RepositoryId`
`_ptr intf);`

8.6.12 create_reference_with_id()

An object reference that encapsulates a POA-generated object ID value and the specified Interface Repository ID is created by this method. An activation does not take place with this method. The resulting reference may be passed to clients, so that subsequent requests to those references will cause the object to be activated if necessary, or the default servant used, depending on the applicable policies. A BAD_PARAM system exception is raised if the POA has the SYSTEM_IS policy and detects that the object ID value was not generated but the system or for this POA.

CORBA definition Object create_reference_with_id(in ObjectId oid,

In CORBA::RepositoryId intf);

C++ mapping `Object_ptr create_reference_with_id(`
`CORBA::Object_ptr oid,`
`CORBA::RepositoryId_ptr intf);`

8.6.13 servant_to_id()

With the UNIQUE_ID policy, and the specified servant is active, the object ID that is associated with that servant is returned. With the IMPLICIT_ACTIVATION policy, and either the POA has the MULTIPLE_ID policy or the specified servant is not active, the servant is activated using a POA-generated object ID and the interface ID associated with the servant, and a corresponding object ID is returned. A ServantNotActive exception is raised otherwise. Therefore this method requires the use of the RETAIN and either UNIQUE_ID or IMPLICIT_ ACTIVATION policies, otherwise a WrongPolicy exception is raised.

CORBA definition Object servant_to_id(in Servant p_servant)

raises (ServantNotActive, WrongPolicy);

C++ mapping `Object_ptr servant_to_id(Servant_ptr p_servant);`

8.6.14 servant_to_reference()

With the UNIQUE_ID policy, and the specified servant is active, an object reference encapsulating the information used to activate the servant is returned. With the IMPLICIT_ACTIVATION policy, and either the POA has the MULTIPLE_ID policy or the specified servant is not active, the servant is activated using a POA generated object ID and the interface ID associated with the servant, and a corresponding object reference is returned. A

ServantNotActive exception is raised otherwise. Therefore this method requires the use of the RETAIN and either UNIQUE_ID or IMPLICIT_ACTIVATION policies, otherwise a WrongPolicy exception is raised.

CORBA definition   Object servant_to_reference(in Servant p_servant)

raises (ServantNotActive, WrongPolicy);

C++ mapping
```
Object_ptr servant_to_reference(
        Servant_ptr p_servant);
```

8.6.15 reference_to_servant()

This method returns the servant associated with that object in the active object map if the POA has the RETAIN policy and the specified object is present in the active object map. Otherwise this method returns the default servant if the POA has the USE_DEFAULT_SERVANT policy and a default servant has been registered with the POA. The WrongAdapter exception is raised if the object reference was not created by this POA. The WrongPolicy exception is raised if either the RETAIN or USE_DEFAULT_SERVANT policy is not present.

CORBA definition   Servant reference_to_servant(Object reference)

raises (ObjectNotActive, WrongAdapter,

WrongPolicy);

C++ mapping
```
Servant_ptr reference_to_servant(
            CORBA::Object_ptr reference);
```

8.6.16 reference_to_id()

The object ID value encapsulated by the specified reference is returned by this method. A WrongAdapter exception is raised if the reference was not created by the POA on which the operation is being performed. The object denoted by the reference does not have to be active for this method to succeed. Currently, the WrongPolicy exception is declared to allow for future extensions.

CORBA definition   ObjectId reference_to_id(in Object reference)

raises (WrongAdapter, WrongPolicy);

C++ mapping
```
ObjectId_ptr reference_to_id(
            CORBA::Object_ptr reference);
```

8.6.17 id_to_servant()

The active servant associated with the specified object ID value is returned by this method. An ObjectNotActive exception is raised if the object ID value is not active in the POA. A WrongPolicy exception is raised if this method does not use the RETAIN policy.

CORBA definition   Servant id_to_servant(in ObjectId oid)

raises (ObjectNotActive, WrongPolicy);

C++ mapping   `Servant_ptr id_to_servant(ObjectId_ptr oid);`

8.6.18 *id_to_reference()*

A reference encapsulating the information used to activate the object is returned by this method if an object with the specified object ID value is currently active. An ObjectNotActive exception is raised if the object ID value is not active in the POA. A WrongPolicy exception is raised if this method does not use the RETAIN policy.

CORBA definition   Object id_to_reference(in ObjectId oid)

raises (ObjectNotActive, WrongPolicy);

C++ mapping   `Object_ptr id_to_reference(const ObjectId& oid);`

8.7   Current Operations

Derived from CORBA::Current, the PortableServer::Current interface provides method implementations with access to the identity of the object on which the method was invoked.

8.7.1 *get_POA()*

A reference to the POA implementing the object in whose context is called is returned by this operation. A NoContext exception is raised if `get_POA()` is called outside the context of a POA-dispatched operation.

CORBA definition   POA get_POA()

raises (NoContext);

C++ mapping   `CORBA::Current::POA_ptr get_POA();`

8.7.2 *get_object_id()*

The object ID identifying the object whose context is called is returned by this operation. A NoContext exception is raised if `get_object_id()` is called outside the context of a POA-dispatched operation.

CORBA definition   ObjectId get_object_id()

raises (NoContext);

C++ mapping   `CORBA::Current::ObjectId_ptr get_object_id();`

5

Discovering Services

This chapter provides an overview of mechanisms for discovering CORBA objects. We explain the two most important CORBA services for locating objects: the Naming Service (Section 2), which finds objects by name, and the Trading Service (Section 3), which finds objects by type and properties. However, there is still the question of how to find initial references to instances of those services. In Section 1 we explain the operations on the ORB pseudo-interface that can be used for bootstrapping.

In Section 4, Naming and Trading domains are introduced. This section discusses which object instance is returned by the bootstrapping operations.

Finally, Section 5 explains how ORBs name and locate servers and objects by using proprietary mechanisms. Although these mechanisms are not standardized, and hence not portable or interoperable, they are quite popular due to their simplicity.

1   *Bootstrapping*

CORBA solves the bootstrapping problem by providing a pair of operations on the ORB pseudo-interface: list_initial_services()—list the names of initial services which are available from the ORB; resolve_initial_references()—returns an initial object reference to a named service. For example, a naming context is returned when a Naming Service reference is requested.

We have already introduced these operations in Chapter 2 and have explained their C++ mapping in Chapter 7. We show how to use these operations in the Naming Service example in the following section.

These two operations only provide a bootstrapping mechanism for the services offered by a particular ORB implementation because the mechanism for registering services with the ORB is not defined by CORBA. However, the standard interface to the ORB ensures the portability of application code.

These two operations do not provide full bootstrap support. The problem is that it is not clear which object instance is returned when several are available. We discuss this problem in more detail in Section 4 where we introduce the concept of domains as a solution.

An alternative way to bootstrap applications is to use proprietary mechanisms provided by various ORB implementations. We have a closer look at some of the options in Section 5.

2 The CORBA Naming Service

The Naming Service allows object implementations to be identified by name and is thus a fundamental service for distributed object systems. This section is organized as follows:

◆ We give an overview and explain how to use the Naming Service (Section 2.1).
◆ We explain the interface specification in detail (Section 2.2).
◆ We provide an example (Section 2.3).

2.1 Overview of the Naming Service

The Naming Service provides a mapping between a name and an object reference. Storing such a mapping in the Naming Service is known as *binding an object* and removing this entry is called *unbinding*. Obtaining an object reference bound to a name is known as *resolving the name*.

Names can be hierarchically structured by using contexts. Contexts are similar to directories in file systems and they can contain names as well as subcontexts.

The use of object references alone to identify objects has two problems. First, object references are difficult for human users, as they are opaque datatypes, and second, their string form is a long sequence of numbers. When a service is restarted, its objects typically have new object references. However, in most cases clients want to use the service repeatedly without needing to be aware that the service has been restarted.

The Naming Service solves these problems by providing an extra layer of abstraction for the identification of objects. It provides readable object identifiers for the human user—users can assign names that look like structured file names—and a persistent identification mechanism—objects can bind themselves under the same name regardless of their object reference.

The typical use of the Naming Service involves object implementations binding to the Naming Service when they come into existence and unbinding before they terminate. Clients resolve names to objects, on which they subsequently invoke operations. Figure 5.1 illustrates this typical usage scenario.

2.2   Interface Specification

The central interface is called NamingContext and it contains operations to bind names to object references and to create subcontexts. Names are sequences of NameComponents. NamingContexts can resolve a name with a single component and return an object reference. They resolve names with more than one component by resolving the first component to a subcontext and passing the remainder of a name on to that subcontext for resolution.

2.2.1   *The Name Type*

The CosNaming module provides type definitions used to identify objects by names:

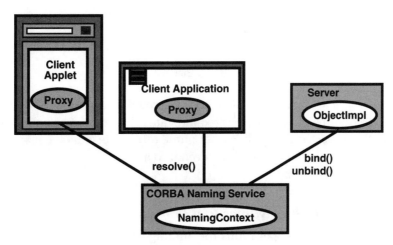

FIGURE 5.1   Typical use of the CORBA Naming Service.

```
module CosNaming {

    typedef string Istring;

    struct NameComponent {
        Istring id;
        Istring kind;
    };

    typedef sequence <NameComponent> Name;
```

The type Istring is used to define the Name type for future compatibility with internationalized strings. At the time of writing, this type is defined to be string. A NameComponent has two fields: id contains the string that is actually matched when a name is resolved; kind is available for application-specific purposes and may or may not be interpreted by the Naming Service. We recommend that the kind field always be initialized to the empty string.

The Name type is a sequence of component, or atomic, names and no syntax is given for the textual representation of names. This allows application programs to use separators such as the UNIX file system "/" character to separate components when printing names for users.

2.2.2 Bindings

The Binding type provides information about the bindings in a context:

```
// module CosNaming

enum BindingType {nobject, ncontext};

struct Binding {
    Name binding_name;
    BindingType binding_type;
};

typedef sequence < Binding > BindingList;
```

The type CosNaming::Binding provides a name and a flag of type BindingType. The value ncontext indicates that an object bound to a name is a NamingContext at which further name resolution can take place. The value nobject means that the binding, even if to a NamingContext, cannot be used for further resolution.

2.2.3 Adding Names to a Context

There are two operations for binding an object to a name in a context and two for binding another context to a name.

```
// module CosNaming

interface NamingContext {

// we elide the exceptions declared here

void bind(in Name n, in Object obj)
    raises(NotFound, CannotProceed, InvalidName, AlreadyBound);
void rebind(in Name n, in Object obj)
    raises(NotFound, CannotProceed, InvalidName);

void bind_context(in Name n, in NamingContext nc)
    raises(NotFound, CannotProceed, InvalidName, AlreadyBound);
void rebind_context(in Name n, in NamingContext nc)
    raises(NotFound, CannotProceed, InvalidName);
```

The bind() and bind_context() operations associate a new name with an object. In the case of bind_context() the object must be of type NamingContext. We will see how to create new contexts below. If the name used has more than one component, the NamingContext will expect that all but the last component refers to a nested context, and it will make the binding in the context resolved by the first part of the name. For example, consider Figure 5.2.

We use the "/" character as a separator for NameComponents. In our example we invoke the bind() operation on the NamingContext object we have called "Context1" with the parameters "Context2/Context5/MyName" and some object reference. This results in a new atomic name, "MyName," being bound to the object in the "Context5" context (see Figure 5.3). The BindingType of the resulting binding will be nobject.

If we invoked bind_context with the same parameters (although the object reference must be to a NamingContext) then the same situation would result. However, the BindingType will be ncontext, and the "Context5" context would then be able to resolve names like "MyName/x/y/z" by passing the remainder, "x/y/z," to the new "MyName" context.

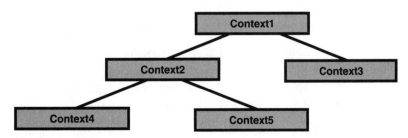

FIGURE 5.2 NamingContext structure—before binding.

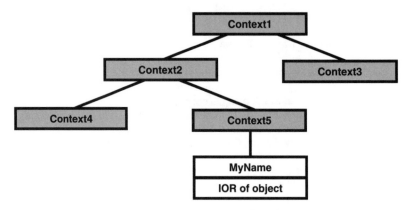

FIGURE 5.3 NamingContext structure—after binding.

The rebind() and rebind_context() operations work the same as bind() and bind_context(), but rather than raising an exception if the name already exists, they simply replace the existing object reference.

2.2.4 Removing Names from a Context

The operation unbind() will remove a name and its associated object reference from a context or one of its subcontexts.

```
void unbind(in Name n)
    raises(NotFound, CannotProceed, InvalidName);
```

2.2.5 Name Resolution

The resolve() operation returns an object reference bound to a name supplied as its argument.

```
Object resolve (in Name n)
    raises(NotFound, CannotProceed, InvalidName);
```

The resolve() operation behaves as follows:

It resolves the first component of the name, n, to an object reference.

If there are no remaining components then it returns this object reference to the caller.

Otherwise it narrows the object reference to a NamingContext and passes the remainder of the name to its resolve() operation.

Implementations of the Naming Service will probably optimize this process so that the narrow() and resolve() operations are not called repeatedly.

However, the result will logically be the same as that produced by the algorithm above.

2.2.6 Exceptions

Here are the exceptions omitted above:

```
// interface NamingContext

enum NotFoundReason {missing_node, not_context, not_object};

exception NotFound {
    NotFoundReason why;
    Name rest_of_name;
};

exception CannotProceed {
    NamingContext cxt;
    Name rest_of_name;
};

exception InvalidName{};
exception AlreadyBound {};
exception NotEmpty{};
```

The NotFound exception indicates that the name does not identify a binding. It may be raised by any operation that takes a name as an argument. The Naming Service specification does not explain the meaning of the why member of this exception, but we make the following interpretation: At some stage of tracing the leading name components down to the context in which the final component is bound to a (possibly noncontext) object reference one of these situations occurs:

♦ A NameComponent does not exist in the context expected (missing_node).
♦ A leading NameComponent is bound to an object with a binding type of nobject rather than ncontext, or an ncontext binding is bound to an object of a type other than NamingContext (not_context).
♦ The object reference bound to a NameComponent denotes a destroyed object (not_object).

If this happens, the rest_of_name member returns the rest of the sequence from the unresolvable name onward. This is not explicitly specified in the Naming Service.

The CannotProceed exception returns a NamingContext object reference and a part of the original name. It indicates that the resolve() operation has given up, for example, for security or efficiency reasons. However, the client may be able to continue at the returned context. The rest_of_name member returns the part of the name that should be passed to the returned context ctx for resolution.

The InvalidName exception indicates that the name is syntactically invalid. For example, it might contain a zero length NameComponent. The names acceptable to different Naming Services may vary.

The AlreadyBound exception may be raised by bind operations. It informs the caller that a name is already used and cannot be overridden without using a rebind operation.

NotEmpty is an exception raised by the destroy() operation defined below. Contexts that still contain bindings cannot be destroyed.

2.2.7   Context Creation

There are operations to create new contexts defined in the NamingContext interface.

```
// interface NamingContext

NamingContext new_context();
NamingContext bind_new_context(in Name n)
    raises(NotFound, AlreadyBound, CannotProceed, InvalidName);
```

New NamingContexts may be created and later used alone or bound into other contexts using bind_context(). They can also be created with a particular name and bound in a single operation. new_context() produces an empty NamingContext that can be used anywhere. bind_new_context() also creates a new context, but binds it into a subcontext of the context on which the operation is invoked. It can raise the usual exceptions for an operation that takes a name as an argument.

2.2.8   Context Destruction

When a context is no longer used, and all the bindings it contained have been unbound, it can be destroyed.

```
// interface NamingContext

void destroy()
    raises(NotEmpty);
```

The destroy() operation will delete a context as long as it contains no bindings. Be sure at the same time to remove any bindings that may refer to this context.

2.2.9   Browsing Contexts

A NamingContext supports browsing of its contents by use of the list() operation.

```
// interface BindingIterator; has been forward declared

// interface NamingContext

void list ( in unsigned long how_many,
          out BindingList bl, out BindingIterator bi);

}; // end of interface NamingContext
```

The parameters of the list() operation allow the caller to specify how many bindings to return in a BindingList sequence. The rest will be returned through an iterator object (which are explained below) referred to by the bi parameter, which will be a nil object reference if there are no further bindings.

2.2.10 Binding Iterators

A BindingIterator object will be returned if the number of bindings in a context exceeds the how_many argument value of the list() operation invoked on the context.

```
// module CosNaming

interface BindingIterator {
    boolean next_one(out Binding b);
    boolean next_n( in unsigned long how_many,
                    out BindingList bl);
    void destroy();
  };
}; //end of module CosNaming
```

If there are remaining bindings, the next_one() operation returns TRUE and places a Binding in its out parameter. The Naming Service specification is ambiguous about whether it should return FALSE if this is the last binding in the iterator or on the next call.

The next_n() operation returns a sequence of at most how_many bindings in the out parameter bl. It also returns FALSE if there are no further bindings to be iterated over. It is not specified whether the FALSE value should be returned with the last binding or on the next call.

The destroy() operation allows the iterator to deallocate its resources and it will render the object reference invalid. Iterators may sometimes be implemented so that they time out or are deleted on demand for resource recovery.

2.2.11 The Names Library

The Naming Service also defines some pseudo-IDL for a Names Library. This is a set of operations intended to ease the creation and manipulation of names. To our knowledge it has not been implemented in any Naming Service product, and so we will omit details of this part of the specification.

Users typically type in strings to nominate objects. In our examples we use a C++ class library, introduced in Section 2.3, which allows the use of strings in a convenient syntax to access the Naming Service.

2.3   Using the Naming Service from a C++ Client

This subsection contains some of the methods for an EasyNaming class that will be used in subsequent chapters. This class allows applications to obtain a stringified object reference to a NamingContext and then use string arguments with the "/" character as a name separator to identify objects relative to that context.

First let's look at the declaration of the class, its private fields, and constructors. There are two constructors, one of which obtains a root context via the ORB, the other which uses a stringified object reference for bootstrapping.

```
// EasyNaming.C
#include "EasyNaming.h"

// constructors
EasyNaming::EasyNaming( const CORBA::ORB_var& orb ) {
  // initialize Naming Service via ORB
  try {
    cout << "Initial Services: " << endl;
    CORBA_StringSequence_var services;
    services = orb->list_initial_services();
    if ( services->length() == 0 )
      cout << "No services available" << endl;
    for( int i = 0; i < services->length(); i++ )
      cout << services[i] << endl;

    CORBA::Object_var obj =
      orb->resolve_initial_references("NameService");

    root_context = CosNaming::NamingContext::_narrow( obj );
    if ( root_context == CosNaming::NamingContext::_nil() ) {
      cerr << "Returned IOR is not a Naming Context" << endl;
      cerr << "Giving up ..." << endl;
      exit(1);
    }
    cout << "Its IOR is: " <<
          orb->object_to_string( root_context ) << endl;
  }
  catch( const CosNaming::NamingContext::InvalidName& inex ) {
    cerr << inex << endl;
  }
  catch( const CORBA::SystemException& corba_exception ) {
```

```
        cerr << corba_exception << endl;
    }
}
```

We first list all available initial services by calling `list_initial_ser-vices()`. This is not needed to initialize the object, but we use the opportunity to demonstrate the use of the ORB bootstrap operation. We then try to obtain a reference to a root context of the naming service by calling `resolve_initial_references()` on the ORB. We obtain an object reference of the type CORBA::Object which we narrow to a NamingContext. If the `root_context` is nil, the obtained object is of the wrong type and we give up.

Alternatively, there is a constructor which initializes the EasyNaming object with a stringified object reference for a root context. This constructor can be used for cross-ORB bootstrapping.

```
const CORBA::String_var& ior_string ) {
// Initialize Naming Service via stringified IOR
try {
  CORBA::Object_var obj = orb->string_to_object( ior_string );
  root_context = CosNaming::NamingContext::_narrow( obj );
  if ( root_context == CosNaming::NamingContext::_nil() ) {
    cout << "Could not narrow down object to root_context" << endl;
    cout << "Narrowing down to Extended Naming " <<
    cout << "Context Factory" << endl;
    CosNaming::ExtendedNamingContextFactory_var
        ext_naming_factory =
          CosNaming::ExtendedNamingContextFactory::_narrow( obj );
    if ( ext_naming_factory ==
      CosNaming::ExtendedNamingContextFactory::_nil() ) {
      cout << "Extended Naming Context Factory is NULL" << endl;
      cout << "Narrowing down to Naming Context Factory" << endl;
      CosNaming::NamingContextFactory_var naming_factory =
      CosNaming::NamingContextFactory::_narrow( obj );
      if ( naming_factory ==
        CosNaming::NamingContextFactory::_nil() ) {
        cout << "Naming Context Factory is NULL" << endl;
        cout << "Giving up" << endl;
        exit (1);
      }
      else {
        // Creating a new root context
        cout << "Creating root context" << endl;
        root_context = naming_factory->create_context();
      }
    }
    else {
     cout << "Get root_context from Extended Naming Context "
         << "Factory" << endl;
     root_context = ext_naming_factory->root_context ();
    }
```

Both constructors will create an object with a properly initialized root_context private field. We can now look at the methods provided by the EasyNaming class.

A method called str2name() takes a UNIX file name string format (always starting with a "/" character, as all names are relative to our root context) and produces a CosNaming::Name, which is mapped to CosNaming::NameComponent. The method's signature is defined below, and the implementation of the class EasyNaming can be found in the examples associated with this chapter.

```
CosNaming::Name_var EasyNaming::str2name( const
                                    CORBA::String_var& str ) {

}
```

The EasyNaming class provides methods equivalent to the operations on naming contexts, but accepts string arguments. The bind_from_string() and rebind_from_string() methods also allow the use of names that refer to nonexistent contexts, and create subcontexts as necessary. This allows us to exercise the bind() or rebind() operations, as well as resolve(), to check the existence of a subcontext and bind_new_context() to create the subcontexts that don't already exist. This is how we implement bind_from_string():

```
CORBA::Object ptr obj ) {
CosNaming::Name_var name;
try {
  name = EasyNaming::str2name( str );
}
catch( const CosNaming::NamingContext::InvalidName& excep ) {
  cerr << "Caught Invalid name exception" << endl;
  cerr << "String was: " << str << endl;
  return;
}

CosNaming::NamingContext_var context = root_context;
CosNaming::Name _name;
_name.length(1);

try {
  root_context->bind( name, obj );
}
catch( const CosNaming::NamingContext::NotFound& not_found ) {
  // bind step by step

  // create and bind all nonexistent contexts in the path
  for( int i = 0; i < name->length() - 1; i++ ) {
    _name[0] = name[i];
    try {
      // see if the other context exists
      context = CosNaming::NamingContext::_narrow(
```

```
                    context->resolve( _name ) );
      cout << "Resolved " << _name[0].id << endl;
    }
    catch( const CosNaming::NamingContext::NotFound& not_found ) {
      // if not then create a new context
      cout << "Creating " << _name[0].id << endl;
      context = context->bind_new_context( _name );
    }
    // let other exceptions propagate to the caller
```

First the `str` argument is converted to a Naming Service name and an attempt is made to bind the `obj` argument using the bind() operation. If one of the contexts in the name path is not found, the method `bind_from_string()` descends the context hierarchy, one `NameComponent` at a time. If a component resolves correctly to a context then that context is used to test the name of the next component. If the resolve() operation fails then the name component is used to create a new subcontext. This continues until the final component, which is then bound in the final subcontext to the object reference passed as an argument.

Similarly, we have implemented a more convenient method for resolving names. Below we show the implementation of the method `resolve_from_string()`, which directly calls the resolve operation on the root context after having converted the string name into a Naming Service name.

```
CORBA::Object_var EasyNaming::resolve_from_string(
                            const CORBA::String_var& str ) {
  return root_context->resolve( EasyNaming::str2name( str ) );
}
```

We have implemented other methods, matching the operations on naming contexts, which use string names instead of Naming Service names. The complete implementation of `EasyNaming` is shown in the set of examples associated with this chapter.

3 *Trading Service*

The Trading Service (see Figure 5.4) has its basis in the ISO Open Distributed Processing (ODP) standards. The trader work in this group had reached a Draft International Standard (DIS) level within ISO when responses were due for OMG's Object Services RFP 5. The submitters to the RFP were mostly people who had been working on the ODP standard, which enabled the convergence of the Trading Standards from both groups. Even though ODP uses OMG IDL as an interface specification language,

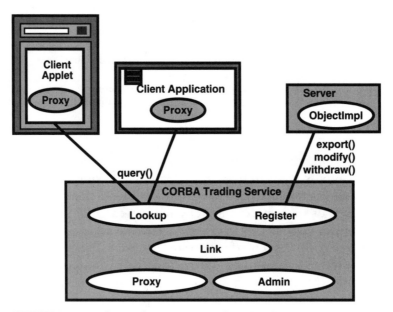

FIGURE 5.4 Typical use of a CORBA Trading Service.

implementations of ODP standards may use any technology. However, the common underlying semantics of the two efforts greatly enhances the prospects for future cross-platform interoperability.

3.1 Overview of Trading

Traders are repositories of object references that are described by an interface type and a set of property values. Such a description of an interface is known as a *service offer*. Each service offer has a *service type,* which is a combination of the interface type of the object being advertised and a list of properties that a service offer of this service type should provide values for.

An *exporter* is a service or some third party acting as an agent for the service which places a service offer into a trader. That service offer can then be matched by the trader to some client's criteria.

A client which queries a trader to discover a service is called an *importer.* An importer provides the trader with a specification of a service type and a constraint expression over the properties of offers of that type. The constraint expression describes the importer's requirements.

A long-standing example of a trading scenario is that of printing services. Currently system administrators configure new printers in a network by providing a unique name for a new device and then notifying potential users by email, news, or notice board. Then each user must remember the printer's name and type it into a dialog box in an application. A better way to discover new printers is to allow applications or users to provide their requirements to the application, which then sends the print job to the most appropriate printer. This is achieved as follows:

We assume that new printers are provided with an implementation of a standard printing interface, specified in IDL. For example

```
module Printing {
    interface Printer {
        typedef string filename;

        exception PrinterOffLine {};

        void print_file(in filename fn)
            raises(PrinterOffLine);

        short queue_length()
            raises(PrinterOffLine);
    };
};
```

Then we define a service type that nominates the Printer interface and a number of property names and types. For example, the printer's location, its language (ASCII, PostScript, HP Laser Jet, etc.), its resolution in DPI, its color properties, its print queue length, and its name.

Each printer is then advertised by exporting a service offer to the trader. For convenience we will refer to the example printers below by their "name" property:

Property	*Value*
building	"A Block"
floor	2
language	postscript
resolution	150
color	black
queue_len	——> [PrinterObjectRef]->queue_length()
name	"12ps"

Property	Value
building	"A Block"
floor	3
language	postscript
resolution	300
color	black
queue_len	——> [PrinterObjectRef]->queue_length()
name	"monster"

Property	Value
building	"A Block"
floor	7
language	postscript
resolution	150
color	256color
queue_len	——> [PrinterObjectRef]->queue_length()
name	"rib"

Applications configure print requests based on user preferences, either from a user's environment, a dialog box, or a text query. This results in a constraint expression that can be passed to the trader in an import query. For example,

```
building == "A Block" && floor <= 5 && language == postscript
```

This query would result in matching two printers ("12ps" and "monster"). The query can ask for the resulting service offers to be ordered according to a *preference expression*. This provides the matched service offers in order based on some minimal, maximal, or boolean expression. For example, a preference to give us the highest resolution printers first would be expressed as

```
max resolution
```

The "queue_len" property is a *dynamic property,* which means that its value is not stored but looked up each time a query is made. So we would probably have a default preference criterion of "min queue_len". This would sort the printers which are returned so that we print to the one that matches the constraint expression, and has the shortest queue.

Let's imagine that a new color printer is installed in Block A and that it is higher in resolution than the "rib" printer. All users who want high resolution will have this maximized in their preferences, and when they next require a color printer the new printer is automatically selected when their application does an import. If, on the other hand, a new printer is installed on floor 1 of the building, then people who used to walk upstairs to collect printouts will have their ordinary black-and-white postscript print jobs directed to the new printer on their floor, without having to change their environment, or even know the name of the printer. In this way they will be informed of a new device as soon as they trade for a printer and the new one meets their requirements.

Of course it is hard to set requirements and preferences when you don't know what is available. Some applications that regularly use the Printer interface will have browsers built in to allow users to see all available printers and their properties by querying the trader with a simple constraint such as

```
building == "A Block"
```

3.1.1 Service Types and Service Offers

Service types are templates from which service offers are created. They ensure that groups of services that offer the same interface, and have the same nonfunctional considerations, are grouped together. This allows efficient searching and matching of service offers in the trader. Most importantly it allows exporters and importers to use the same terminology (property names) to describe a common set of features so that expressions written in terms of those properties will always be evaluated correctly.

3.1.2 Export and Lookup of Service Offers

Any program may export a service offer to a trader if it has an object reference to some application object and knowledge of the implementation behind the reference so that it can describe the properties of that object. Often services will advertise themselves by exporting a service offer.

Any client that is compiled using a set of IDL stubs for a particular interface may assign any valid object reference to a variable at run time and execute operations on that object. As new implementations of servers become available, a client may wish to select objects based on some proximity, quality of service, or other characteristics. To do this, it formulates a constraint expression in terms of the property names of a service type. This expression determines which service offers of that type match the client's requirements.

A client may also ask a trader to sort the matching service offers based on some preference expression that emphasizes the values of particular properties. The trader will return a sorted list of matching service offers, and the client will then use the object reference extracted from one of these.

3.1.3 Trader Federation

Each trader contains a database of service offers which it searches when it receives an import request. It may also store a number of *links* to other traders to which it can pass on queries to reach a larger set of service offers. Links are named within a trader and consist of an object reference to the Lookup interface of another trader, as well as some rules to determine when to use the link to satisfy an importer's request. Traders which are linked in this manner are said to be interworking, or *federated*.

Federated queries are import requests passed from one trader via its links to other traders, and perhaps by them to other traders and so forth. These queries can be constrained by policies passed in by the initial importer, by the policies of each trader, and by the rules stored in the links themselves.

3.2   Overview of the Trading Service Interfaces

In this section we give an overview about the specification of the CORBA Trading Service. The specification includes the following interface definitions:

- Service Type Repository
- Trader Components
- Lookup
- Iterators
- Register
- Link
- Admin
- Proxy
- Dynamic Properties

We will look at each of these in a separate subsection.

3.2.1   Service Type Repository

We have seen the importance of service types in the scenario presented in Section 3.1. If a service offer does not provide an object reference of a known type then it is impossible for an importer to invoke operations on the object references it gets back. In the same way, service types are important for writing constraint expressions. If a service offer's property names and types vary then the constraint and preference expressions that express the requirements of an importer will fail to match relevant service offers. For example, if one service offer for a Printer described its floor via the property

("Floor", "ground"), and another as the property ("level", 4), then it would be impossible to compare them for proximity.

Service types are stored in the Service Type Repository. A service type consists of a name, an interface type, and a set of property specifications. A property specification gives the name and TypeCode of properties that will occur in service offers of this type. Properties are also given modes which allow them to be specified as read-only and/or mandatory. Read-only properties may not be modified after export. Mandatory properties must be included in a service offer to be accepted as an instance of this service type.

The datatypes and operations for the Service Type Repository are contained in the CosTradingRepos::ServiceTypeRepository interface. Most traders will implement a compiler for a service type language (for which there is no standard syntax) and browsing tools to enable importers to compose queries to a trader without needing to write clients to the Service Type Repository. The only type needed when importing using a trader is ServiceTypeName, which is a string.

```
typedef sequence <CosTrading::ServiceTypeName> ServiceTypeNameSeq;

enum PropertyMode {
    PROP_NORMAL, PROP_READONLY,
    PROP_MANDATORY, PROP_MANDATORY_READONLY
};

struct PropStruct {
    CosTrading::PropertyName name;
    CORBA::TypeCode value_type;
    PropertyMode mode;
};

typedef sequence <PropStruct> PropStructSeq;

typedef CosTrading::Istring Identifier; // IR::Identifier

struct IncarnationNumber {
    unsigned long high;
    unsigned long low;
};

struct TypeStruct {
    Identifier if_name;
    PropStructSeq props;
    ServiceTypeNameSeq super_types;
    boolean masked;
    IncarnationNumber incarnation;
};
```

Substitutability of Service Types.   Service types, like IDL interfaces are substitutable via an inheritance relationship. For IDL interfaces this simply means that all the attributes and operations defined in the base interface become part of the derived interface. However, in service types there are three aspects to substitutibility:

The interface type of a derived service type may be a subtype of the interface type in the base service type.

The property set may be extended in a derived service type with new property names (and their associated type and mode specifications).

Inherited properties may be strengthened. That is, nonmandatory properties may be made mandatory, and modifiable properties may be made read-only. However, the datatype of an inherited property must remain the same.

When an importer queries the trader it may receive service offers of a subtype of the requested service type in the same way that object references to subtypes of a required interface type may be passed where a base type is required.

The masked member of the TypeStruct allows service types to be declared as abstract base service types. The incarnation member is assigned an increasing index so that queries on service type definitions can be restricted to those that were defined after some other service type which has a lower incarnation number.

Creating and Deleting Service Types.   Exporters and trader administrators will often want to write code to define a new service type. This is done by populating a PropStructSeq and then calling the add_type() operation.

```
IncarnationNumber add_type (
      in CosTrading::ServiceTypeName name,
      in Identifier if_name,
      in PropStructSeq props,
      in ServiceTypeNameSeq super_type,
) raises (
      CosTrading::IllegalServiceType,
      ServiceTypeExists,
      InterfaceTypeMismatch,
      CosTrading::IllegalPropertyName,
      CosTrading::DuplicatePropertyName,
      ValueTypeRedefinition,
      CosTrading::UnknownServiceType,
      DuplicateServiceTypeName
);
```

The name parameter is the name of the service type, which is used by importers to nominate the types of service offers they wish to search over. The if_name parameter is a Repository ID that identifies the type of the object to be advertised by service offers of this type. The properties expected in service offers of this type are given in the props parameter. The final parameter specifies a list of existing service types which are being subtyped by the new service type. The rules for inheritance of service types are explained above. The exceptions are mostly self-explanatory, and many of them relate to conditions in which the properties added or modified in a subtype do not follow the compatibility rules.

Service types should not be removed from a repository unless no service offers of this type are currently exported to the trader. Even in this case it is probably better to mask service types (see below) than delete them, as this avoids the reuse of old service type names, which can lead to confusion. On the rare occasions when a service type should be deleted, the operation remove_type() performs this action.

```
void remove_type (
    in CosTrading::ServiceTypeName name
) raises (
    CosTrading::IllegalServiceType,
    CosTrading::UnknownServiceType,
    HasSubTypes
);
```

A known service type cannot be removed if it has subtypes, and the exception HasSubTypes is raised in these circumstances.

Obtaining Service Type Information. The repository has operations to list the service types it holds. It can also describe them, either in terms of their supertypes and additional or modified properties, or in terms of the properties that must go into a service offer to conform to this type.

The operation `list_types()` returns all the service type names in the repository:

```
ServiceTypeNameSeq list_types (
    in SpecifiedServiceTypes which_types
);
```

The operation describe_type() returns a TypeStruct which contains the service type's definition as it was added to the repository. It does not include any properties inherited from its supertypes.

```
TypeStruct describe_type (
    in CosTrading::ServiceTypeName name
) raises (
```

```
        CosTrading::IllegalServiceType,
        CosTrading::UnknownServiceType
);
```

The fully_describe_type() operation, on the other hand, gives a full list of properties derived from all of a type's supertypes. This operation would usually be called by importers and exporters who want to know what properties to expect in a service offer of this type.

```
TypeStruct fully_describe_type (
        in CosTrading::ServiceTypeName name
) raises (
        CosTrading::IllegalServiceType,
        CosTrading::UnknownServiceType
);
```

Masking Types.   Masking a service type is used to either deprecate an existing service type, for which there are already offers in the trader, or to declare an abstract base service type which must be subtyped before service offer instances will be accepted by the trader.

As a service type becomes widely used, people think of additional properties of a service that they wish to describe. So rather than simply adding nonstandard extra properties to their service offers, they create a new service type that subtypes the existing type. If the new properties become important, or widely accepted, then the old type can be masked to prevent new service offers being created without the extra properties.

The operation mask_type() indicates that this type is no longer used, at least in its base form:

```
void mask_type (
        in CosTrading::ServiceTypeName name
) raises (
        CosTrading::IllegalServiceType,
        CosTrading::UnknownServiceType,
        AlreadyMasked
);
```

The unmask_type() operation reverses this masking, and the trader will once again accept offers of this type. The Trading Service authors think that this operation will seldom be used.

```
void unmask_type (
        in CosTrading::ServiceTypeName name
) raises (
        CosTrading::IllegalServiceType,
        CosTrading::UnknownServiceType,
        NotMasked
);
```

3.2.2 TraderComponents—Finding the Right Interface

The trader defines five separate interfaces:

- Lookup—where importers make queries
- Register—where exporters advertise new service offers
- Link—where links to federated traders are administered
- Admin—where policies of the trader are administered
- Proxy—where legacy mechanisms for advertising services are added so that they look like service offers

A single interface, TraderComponents, is inherited by all the interfaces listed above. This allows users to locate the other interfaces supported by a particular trader implementation.

```
interface TraderComponents {

    readonly attribute Lookup lookup_if;
    readonly attribute Register register_if;
    readonly attribute Link link_if;
    readonly attribute Proxy proxy_if;
    readonly attribute Admin admin_if;
};
```

3.2.3 Lookup

The Lookup interface is used by importers to find service offers that meet their needs. It offers a single operation, query(), that requires a specification of the service type and matching constraint expression, and returns a list of service offers. The signature for query() is significantly more complex than this simple explanation would indicate:

```
void query (
    in ServiceTypeName type,
    in Constraint constr,
    in Preference pref,
    in PolicySeq policies,
    in SpecifiedProps desired_props,
    in unsigned long how_many,
    out OfferSeq offers,
    out OfferIterator offer_itr,
    out PolicyNameSeq limits_applied
) raises (
    IllegalServiceType,
    UnknownServiceType,
    IllegalConstraint,
    IllegalPreference,
    IllegalPolicyName,
    PolicyTypeMismatch,
```

```
        InvalidPolicyValue,
        IllegalPropertyName,
        DuplicatePropertyName,
        DuplicatePolicyName
    );
```

The third parameter, pref, is a minimizing, maximizing, or boolean sorting expression that tells the trader which matched offers to return first. The policies parameter allows the importer to influence the way in which the trader searches its service offers, and the way in which it propagates the query to other traders. Often query invocations will be given an empty PolicySeq as the trader administrator will configure the trader to allow a trade-off between search space and resource usage that will deliver appropriate services to users.

A desired_props argument must be provided so that the trader knows whether to return properties of the service offers that matched, or simply the object references to the services. The SpecifiedProps type is defined as follows:

```
    enum HowManyProps { none, some, all };

    union SpecifiedProps switch ( HowManyProps ) {
        case some: PropertyNameSeq prop_names;
    };
```

Sometimes a service type will contain many properties that do not interest a particular importer. In this case the importer will need to specify in the prop_names field of the desired_props which property values to return. In many cases the choice to ignore the property values or to require all the values is sufficient.

The how_many parameter specifies that the importer wishes to receive a certain number of offers back in the form of a sequence (in the offers out parameter). The rest of the offers will be obtained through an iterator, whose object reference is returned in the offer_itr out parameter (see Section 3.2.4). Typically, importers are interested in one of these:

♦ Getting back a small number of offers so that they can ensure that one service is actually available at the time

♦ Examining a large number of service offers for direct comparison outside the trader

In the first case, an importer may save the trader the time and resources of creating an iterator by specifying a policy called "return_card." This policy instructs the trader only to return the number of matching service offers specified by the policy. Making its value the same as the how_many argument will prevent the creation of an iterator. The creation of policies is dealt with in Section 3.2.

3.2.4 Iterators

An iterator is an object that controls a logical list of objects or data items and can return them to a client a few at a time. We use the term logical list because the object supporting the iterator may produce new items for the list as they are required. This is a common style used in many OMG specifications. In the trader two iterators are specified:

- ◆ OfferIterator is used when a large number of service offers are returned from the Lookup::query operation.
- ◆ OfferIdIterator is used to return all of the OfferIds held in a particular trader from the Admin::list_offers operation.

They have essentially the same interface, so we will look at only one of them here.

```
interface OfferIterator {

    unsigned long max_left (
    ) raises (
        UnknownMaxLeft
    );

    boolean next_n (
        in unsigned long n,
        out OfferSeq offers
    );

    void destroy ();
};
```

The max_left() operation provides an upper bound on the number of offers that the iterator contains. If the offers are being constructed a few at a time, then the upper bound may not be easily calculated, so the UnknownMaxLeft exception will be raised. The next_n() operation will return up to *n* offers in the offers out parameter, and a return value of FALSE indicates that no other offers are contained in the iterator.

Although the trader may clean up iterators from time to time to reclaim resources, responsible clients will call destroy() on iterators as soon as they have extracted enough offers.

3.2.5 Register

The Register interface provides operations for advertisers of services. The most important operations are

- export() advertises a service offer in the trader and returns an identifier for it.
- withdraw() removes an identified service offer from the trader.
- describe() returns the properties of an identified service offer.
- modify() allows an exporter to change the values of non-read-only properties of a service offer.

Other operations allow exporters to withdraw all service offers matching a particular query and to obtain the Register interface of a linked trader by name.

```
OfferId export (
    in Object reference,
    in ServiceTypeName type,
    in PropertySeq properties
) raises (
    InvalidObjectRef,
    IllegalServiceType,
    UnknownServiceType,
    InterfaceTypeMismatch,
    IllegalPropertyName, // e.g. prop_name = "<foo-bar"
    PropertyTypeMismatch,
    ReadonlyDynamicProperty,
    MissingMandatoryProperty,
    DuplicatePropertyName
);
```

The export() operation takes three parameters that describe a service and places that service offer in the trader's database for return as a result of an importer's query. The reference parameter must contain an object reference of the type specified in the service offer named by the second parameter, type. The properties parameter must contain a value for each mandatory property in the service type and may contain values for other properties. All values provided for property names specified in the service type must be of the property type specified, and additional properties of any other name and type may also be included. Any non-read-only property value may be replaced by a structure of the following type:

```
struct DynamicProp {
    DynamicPropEval eval_if;
    TypeCode returned_type;
    any extra_info;
};
```

This will cause the property's value to be determined at import time, which means that the constraint will be evaluated on up-to-date information. The printer example above has a property that reflects the length of the current print queue. The eval_if member is an object reference to a standard interface that has a single operation which returns an any. The returned_type member is the type of the value expected in that any, and must match the type specified for this property in the service type.

The exceptions that may be returned are mostly self-explanatory. The ReadonlyDynamicProperty exception indicates that it is illegal for a read-only property to change after export.

The withdraw() operation passes the trader an OfferId returned from a previous export(), and the trader will remove the corresponding service offer from its database.

```
void withdraw (
    in OfferId id
) raises (
    IllegalOfferId,
    UnknownOfferId,
    ProxyOfferId
);
```

The other withdraw operation, withdraw_using_constraint(), will remove all service offers that match a particular constraint expression. This should generally only be used by the administrator.

The describe() operation returns an OfferInfo structure corresponding to the id parameter. OfferInfo contains exactly the same information as the three parameters to export(): an object reference, a service type, and a sequence of properties.

```
struct OfferInfo {
    Object reference;
    ServiceTypeName type;
    PropertySeq properties;
};

OfferInfo describe (
    in OfferId id
) raises (
    IllegalOfferId,
    UnknownOfferId,
    ProxyOfferId
);
```

The modify() operation allows exporters to change the properties contained in a particular service offer. Some traders do not allow the modification of service offers and will raise the NotImplemented exception. Traders that implement this operation must succeed on all modifications, or fail on all. Properties listed in the del_list parameter will be deleted if possible, and property values in modify_list will replace current values in the identified service offer, if this is allowed. The reasons the operation may fail are reflected in its long raises clause. In short, the two list parameters may be inconsistent, or the caller may be trying to modify something read only, or delete something mandatory.

```
void modify (
    in OfferId id,
    in PropertyNameSeq del_list,
    in PropertySeq modify_list
) raises (
    NotImplemented,
    IllegalOfferId,
    UnknownOfferId,
    ProxyOfferId,
    IllegalPropertyName,
    UnknownPropertyName,
    PropertyTypeMismatch,
    ReadonlyDynamicProperty,
    MandatoryProperty,
    ReadonlyProperty,
    DuplicatePropertyName
);
```

The resolve() operation is for obtaining a reference to the Register interface of another trader, to which this trader has a named link. This is how one exports service offers to and withdraws them from federated traders.

```
Register resolve (
    in TraderName name
) raises (
    IllegalTraderName,
    UnknownTraderName,
    RegisterNotSupported
);
```

3.2.6 Link

Links can be considered a specialization of service offers. They advertise other traders that can be used to perform federated queries. The Link interface therefore looks much the same as the Register interface, with operations to add and remove as well as describe and modify links. Each link has four associated pieces of information: its name, its object reference (to a Lookup interface), and two policies on link following. Most users of traders do not need to know what links a trader has or how they are followed. The trader administrator sets up link policies and trader defaults.

3.2.7   *Admin*

The Admin interface contains a large number of operations to set the policies of a trader and operations to list the OfferIds of service offers contained in the trader. Ordinary trader users can query the attributes of the other interfaces to determine the current policies of a trader but will never need to use the Admin interface. Some traders will not even offer this interface, as all policy will be determined by the implementation.

3.2.8   *Proxies and Dynamic Properties*

Proxies are objects that sit alongside service offers but hide some legacy mechanism of service creation or discovery. Most traders will not support the Proxy interface. Traders that do, return identical results from a proxy as from a normal service offer.

Dynamic properties are a mechanism to allow a service to provide a property value at import time that reflects the current state of the service. We have seen in the explanation of the export operation above that the value of a non-read-only property may be replaced by a DynamicProp structure. This will cause the trader to call back to an interface supported by the service (or some associated server) to obtain the property value when the constraint expression of a query is being evaluated. The object reference provided in that structure must be of the following interface type:

```
interface DynamicPropEval {

    any evalDP (
        in CosTrading::PropertyName name,
        in TypeCode returned_type,
        in any extra_info
    ) raises (
        DPEvalFailure
    );
};
```

When evaluating a dynamic property, the trader invokes the evalDP() operation of the eval_if member of the DynamicProp, passing the property name and the returned_type and extra_info members of the structure. It receives an appropriate value in return.

The evaluation of a query which involves calling back to several services to determine the dynamic value of a property can be very costly, and some traders will not support dynamic properties, as indicated by the SupportAttributes::supports_dynamic_properties boolean attribute. However, for some services the information is invaluable for determining their suitability for a purpose. For example, a printer that is one floor up from me and has a zero-length queue is much more useful than one in the same room that has thirty jobs queued or is out of toner.

3.3 Exporting a Service Offer

In this section we will provide an example implementation of the Printer interface introduced in Section 3.1. The server that supports objects of this type will export service offers describing the printer objects to the trader. In this way printer clients can choose printers using an expression of their requirements rather than the usual method of choosing the name of a printer they know.

The Printer interface is very simple and emulates the kind of command line interface provided by UNIX print commands such as 1pr. The purpose of this implementation is to show how a minimal wrapper of this kind of service, which describes printer attributes in service offers, can allow users more flexibility. They can not only choose a printer based on some capability that it has, such as high resolution, but they can also choose it based on its current state, such as the length of its print queue. In addition, users can discover new printers that they were previously unaware of.

The environment in which we implemented this server is one in which many different operating systems run on different machines. Although they all have access to the same file systems via NFS, it is too complex to integrate all the different printing services, and printing is only available on some machines. One way of extending printer availability is installing this server on one of the printing machines and using a CORBA client on the other machines which passes the name of the file to be printed.

The implementation of the Printer Server has the usual steps. The first of these, specifying the interface of a CORBA object, has already been done in Section 3.1, although we will extend this IDL to facilitate the evaluation of dynamic properties. The second is to compile the IDL. Following that we need to implement the Printer interface and write a server which creates instances of the implementation class. Our server will also create service offers for the printers it creates and export these to the trader.

3.3.1 *Implementing the Printer Interface*

We intend to allow the trader to use its dynamic property evaluation to get the printer queue length at query time, so that clients of the trader can sort their returned printer service offers according to the length of the queue. In order to do this we need to implement the interface CosTradingDynamic:: DynamicPropEval so that the trader can call its evalDP() operation to get the queue_len property of each printer service offer. The best way to do this is to create a new interface that multiply inherits from the printer and the dynamic property evaluation interfaces. We reopen the Printing module and define a new interface as follows:

```
module chapter8 {
module Printing {
   interface TradingPrinter : Printer,
              CosTradingDynamic::DynamicPropEval {};
};
};
```

The IDL compiler generates the following files: `printingC.hh`, `printingC.cc`, `printingS.hh`, and `printingS.cc`.

Our implementation of the TradingPrinter interface is done in the servant class `PrinterImpl`, which inherits from the POA class generated from IDL, `POA_Printing::POA_TradingPrinter`.

```
// PrinterImpl.C

#include "printingS.hh"

class PrinterImpl : public POA__Printing::POA_TradingPrinter {
```

Because the printer interface is so simple, we only need `PrinterImpl` to know the command we will use to find the queue length, the command to print files, and the name of the printer to which it will send them. Therefore we define three private string members to store the commands and the name, and a constructor which accepts three corresponding string arguments.

```
// PrinterImpl.C

#include "PrinterImpl.h"
...
char              **print_command;
char              **queue_command;
CORBA::String_var   printer_name;
CORBA::TypeCode_var ret_type;

// constructor
PrinterImpl::PrinterImpl (const char *p_command,
          const char *q_command,
          const char *name,
          CORBA::TypeCode_ptr dp_eval_ret_type) {

    print_command = new char *[4];

    print_command[0] = new char[256];
    strcpy(print_command[0], p_command);
```

```
            print_command[1] = new char[256];
            strcpy(print_command[1], " -P ");
            strcat(print_command[1], name);
            print_command[2] = new char[256];
            strcpy(print_command[2],"");
            queue_command = new char *[2];

queue_command[0] = new char[256];
            strcpy(queue_command[0], q_command);
            queue_command[1] = new char[256];
            strcpy(queue_command[1], "-P");
            strcat(queue_command[1],name);
            queue_command[2] = new char[256];
            strcpy(queue_command[2],"");

            printer_name = CORBA::strdup(name);
            ret_type = dp_eval_ret_type;
}
```

We could have chosen to initialize printer objects with all the characteristics which we will export in their service offers, but because we don't define any attributes or operations to retrieve these properties, there is no point in doing so. Instead we make the server aware of these characteristics, and it exports service offers with corresponding property values on the objects' behalf.

The remainder of the implementation consists of the methods mapped from the IDL operations. The first of these is print_file():

```
void PrinterImpl::print_file (const char *fn) {

        strcpy( print_command[2], " ");
        strcat( print_command[2], fn );
        print_command[3] = new char [256];
        strcpy( print_command[3], "" );

        cout << "print command: " << endl;
        for( int i = 0; i < 4; i++ )
          cout << print_command[i];
          cout << endl;

        cout << "Invoking print command" << endl;
        if (execvp((const char *)print_command[0],
              (char *const *) print_command) < 0) {
          cout << "execvp to print file failed " << endl;
          throw Printing::Printer::PrinterOffLine();
        }


}
```

The method is implemented very simply by concatenating the print command, the printer name, and the file name and executing it via the system call, execvp().

The queue_len() method is also implemented by making a call to a UNIX executable, which makes the crude assumption that the output of the queue command lists two lines of header information of 80 characters, followed by a line of 80 characters for each queued job.

```cpp
CORBA::Short PrinterImpl::queue_length() {

    const int MAXLINE = 1024;
    char line[ MAXLINE ], command[ MAXLINE ];
    CORBA::UShort len = 0;
    int line_num = 0;
    FILE *fp;

    // Execute the lpq command
    strcpy( command, queue_command[0] );
    for( int i = 1; i < 3; i++ ) {
      strcat( command, " " );
      strcat( command, queue_command[i] );
    }

    // Print the command actually being invoked
    cout << "Invoking command: ";
    cout << command << endl;

    if ((fp = popen( command, "r" )) == NULL )
      throw Printing::Printer::PrinterOffLine();

    // sleep while the queue command produces
    // output
    VISPortable::vsleep(1);

    // read lpq output
    while ((fgets( line, MAXLINE, fp )) != NULL)
      ++line_num;

    // close file
    fclose (fp);

    // check the length of the output available
    // and use this to calculate the number of
    // lines of queue output, then subtract the
    // header lines to give queue length
    len = (CORBA::UShort) (line_num / 80 - 2);
    len = (len ? len : 0);
    cout << "Printer " << printer_name <<
      " queue_len:" << len << endl;
```

```
        return len;
}
```

The other method which must be implemented is for the dynamic property evaluation operation evalDP(). Its parameters are extracted from the value of any dynamic property in a service offer. This value will always be of type

```
struct DynamicProp {
        DynamicPropEval eval_if;
        TypeCode returned_type;
        any extra_info;
};
```

The eval_if member of this struct will be a reference to our PrinterImpl object, and the other two parameters will be passed to the evalDP() operation on that interface. This is what we implement here:

```
CORBA::Any_ptr PrinterImpl::evalDP ( const char *name,
                    CORBA::TypeCode_ptr returned_type,
                    const CORBA::Any& extra_info ) {

  cout << "Printer " << printer_name << " DPEval" << endl;
  if ( strcmp( name, " queue_len" ) == 0 ) {
    throw CosTradingDynamic::DPEvalFailure();
  }

  if ( returned_type != ret_type ) {
    throw CosTradingDynamic::DPEvalFailure();
  }

  CORBA::Any_var ret_val;

  try {
    (*ret_val) <<= this->queue_length();
  }

  catch (const Printing::Printer::PrinterOffLine& pol) {
    throw CosTradingDynamic::DPEvalFailure();
  }

  return CORBA::Any::_duplicate(ret_val);
}
```

The name argument to the evalDP() method is the name of the property in the service offer which is being evaluated. We are expecting only one such name, queue_len, and if we receive any other we will throw the DPEvalFailure exception. The result of the evaluation must be an any with the TypeCode passed in the returned_type argument. If the TypeCode expected is not the typecode for an IDL short then we also raise an exception. We are not expecting any extra information (such as arguments to supply to a method call), so we then create an `any` object and place the result of the call to `queue_length()` into it and return the `any`. The last failure condition may occur when the printer is off-line and cannot return a queue length value. In this case we also throw the `DPEvalFailure` exception.

3.3.2 *Implementing the Printer Server*

Now that we have an implementation of a `PrinterImpl` servant class that satisfies the requirements of printer clients and the trader, we will implement a server that creates printer objects and service offers that represent their characteristics and then exports them to the trader. We have used the Inprise VisiTrader implementation for testing. As it was not incorporated into C++ ORB products at the time of writing, the ORB bootstrap resolve_initial_reference() could not be used to obtain a reference to a trader by passing it the string "`TradingService`". Instead, the application uses a helper class called `IORFile` that reads an Interoperable Object reference from a file and produces a string that we can pass the ORB::string_to_object() operation.

Our server will take the following command line arguments:

◆ A filename where the trader's object reference is kept
◆ A command to send a file to the printer that takes the printer name and a filename
◆ A command to check the printer queue length that takes a printer name
◆ The characteristics of one or more printers including the printer's name, resolution in DPI, building location, and floor number

The `PrinterServer` **program is in** `PrinterServer.C`:

```
// PrintServer.C

#include "CosTradingC.hh"
#include "CosTradingReposC.hh"
#include "PrinterImpl.h"
#include "IORFile.h"

const int NAME = 0;
const int BUILDING = 1;
const int FLOOR = 2;
const int RESOLUTION = 3;
const int QUEUE_LEN = 4;
const int COLOR = 5;
const int LANGUAGE = 6;
```

The server's main function is as follows:

```
int main( int argc, char *const *argv ) {

  int                num_printers;
  PrinterImpl        **printers;
  CORBA::String_var  printer_name;
  if ( (argc < 8) ||( (argc-4)%4 != 0) ) {
    cout << "Usage: " << argv[0]
         << " TraderIORFile print_command ";
    cout << "queue_len_command name "
         << "resolution building floor ";
    cout << " [ name res build floor ... ]"
         << endl;
    exit(1);
  }
}
```

An array is declared for storing pointers to the printer object references. Various ORB and trader variables are declared and then the usual ORB initialization is carried out.

```
// allocate an array to store Printer Implementation Objects

num_printers = (argc - 4)/4;
printers = new PrinterImpl *[num_printers];

cout << "number of printers: " << num_printers << endl;

CORBA::ULong i = 0;
```

We initialize the ORB, obtain a reference to preinitialized root POA.

```
try {

  CORBA::ORB_var orb;

  // initialize the Object Request Broker
  orb = CORBA::ORB_init( argc, argv );

  // get the root POA object reference
  CORBA::Object_var obj =
    orb->resolve_initial_references("RootPOA");

  // narrow the object reference to a POA reference
  PortableServer::POA_var poa =
              PortableServer::POA::_narrow( obj );
```

We then proceed with the trader-related declarations.

```
// Trader object reference declarations
CosTrading::LookupRef                        lookup;
CosTrading::Register_ptr                     p_register;
CosTradingRepos::ServiceTypeRepository_var st_repos;
```

```
// get the trader reference from the command line
// and initialize the ServiceTypeRepository and Register
// interface references from the Initial Lookup interface

IORFile trader_ref( argv[1] );
CORBA::Object_var obj =
orb->string_to_object( trader_ref.get_ior_string() );

lookup = CosTrading::Lookup::_narrow( obj );
if ( lookup == CosTrading::Lookup::_nil() ) {
  cerr << "lookup narrowed incorrectly" << endl;
  exit(1);
}
cout << "lookup narrowed" << endl;

p_register = lookup->register_if();
cout << "register obtained" << endl;

obj = p_register->type_repos();
st_repos =
   CosTradingRepos::ServiceTypeRepository::_narrow( obj );

if ( st_repos ==
   CosTradingRepos::ServiceTypeRepository::_nil() ) {
     cerr << "ServiceTypeRepository narrowed incorrectly"
          << endl;
     exit(1);
   }
```

The trader's reference is obtained from the file supplied on the command line using an instance of the IORFile class. The first reference for a trader is to a Lookup interface, from which we obtain references to its Register interface and the service type repository. The service type repository reference returned from the attribute type_repos is specified as type Object in the standard, in anticipation of the interface ServiceTypeRepository being replaced by a repository specified by the Meta Object Facility, which was adopted by the OMG in September 1997. This is why the returned reference must be narrowed.

The next thing we need to do is to check if the service type that we want to use is already defined in the service type repository. We do this by checking the result of a call to the describe_type() operation, which will raise the UnknownServiceType exception if it is not yet created.

```
// check for Service Type existence
// and create a new Service Type if it does not exist

CORBA::Boolean type_exists = (CORBA::Boolean)0;
CORBA::String_var repos_id = (const char *)
                   "IDL:Printing/Printer:1.0";
```

```
CORBA::String_var serv_type_name = repos_id;
CosTradingRepos::ServiceTypeRepository::IncarnationNumber
                            incarn_num;

CosTradingRepos::ServiceTypeRepository::TypeStruct_var
                            type_desc;
try {
  type_desc = st_repos->describe_type(
                CORBA::strdup(serv_type_name) );
  cout << "called describe_type - returned typedesc"
      << endl;
  type_exists = (CORBA::Boolean)1;
}
catch( const CosTrading::UnknownServiceType& ust ) {
  cerr << "called describe_type - raised UnknownServiceType"
      << endl;
  type_exists = (CORBA::Boolean)0;
}
catch( const CosTrading::IllegalServiceType& ist ) {
  cerr << ist << endl;
  exit(1);
}
catch( CORBA::SystemException& se ) {
  cerr << se << endl;
  exit(1);
}
```

If the service type is not present then we must create it. We will use the same properties as shown when we introduced the printing example in Section 3.1. We make all the properties mandatory, so that we can be sure that a query using any property name in the service type will be evaluated on all service offers of this type.

```
if ( type_exists == (CORBA::Boolean)0 ) {
  cout << "service type does not exist" << endl;

// we will create a new service type

// create a prop struct list with the property names
// for a printer service type

CosTradingRepos::ServiceTypeRepository::PropStructSeq_var
st_props = new
  CosTradingRepos::ServiceTypeRepository::PropStructSeq();
st_props->length(6);

st_props[NAME].name = (const char *)"name";
st_props[NAME].value_type = CORBA::_tc_string;
st_props[NAME].mode =
  CosTradingRepos::ServiceTypeRepository::PROP_MANDATORY;
```

```
st_props[BUILDING].name = (const char *)"building";
st_props[BUILDING].value_type = CORBA::_tc_ushort;
st_props[BUILDING].mode =
  CosTradingRepos::ServiceTypeRepository::PROP_MANDATORY;

st_props[FLOOR].name = (const char *)"floor";
st_props[FLOOR].value_type = CORBA::_tc_ushort;
st_props[FLOOR].mode =
  CosTradingRepos::ServiceTypeRepository::PROP_MANDATORY;

st_props[RESOLUTION].name = (const char *)"resolution";
st_props[RESOLUTION].value_type = CORBA::_tc_ushort;
st_props[RESOLUTION].mode =
  CosTradingRepos::ServiceTypeRepository::PROP_MANDATORY;

st_props[QUEUE_LEN].name = (const char *) "queue_len";
CosTradingDynamic::DynamicProp dynamicProp;
st_props[QUEUE_LEN].value_type = dynamicProp.returned_type;
st_props[QUEUE_LEN].mode =
  CosTradingRepos::ServiceTypeRepository::PROP_MANDATORY;

st_props[COLOR].name = (const char *)"color";
st_props[COLOR].value_type = CORBA::_tc_string;
st_props[COLOR].mode =
  CosTradingRepos::ServiceTypeRepository::PROP_MANDATORY;
```

The other arguments required by the repository's **add_type()** operation are a service type name, an interface's Repository ID, and a list of supertypes. We are using the interface's Repository ID as the service type name, and will not use any supertypes.

```
// create an empty super type list
CosTrading::STSeq_var super_types =
                      new CosTrading::STSeq();

// add the new Service Type
// we use the Interface type string as the service
// type name
cout << "about to add_type" << endl;
cout << "serv_type_name = " << serv_type_name << endl;
cout << "repos_id = " << repos_id << endl;

incarn_num = st_repos->add_type( serv_type_name,
                                 repos_id,
                                 st_props,
                                 super_types );

cout << "Created Service Type: " << serv_type_name
     << endl;
cout << "Incarnation Number: high= "
```

```
        << incarn_num.high << endl;
cout << "                    low= "
    << incarn_num.low << endl;
}
```

Now we are ready to create a template service offer, which we can reuse for all the printers that we will export. This server is only going to support printers that are black and white and use postscript, so we can set the values for the "color" and "language" properties now. The other property that will share a value for all service offers is `"queue_len"`, which will contain a `DynamicProp`. It will be initialized with the type expected from the dynamic evaluation, but the actual object reference will be added once the printer object is created.

```
// create Service Offer Property Seq to use for export
CosTrading::PropertySeq_var so_props = new
                            CosTrading::PropertySeq();
so_props->length(7);

// create a Dynamic Property for queue length evaluation
CosTradingDynamic::DynamicProp_var queue_prop =
            new CosTradingDynamic::DynamicProp();

queue_prop->eval_if =
  CosTradingDynamic::DynamicPropEval::_nil();
queue_prop->returned_type = CORBA::_tc_ushort;
// The first five properties will be different for each
// printer, so we initialize them in the loop below

so_props[NAME].name = (const char *)"name";
so_props[BUILDING].name = (const char *)"building";
so_props[FLOOR].name = (const char *)"floor";
so_props[RESOLUTION].name = (const char *)"resolution";
so_props[QUEUE_LEN].name = (const char *)"queue_len";

// the last twp properties' values are assumed by this
// server
// so we initialize them for all printers

so_props[COLOR].name = (const char *)"color";
so_props[COLOR].value <<= (const char *)"black";
so_props[LANGUAGE].name = (const char *)"language";
so_props[LANGUAGE].value <<= (const char *)"postscript";

// create printer object(s) and export
```

The next step is to process the command line arguments and create printers with the corresponding characteristics. We do this in a loop, creating the `PrinterImpl` objects, making them available to the ORB, and then updating the creating service offer to advertise them

```
for( CORBA::ULong i = 0; i < num_printers; i++ ) {

    cout << "about to create printer" << endl;
    // create a Printer object
    printers[i] = new PrinterImpl(
                            argv[2],
                            argv[3],
                            argv[i*4 + 4],
                            CORBA::_tc_ushort
                    );

    // activate the object created
    PortableServer::ObjectId_var oid =
                    root_poa->activate( printers[i] );

    // activate the POA to wait for requests
    root_poa->the_POAManager ()->activate();

    // create Printer Object Reference
    CORBA::Object_var printerRef =
                    root_poa->id_to_reference ( oid );

    cout << "Printer IOR: "
         << orb->object_to_string( printerRef ) << endl;

    cout << "Created printer: " << argv[i*4 + 4] << endl;
```

We activate each printer object using the root POA and have the root POA create object references for each of them, which will then be published through the TraderService.

```
    // initialize the properties we get from the
    // command line

    // name
    so_props[NAME].value <<= argv[i*4 + 4];

    // resolution
    cout << "Resolution: " << argv[i*4 + 5] << endl;
    so_props[RESOLUTION].value <<=
                        (CORBA::UShort)atoi(argv[i*4 +5]);

    // building
    cout << "Building: " << argv[i*4 + 6] << endl;
    so_props[BUILDING].value <<= argv[i*4 + 6];

    // floor
    cout << "Floor: " << argv[i*4 + 7] << endl;
    so_props[FLOOR].value <<=
                    (CORBA::UShort)atoi(argv[i*4 + 7]);
```

```
        // update the dynamic prop struct and insert into
        // the queue_len property of the service offer
        queue_prop->eval_if = printers[i];
        so_props[4].value <<= queue_prop;

        // export the service offer
        cout << "about to export" << endl;
        p_register->export( printers[i],
                            serv_type_name,
                            so_props );

        cout << "Exported printer: " << argv[i*4 + 4] << endl;
    } // end for loop
```

Once the printers are all created and their offers exported, we call `orb->run()` to enter the ORB's event loop. We also have to catch the various CORBA user and system exceptions that can be raised.

```
        // start ORB's event loop
        orb->run();
    }
    catch( const CosTrading::PropertyTypeMismatch& pm ) {
        cerr << pm << endl;
        cerr << pm.type << endl;
        cerr << pm.prop.name << endl;
        cerr << pm.prop.value << endl;
    }
    catch( const CORBA::UserException& ue ) {
        cerr << "User Exception caught" << endl;
        cerr << ue << endl;
        exit(1);
    }
    catch( const CORBA::SystemException& se ) {
        cerr << "System Exception caught" << endl;
        cerr << se << endl;
        exit (1);
    }

    return 0;
}
```

3.4   Finding an Object Using a Trader

In this section we use VisiBroker for C++ to implement a simple C++ application client that trades for a suitable Printer object to send its print job to. The application expects two mandatory and two optional arguments:

♦ A name of the file where the IOR to a CosTrading::Lookup object is stored
♦ The name of the file we wish to print

♦ A constraint expression to select suitable printers
♦ A preference expression to order the printer service offers returned

The structure of the application is as follows:

The program usage is checked for an appropriate number of arguments.
We obtain an object reference to a Lookup object.
The command line arguments to the application are processed.
Some basic policies for a trader query are established.
The query is made.
The returned Printer objects are tried in order until one successfully
prints the file.

Let's look at the code starting with the included files, the main function, and command line argument check:

```
// PrintClient.C

#include "CosTradingC.hh"
#include "IORFile.h"
#include "printingC.hh"

int main(int argc, char *const *argv) {

  if ( argc < 3 || argc > 5) {
    cout << "usage: PrintClient trader_ior_file printfile "
         << "[constraint [preference]]" << endl;
    exit( 1 );
  }
```

The application exits if it has not been run with the two mandatory arguments.

The next piece of code declares some variables and then initializes the
ORB and obtains a reference to the trader's Lookup interface.

```
CORBA::ORB_var orb;

// initialize the ORB
try {
  orb = CORBA::ORB_init (argc, argv);
}
catch( const CORBA::SystemException& excep ) {
  cerr << "System Exception caught while "
       << "initializing ORB" << endl;
  exit(1);
}
```

```
// some general purpose variables
CORBA::Any_var policy_any = new CORBA::Any;
CORBA::Object_ptr obj;

// get reference to trader lookup interface
CosTrading::LookupRef my_lookup;
try {
  IORFile ior_file( CORBA::strdup (argv[1]) );
  obj = orb->string_to_object( ior_file.get_ior_string() );
  my_lookup = CosTrading::Lookup::_narrow( obj );

  if ( my_lookup == CosTrading::Lookup::_nil() ) {
    cerr << "NIL Trader Reference" << endl;
    exit(1);
  }
}
catch( const CORBA::SystemException& se ) {
  cerr << "Caught CORBA System Exception" << endl;
  cerr << se << endl;
  exit(1);
}
cout << "trader narrowed" << endl;
```

The IORFile class opens and reads the file given as a command line argument and produces a string for use with the ORB's string_to_object() method. We then narrow the reference obtained.

The next step is to prepare the query for a printer. We use any constraint and preference strings received from the command line and provide suitable defaults when they are not provided.

```
// determine the constraint
CORBA::String_var constr;

if ( argc > 3 )
  constr = (const char *)argv[3];
else
  constr = (const char *)"";

// determine the prefs
CORBA::String_var prefs;

if ( argc > 4 )
  prefs = (const char *)argv[4];
else
  // if no preference, compare the offers for shortest queue
  prefs = (const char *)"min queue_len";
```

An empty constraint string will match all service offers of the right type. If the user does not supply a preference then we use a default which orders the returned printers by shortest queue length. Now we set parameter values and some policies which will ensure that we get a reasonable result.

```
// set some basic policies
CosTrading::PolicySeq_var query_pols = new
                              CosTrading::PolicySeq();

query_pols->length (2);

//declare variables needed in the query()
CORBA::Short num_offers = 3;
CORBA::String_var service_type_name =
    (const char *)"IDL:Printing/Printer:1.0";
CosTrading::Lookup::SpecifiedProps_var desired_props;
CosTrading::OfferSeq_var return_offers;
CosTrading::OfferIterator_var iter;
CosTrading::PolicyNameSeq_var limits;
```

We will ask for at most three offers back, as this provides a reasonable likelihood of one printer being operational. We initialize a short variable
num_offers to the value 3. This is used in the policy "return_card", which specifies the maximum number of service offers to return from a query. If we
then pass the same value to the query() operation's how_many parameter, we
can ensure that all of the results will come back in the offers out parameter,
and we will not have to process an iterator.

```
try {
  // we want at most 3 offers back
  (*policy_any) <<= num_offers;
  CosTrading::PolicyName_var policy_name =
    (const char *) "return_card";
  CosTrading::Policy policy;
  policy.name = policy_name;
  policy.value = *(policy_any);

  query_pols[0] = policy;
```

The other policy we will pass to the trader is "use_dynamic_properties", which
tells the trader to evaluate the "queue_len" property dynamically so that the
value used is up to date.

```
// we want to use dynamic props to find
// printer queue length
(*policy_any) <<=
      CORBA::Any::from_boolean( (CORBA::Boolean)1 );
policy_name = (const char *)"use_dynamic_properties";
policy.name = policy_name;
policy.value = *(policy_any);
query_pols[1] = policy;
```

The desired_props parameter to query() lists the property names whose
values we want returned with the query result. For easy processing in this

example we will ask for only the printer name, which assumes that users of our application know their printers by name so that they can go and pick up a print-out from the right location. Remember that using the trader we can discover new printers that only the systems administrator knows about. A more advanced printing application would probably ask for all the properties and provide the user with information on the location of printers, which would enable newly discovered printers to be found by location.

```
// we want back only the name property
CosTrading::PropertyNameSeq_var desired_prop_names;

desired_prop_names = new CosTrading::PropertyNameSeq(1);
desired_prop_names->length(1);
desired_prop_names[0] = "name";
desired_props = new CosTrading::Lookup::SpecifiedProps();
desired_props->prop_names(desired_prop_names);
}
catch (const CORBA::SystemException& se) {
  cerr << "Query failed: " << se << endl;
  exit(1);
}
```

The SpecifiedProps type is a union, so we must initialize its value and discriminator. The C++ mapping specifies that a method corresponding to a union branch name will set the discriminator for us. We use the method prop_names() to set the value of the only branch.

Having created objects or variables for each of the parameters to the query() method, we can now invoke it:

```
// make a query
try {
  my_lookup->query( service_type_name,
                    constr,
                    prefs,
                    query_pols,
                    desired_props,
                    num_offers,
                    return_offers.out(),
                    iter.out(),
                    limits.out());
}
```

Since we have set the value in policy return_card to the value of num_offers (the size of the sequence we are prepared to accept back into our return_offers object), we can ignore the iterator. We also ignore the feedback from the trader about what policy restrictions it applied to our query, which are returned in the limits object. This time we must catch the user exceptions as well as any system exceptions. Rather than catching each of the ten possible user exceptions that the query() operation could raise, we will catch the base class of all of these, CORBA::UserException.

```
// catch some important exceptions
catch (const CORBA::UserException& ue) {
  cerr << "Query failed - User Exception: " << ue << endl;
  exit(1);
}
catch (const CORBA::SystemException& se) {
  cerr << "Query failed: " << se << endl;
  exit(1);
}
```

Having received a response from the trader we will now attempt to use the service offers to print the file. We do this by entering a loop which exits once the print_file() operation has successfully been invoked on one of the objects returned in a service offer. First we declare and initialize some variables, including a string and an Any_var to extract the printer's name from the single returned property in each service offer.

```
..// send job to printer
  CORBA::ULong i = 0;
  CORBA::Boolean printed = (CORBA::Boolean)0;
  char *pname;

  CORBA::Any_var return_any = new CORBA::Any;
```

Then we enter the loop.

```
..// we'll try all the returned printers until one works
  while (i < return_offers->length() - 1 && !printed) {
    try {
      return_any <<= return_offers[i].properties[0];
      *(return_any) >>= pname;
      Printing::Printer_var printer =
        Printing::Printer::_narrow(return_offers[i].reference);

      if ( printer == Printing::Printer::_nil() ) {
        cerr << "Printer " << pname << " not found" << endl;
        i++;
        continue;
      }
}

printer->print_file( CORBA::strdup(argv[2]) );
printed = (CORBA::Boolean)1;
cout << "File " << argv[2] << "sent to printer "
     << pname << endl;
      }
```

If the string extraction from `return_any` and the narrow of the object reference work, we attempt to print the file named in the second command line argument. If the `print_file()` call works, the termination variable is set to true, a message is printed, and the loop will exit. Other possibilities are that the printer is off-line or that the invocation fails for some other reason.

```
catch (const Printing::Printer::PrinterOffLine& pol) {
  cout << "Printer " << pname << " offline!" << endl;
}
catch (const CORBA::SystemException& se) {
  cout << "Printer " << pname << " raised: " << se << endl;
}
i++;
}
}
```

Any failures to print are notified to the user and the next printer is tried.

This is an example of how we might run the application:

```
/Print>PrintClient trader.ior
                /home/dud/myfile.ps \
                language == "postscript" && floor < 4
```

Our constraint expression expresses our need for a postscript printer somewhere on the lower floors of our building. We do not specify a preference, as the default preference for the shortest print queue length is suitable. The execution above may result in the following output:

```
..Printer 12ps offline!
..File /home/dud/myfile.ps sent to printer monster
```

3.4.1 Possible Enhancements to the PrintClient

The example exercises the query() operation, demonstrates how to pass policies and how to specify the properties we want back, and shows how to extract the returned property values. However, it does not deal with the situation where no service offers match the constraint expression.

A more sophisticated printer query might look up the user's default printer constraint expression and preferences from a file if none were supplied on the command line. It could also check that at least one working printer offer is returned, and if not, it could make a less specific query with an empty constraint string to match all available offers of the service type.

In the case where the first attempt fails, it could query for all printers and ask for all of their properties to be returned, then display a list and allow the user to select an appropriate printer. This would require that the `return_card` policy not be set and that an iterator be used, as the number of offers returned would be unpredictable. When making a query that might match a large number of offers, it is often best to set the how_many argument to zero and have a single loop to process the iterator. This avoids having to have two loops, one for the returned sequence of offers and the other to invoke the next_n() operation on the returned iterator.

4 Domains

As we saw in Section 1, the operation resolve_initial_references() returns an object of type CORBA::Object, but this object is expected to be of a specific type, depending on the service name specified as parameter. For the Naming Service, you narrow the object to a NamingContext. The question we want to discuss in this section is which object instance the method `resolve_initial_references()` returns for a given service name.

It might appear that the answer is the root context of the Naming Service. However, there are a number of problems with this answer.

First of all, what is the Naming Service. CORBA does not define an association between the ORB and Services, and there is also no such thing as the ORB. When you obtain an ORB pseudo-object by calling CORBA::ORB_init() a local instance of the class CORBA::ORB is created which implements the operations defined in the pseudo-interface CORBA::ORB. Furthermore, novice users sometimes assume that an ORB is associated with an IP subnet—this is not the case! Whenever your ORB is initialized locally and obtains a reference to an object, you can invoke operations on that object.

As we see, the ORB does not solve our problem. What we want is something which allows us to share the same instances of initial services among a set of objects and clients. We call this a *domain*. There are multiple kinds of domains. In this context we have a naming domain, that is, a set of objects and clients which share the same Naming Service.

In the case of the Naming Service we face an additional problem. The Naming Service specification does not define a structure for the relationships between naming context objects. Even though you organize your naming contexts as a tree, the Naming Service does not know this. Hence any context may have to be returned by resolve_initial_references(). So a domain is specific to a specific service and identifies which initial object instance provided by such a service is returned. All members of a domain will obtain the same initial object. For the Naming Service, this means that all clients and objects which belong to the same naming domain obtain the same context object when calling `orb->resolve_initial_references("NameService")`.

CORBA only provides a minimal interface for choosing domains. The only hook available is the parameters which can be used to initialize the ORB object. The C++ language binding defines the following ORB's ORB_init() operation:

```
CORBA::ORB_ptr
  CORBA::ORB_init( int argc, char *const *argv );
```

Using the `argc` and `argv` parameters, we can pass command line arguments to initialize the local **ORB** object so that it belongs to a certain naming domain.

We illustrate the use of domains with the VisiBroker Naming Service and a simple client program which can resolve string names and print out stringified object references. This client is defined in the Resolve program. The implementation is shown in the examples associated with this chapter. Domains are implemented with VisiBroker using the ORB's underlying directory service, implemented by the OSAgent (see Section 5 for details). We start the Naming Service using a factory which creates one initial naming context object. We then register this naming context object with the OSAgent under the name ROOT.

```
CosNamingExtFactory ROOT /tmp/ns_log
```

Now we start the resolve client from Section 4 so that it belongs to the naming domain defined by the naming context called ROOT. We do this by setting the command line argument `-DSVCnameroot` to the value ROOT.

```
Resolve -DSVCnameroot=ROOT "/x/y/z"
```

Now when we call `resolve_initial_references()` on the local **ORB** object, it returns a reference to the Naming Service's context object called ROOT.

We can assume that the naming context object, which is named "/x/y" relative to the root context, is registered as "_X_Y" with the OSAgent. We can again start the same resolve client, but this time we want it to belong to a different naming domain and obtain the same object. This time the object's name is different as it is relative to a different naming context:

```
Resolve -DSVCnameroot=_X_Y "/z"
```

Alternatively, you can start a client with another command line argument which passes a stringified IOR to determine the naming domain. This is particularly useful for ORB interoperability.

```
Resolve -DSVCnameIOR="IOR:000.."
        -DSVCnameroot=ROOT -ORBagent 0 "/x/y/z"
```

5 *Proprietary Object Location*

Different ORB implementations provide proprietary mechanisms to locate objects. An example of such mechanisms are the `bind()` methods provided by Visibroker C++. Other ORBs such as Orbix also have implementations of the `bind()` method. Although the similarity of the names and signatures suggests interoperability, this is not the case. The set of bind methods have quite different mechanisms.

Although these bind mechanisms are neither interoperable nor portable between different ORB implementations, they are quite popular among application programmers. In fact these mechanisms ease the bootstrapping of applications and provide additional features. For example, Visibroker provides load balancing, fault tolerance through replicas, and automatic object activation.

We introduce here the binding mechanisms of Visibroker for C++. The mechanisms introduced here are uniform across the product suites of the vendors that implement them. C++ ORB access to CORBA objects implemented in other languages will rely on using the equivalent mechanism in another ORB in the same family. We do not provide any details on how this is achieved, and the reader is referred to the product documentation.

VisiBroker's mechanism for binding objects requires the object implementer to assign names to objects when instantiating them. The name is then used to automatically register the object implementation with a VisiBroker's Smart Agent. Clients of the object can then use their knowledge of these names to bind to the objects.

The Visibroker-generated skeleton classes all have a constructor that accepts a string, which is the implementation name for a particular object, assigned by the object implementer. This name is then used by clients to obtain a reference to an object of a particular type by using the `bind()` methods generated in the stub class for that interface type. Let's have a look at an example constructor for an implementation of an interface X in the BOA model:

```
class Ximpl : public _sk_X {
  // constructor
  Ximpl( const char *object_name ) : _sk_X( object_name ) {
  }
```

The object created using this constructor will now be accessible to any client that uses the generated stub class. The client has to pass the same name to a `bind()` method on that class. The `bind()` method looks like the following:

```
static X_ptr bind( const char *object_name = NULL,
             const char *host_name = NULL,
             const CORBA::BindOptions *_opt = NULL,
             CORBA::ORB_ptr _orb = NULL )
```

Specifying nonnull values for the parameters sets constraints on the `bind()` method in finding implementations. For example, specifying a nonnull host_name restricts the bind() method to finding implementations on the specified host_name.

The _opt parameter allows the client to specify options by creating an object of class CORBA::BindOptions updating its boolean fields:

♦ defer_bind—do not make a connection to the target object until the first invocation
♦ enable_rebind—reconnect to the target object if the connection is lost

Object implementations with the same name are treated as replicas. That is, if a client holds an IOR to an object and this object isn't accessible anymore, the invocation will be automatically rerouted by the Smart Agent. The address information in the run-time representation of the IOR, that is, the client side proxy, will be automatically updated. When multiple object instances match a bind request, the Smart Agent returns object references in a round-robin fashion—a simple but in many cases adequate load balancing mechanism. Finally, as long an object implementation is registered with the object activation daemon, the Smart Agent creates an object instance if there are none of the requested specification available.

6

Building Applications

In this chapter we explain how to build applications using C++ ORBs. We have selected a simple room booking system as an example. Since we want to demonstrate CORBA features rather than prove that we can implement a sophisticated booking system, we have kept the application-specific semantics simple. But as will be seen in the IDL specification, we have chosen a very fine-grain object model which allows the creation of many CORBA objects and the demonstration of invocations between them. We will also demonstrate the use of the CORBA Naming Service.

This chapter covers the development of an entire application including

♦ Interface specification (Section 1).
♦ Implementing objects (Section 2).
♦ Implementing a server (Section 3).
♦ Implementing a factory (Section 4).
♦ Starting servers (Section 5).
♦ Client application (Section 6).

1   *Application Specification*

The room booking system allows the booking of rooms and the cancellation of such bookings. It operates over one-hour time slots from 9 A.M. to 4 P.M. To keep things simple we do not consider time notions other than these slots, so there are no days or weeks. The rooms available to the booking system are not fixed; the number and the names of rooms can change. When booking a room, a purpose and the name of the person making the booking should be given. We do not consider security issues and anyone can cancel any booking.

The following key design decisions were made:

♦ Rooms and meetings are CORBA objects.
♦ A meeting object defines a purpose and the person responsible for the meeting.
♦ A meeting factory creates meeting objects.
♦ A room stores meetings indexed by time slots.
♦ Rooms have a name and register themselves under this name with the naming service.

Figure 6.1 illustrates a typical configuration of the room booking system. There are three room servers that all have one room object implementation. There is also a meeting factory server that has created a meeting factory object. The meeting factory has created several meeting objects that are in the same process space. There is also a naming service that has various naming context objects forming a context tree. The room and the meeting factory object implementations are registered with the naming service.

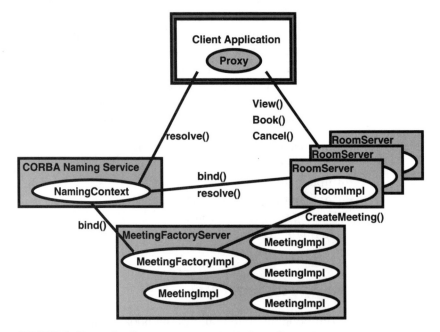

FIGURE 6.1 Room booking system—a typical configuration.

1.1   IDL Specification

The IDL specification of the room booking system is contained in a hierarchy of modules as motivated in Chapter 5. It contains a number of interface specifications: Meeting, MeetingFactory, Room.

The interface Meeting has only two attributes, purpose and participants, which are both of type string and both readonly. The attributes describe the semantics of a meeting.

Meeting objects are created at run time by a meeting factory which is specified in the interface MeetingFactory. It provides a single operation, CreateMeeting(), which has parameters corresponding to the attributes of the meeting object and returns an object reference to the newly created meeting object.

```
module RoomBooking {

  interface Meeting {

      // A meeting has two read-only attributes which describe
      // the purpose and the participants of that meeting.

      readonly attribute string purpose;
      readonly attribute string participants;
  };

  interface MeetingFactory {
      // A meeting factory creates meeting objects.
      Meeting CreateMeeting( in string purpose, in string participants);
  };
```

Within the specification of the interface Room, we start with the definition of some datatypes and a constant. There is the enum Slot which defines the time slots in which meetings can be booked. The constant MaxSlots, of type short, indicates how many slots exist. The typedef Meetings defines an array of length MaxSlots of meeting objects. Then we define two exceptions, NoMeetingInThisSlot and SlotAlreadyTaken, which are raised by operations in the interface. There is also a readonly attribute name of type string which carries the name of the room, for example, "Board Room."

```
  interface Room {

      // A Room provides operations to view, make, and cancel bookings.
      // Making a booking means associating a meeting with a time slot
      // (for this particular room).

      // Meetings can be held between the usual business hours.
      // For the sake of simplicity there are 8 slots at which meetings
      // can take place.
```

```
enum Slot { am9, am10, am11, pm12, pm1, pm2, pm3, pm4 };

// since IDL does not provide means to determine the cardinality
// of an enum, a corresponding constant MaxSlots is defined.

const short MaxSlots = 8;

// Meetings associates all meetings of a day with time slots
// for a room.

typedef Meeting Meetings[ MaxSlots ];

exception NoMeetingInThisSlot {};
exception SlotAlreadyTaken {};

// The attribute "name" names a room.

readonly attribute string name;
```

There are three operations defined in the interface Room. The operation View() returns Meetings, the previously defined array of meeting objects. The meaning is that a meeting object reference indicates that this meeting is booked into the indexed slot. A nil object reference means that the indexed slot is free.

The operation Book() books the meeting a_meeting in the slot a_slot of the room object on which the operation is invoked. The operation raises the SlotAlreadyTaken exception if there is already a meeting booked into the specified slot.

The operation Cancel() removes the meeting at the slot a_slot. It raises the NoMeetingInThisSlot exception if there is no meeting in the slot.

2 Implementing Objects

The servant classes we have to implement are for the IDL interfaces Meeting and Room. We use the POA model for both the meeting and room implementations.

2.1 Implementing the Meeting Object

We implement the meeting object in a class MeetingImpl which extends the IDL-generated implementation base class POA_RoomBooking::POA_Meeting. We define two private variables _purpose and _participants, which correspond to the attributes with the same names. The constructor has two parameters which are used to initialize those two private variables.

```
// MeetingImpl.h
#include "RoomBooking_s.hh";

class MeetingImpl : public POA_RoomBooking::POA_Meeting {

    private:
      CORBA::String_var _purpose;
      CORBA::String_var _participants;

    public:
      // constructor
      MeetingImpl ( const char * purpose,
                    const char * participants ) :
          _purpose( purpose ), _participants ( participants ) {}
```

IDL attributes are mapped to C++ methods. These consist of an accessor method and a modifier method if the attribute is not readonly. Since the attributes of the interface Meeting are readonly we only have to implement the accessors. Their implementation is straightforward, they just return the value of the corresponding private variable.

```
// attributes
char *purpose() { return CORBA::strdup(_purpose); }
char *participants() { return CORBA::strdup(_participants); }
```

2.2   Implementing the Room Object

The room object is implemented in the class RoomImpl, extending the corresponding IDL-generated class POA_RoomBooking::POA_Room. We declare two private variables, _name to hold the name of the room object and meetings to hold the array of booked meetings. Note that the variable meetings is of type RoomBooking::Meetings_var which is a memory-managed type. We also declare a third private variable safetyMutex, which will be used to ensure thread safety. We explain in subsequent sections how we make use of the mutex. Note that the type of the mutex variable is VISMutex_var, which is a convenience class provided by Inprise VisiBroker.

Within the constructor, we assign the only argument, determining the name of the room to be created, to our private variable name.

```
// RoomImpl.h

#include "RoomBooking_s.hh"

class RoomImpl : public POA_RoomBooking::POA_Room {

    private:
      CORBA::String_var        _name;
```

```
        RoomBooking::Meetings_var *meetings;
#if defined(THREAD)
        VISMutex_var     safetyMutex;
#endif

    public:
      // constructor
      RoomImpl( const char *name ) : _name( name ) {
        meetings = RoomBooking::Room::Meetings_alloc();
      }
```

As introduced in Chapter 3, IDL arrays are mapped to C++ arrays. Our variable meetings is an array. We use the constructor to initialize it appropriately. The length of the array is defined in the specification of the interface Room as a constant MaxSlots, which is mapped to a C++ constant MaxSlots of type CORBA::Short.

```
// RoomBooking_c.hh

class Room: public virtual CORBA_Object {
  ...
  static const CORBA::Short MaxSlots; // 8
}
```

The attribute name is read-only and hence only the accessor method needs to be implemented. It returns the value of the corresponding private variable.

```
// attributes
char *name() {
    return CORBA::strdup(_name);
}
```

The operations of IDL interfaces are mapped to C++ methods. Clients can concurrently access room objects. Therefore we have implemented room objects in a thread-safe manner. The particular problem we have to address is that the three methods, View(), Book() and Cancel(), each either access or set the private member variable meetings. These variables are shared between multiple threads. For example, while one thread in the server could be servicing the Book() operation and thus setting an entry in the meetings array, another thread in the server servicing the Cancel() operation could delete the same entry. This leads to an inconsistency in the data structure meetings and to undefined behavior. To prevent this we introduce a private member variable safetyMutex that is locked at the beginning of each of the methods—View(), Cancel() and Book()—and is unlocked when we exit from these methods. The mutex serializes the access to the member variables. Inprise VisiBroker provides us with a convenience class VISMutex_var, which takes care of locking and unlocking in its constructor and destructor, respectively. We simply make use of this class at the beginning of our methods.

The implementation of the method View() is shown below. We lock the mutex safetyMutex to make the View() method thread safe. We simply declare a local variable called lock of type VISMutex_var and pass the safetyMutex as an argument to its constructor. This takes care of locking the safetyMutex. When the VISMutex_var variable goes out of scope, its destructor is called which unlocks the safetyMutex. Hence there is no explicit call to unlock the mutex at the end of the View() method.

We declare a variable new_meetings of type RoomBooking::Meetings_var * and allocate memory to it by making use of the Meetings_alloc() method generated by the IDL compiler. For each element in this array, we assign the corresponding value from the private member variable meetings after invoking _duplicate. The purpose of the _duplicate() method is to increment the reference count of the object reference contained in meetings[i]. Finally, we return new_meetings, which holds the object references to the currently booked meetings. When we return an object reference, we must always invoke _duplicate() on it. Otherwise the skeleton would garbage collect the object. The object reference is returned to the client but the reference on the server side is released. For information on the reference counting mechanism, see Chapter 2.

```
RoomBooking::Meetings_slice *RoomImpl::View() {
  #if defined(THREAD)
     VISMutex_var lock(safetyMutex);
  #endif

  RoomBooking::Meetings_slice *new_meetings =
       RoomBooking::Room::Meetings_alloc();
  for( CORBA::Ulong i=0; i < RoomBooking::Room::MaxSlots; i++ ) {
    new_meetings[i] =
       RoomBooking::Meeting::_duplicate(meetings[i]);
  }
  return new_meetings;
}
```

The method Book() has two parameters, one that determines the slot in which a meeting should be booked and the other that identifies the meeting object. We lock the safetyMutex to make the method thread safe, like we did in the View() method.

We check if the slot is empty, that is, if the object reference indexed by the slot is nil. If the slot is empty we assign the meeting to the slot, otherwise we raise the exception SlotAlreadyTaken. The class for the exception is defined in the class RoomBooking::Room since the corresponding IDL exception was defined in the interface Room.

```
void RoomImpl::Book( RoomBooking::Room::Slot slot,
              RoomBooking::Meeting_ptr meeting ) {
if #defined(THREAD)
  VISMutex_var lock(safetyMutex);
#endif

  if( meetings[slot] == RoomBooking::Meeting::_nil() ) {
        meetings[slot] =
              RoomBooking::Meeting::_duplicate(meeting);
  }
  else {
      cout << "Throwing exception: SlotAlreadyTaken" << endl;
      throw RoomBooking::Room::SlotAlreadyTaken();
  }
}
```

The method `Cancel()` is implemented similarly. We lock the `safetyMutex` to ensure thread safety. We check if the slot is occupied, and if so we assign `RoomBooking::Meeting::_nil()` to the slot. This causes the object reference contained in the `_var` to be released. In the case where there is no meeting object in the indexed slot, we throw the exception `NoMeetingInThisSlot`.

```
void Cancel ( RoomBooking::Room::Slot slot ) {
  if #defined(THREAD)
    VISMutex_var lock(safetyMutex);
  #endif

  if( meetings[slot] != RoomBooking::Meeting::_nil() ) {
      // Assigning _nil releases object reference contained in
      // the _var
      meetings[slot] = RoomBooking::Meeting::_nil ();
  }
  else {
      throw RoomBooking::Room::NoMeetingInThisSlot();
  }
  }
}
```

3   Building Servers

To instantiate the object implementations and to make them available to clients we have to implement a server. The server is code that at run time executes as an operating system process or task. There can be one server per object or a server can host multiple objects. A server has four fundamental tasks:

♦ Initialize the environment, that is, get references to the pseudo-objects for the ORB.
♦ Create objects.
♦ Make objects accessible to the outside world.
♦ Execute a dispatch loop to wait for invocations.

Additional server tasks can include the registration of the objects with the Naming Service or the Trading Service.

The server `RoomServer` does the four fundamental tasks and registers the newly created room with the Naming Service. This is achieved in the `main()` function of the `RoomServer` program. We define two strings which are used when registering the room object with the Naming Service. Then we check that the number of arguments is correct and exit the program if it is not. We expect one argument determining the name of the room object.

To use the Naming Service successfully, objects which want to share information via the Naming Service have to agree on a naming convention. For this example we use the following convention, which is illustrated in Figure 6.2. Under a root context we have a context "BuildingApplications" which contains two contexts called "Rooms" and "MeetingFactories," respectively. We bind room objects into the context "Rooms" and the meeting factory object into the context "MeetingFactories." Following this con-

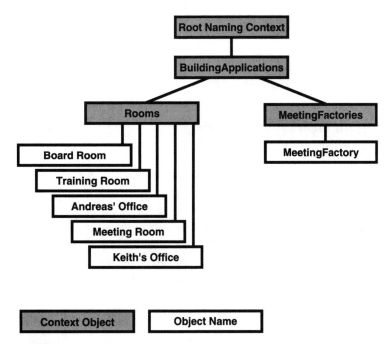

FIGURE 6.2 Naming convention.

vention will ensure that clients can locate the appropriate objects. Note that the Trading Service provides a more formal approach to categorization based on service types (see Chapter 5).

According to this naming convention we initialize the variable `context_name` with a corresponding string version of the room context name.

```
// RoomServer.C

#include "EasyNaming.h"
#include "vpolicy.h"
#include "RoomImpl.h"

int main( int argc, char *const *argv ) {

  CORBA::String_var context_name;
  char str_name[ 256 ];

  if ( argc < 2 ) {
    cerr << "Usage: " << argv[0] << "room_name" << endl;
    exit(1);
  }

  context_name = (const char *)"/BuildingApplications/Rooms/";
```

3.1   Initializing the ORB

The first task is to initialize the ORB. To get a pointer to the ORB, we call the method `ORB_init()` on the class `CORBA`.

```
try {
    //initialize the ORB
    CORBA::ORB_var orb = CORBA::ORB_init( argc, argv );
```

3.2   Creating an Object, Registering with the Root POA

The second task is to create the room object. We create an instance of the class `RoomImpl` and provide the name as a parameter to the constructor (see Section 2.2 for the definition of that class). Then we perform the third task. We use the standard POA model to implement the server. We obtain a reference to the persistent root POA by invoking `resolve_initial_references` on the ORB and `narrow`ing it to a `POA_var`. We then activate the room object by invoking `activate_object` on the root POA and passing the instance of `RoomImpl` as an argument. Following this, we activate the POA manager by invoking `activate()` on the POAManager. We then have the POA manufacture an object reference for the room object so that it can be exported to clients, either in a text file or through the Naming or Trading Service.

```
// create the Room object
RoomImpl room( argv[1] );

// Get the Root POA object reference
CORBA::Object_var obj =
  orb->resolve_initial_references( "RootPOA");

// Narrow the object reference to a POA reference
PortableServer::POA_var root_poa =
  PortableServer::POA::_narrow( obj.in() );

// create a Persistent POA
PortableServer::POA_var persistent_poa = create_persistent_poa(root_poa);
// create an ObjectID
PortableServer::ObjectId_var oid =
  PortableServer::string_to_ObjectID(CORBA::string_dup(argv[1]));

// Register servant with the POA explicitly
persistent_poa->activate_object_with_id(oid,&room);

cout << "activating POA manager ..." << endl;
persistent_poa->the_POAManager()->activate();

cout << "create reference" << endl;
CORBA::Object_var roomRef =
  persistent_poa->id_to_reference( oid );
```

3.3   Registering with the Naming Service

The next step is to register the object with the Naming Service. The class
EasyNaming provides a convenient interface to the Naming Service, as
explained in detail in Chapter 5. Its constructor obtains an initial context of
a Naming Service via the ORB's bootstrap mechanisms. The class EasyNaming
handles simple names including contexts in a notation similar to the notation of file names in various operating systems:

```
/<context1>/<context2>/.../<contextn>/<name>
```

It parses strings in this format and creates Naming Service names of
type CosNaming::Name, which maps to CosNaming::Name in C++.
We initialize such a string in the variable str_name, for example, with a
value "/BuildingApplications/Rooms/Board Room." We then bind the room
object reference to the name corresponding to this string by calling
bind_from_string() on the object easy_naming.

```
// register with naming service
// create EasyNaming object
EasyNaming *easy_naming = new EasyNaming( orb, cosnaming_ior );
```

```
// Copy context_name to str_name
strcpy( str_name, context_name );

// Append string name
strcat( str_name, argv[1] );

// bind str_name to room object
easy_naming->bind_from_string( str_name, roomRef );
```

3.4   Entering the ORB's Event Loop

The fourth task of the server is to enter the ORB's event loop by calling `orb->run()` to wait for incoming invocations.

Finally, we catch exceptions. If an exception of type `AlreadyBound` is raised, we realize that a room with our room's name is already registered with the Naming Service. We handle any exception that is raised in a very simple way. We print it out and exit.

```
    // Enter ORB's Event loop
    orb->run();
}
catch( const CosNaming::NamingContext::AlreadyBound& already_bound ){
  cerr << "Room " << context_name << " " << argv[1]
       << " already bound. " << endl;
  cerr << "Exiting ..." << endl;
  exit(1);
}
catch( const CORBA::UserException& ue ) {
  cerr << ue << endl;
  cerr << "Room " << context_name << " " << argv[1]
       << " already bound. " << endl;
  exit(1);
}
catch( const CORBA::SystemException& se ) {
  cerr << se << endl;
  exit(1);
}
 return 0;
}
```

4   Building Factories

A factory is an object implementation with a particular design pattern. The difference from ordinary objects is that factories provide methods to dynamically create new objects. They perform the same initialization of new objects as a server's `main()` method. That is, they create objects and make them invokable. The process of building factories contains the same steps as building any other server: implementing the object and implementing the server.

4.1 Meeting Factory Object Implementation

The meeting factory implementation, the class MeetingFactoryImpl, is an extension of the corresponding IDL-generated class POA_RoomBooking::POA_MeetingFactory. We declare private variables to hold pointers to the ORB and the POA. In the constructor we pass references to the ORB and POA which have obtained in the server. We also set the name of the object in the POA model.

```
// MeetingFactoryImpl.h

#include "RoomBooking_s.hh"
#include "MeetingImpl.h"

class MeetingFactoryImpl : public POA_RoomBooking::POA_MeetingFactory {
  private:
    CORBA::ORB_var _orb;
    PortableServer::POA_var _poa;

  public:
    // constructor
    MeetingFactoryImpl (
        CORBA::ORB_ptr& orb,
        PortableServer::POA_ptr poa ):
        try {
          _orb = orb;
          _poa = PortableServer::POA::_duplicate (poa);

        } catch( const CORBA::SystemException& excep ) {
          cerr << "MeetingFactoryImpl: exception occurred" << endl;
          cerr << excep << endl;
          exit(1);
        }
    }
```

The implementation of the only method of the meeting factory, CreateMeeting(), is shown below. Its parameters correspond to those of the meeting object's MeetingImpl() constructor. We pass the parameters to the **MeetingImpl** constructor which creates a new instance of a meeting object. We store the reference to this object in the variable newMeeting. Once the object is created we follow the usual procedure to activate an object in the POA model. We activate the object, and have the POA manufacture an object reference that can then be returned to the caller. We must duplicate the object reference before returning to the caller, in accordance with the CORBA reference counting and IDL to C++ mapping rules for returning object references.

```
// MeetingFactoryImpl.C

#include "MeetingFactoryImpl.h"

// operations
RoomBooking::Meeting *MeetingFactoryImpl::CreateMeeting(
            const char * purpose, const char * participants ) {
    MeetingImpl *newMeeting;

    try {
      newMeeting = new MeetingImpl(purpose, participants );

      if (newMeeting == RoomBooking::Meeting::_nil()) {
        cerr << "newMeeting created is nil" << endl;
      }

      cout << "activating obj ..." << endl;
      PortableServer::ObjectId_var oid =
            _poa->activate_object( newMeeting );

      cout << "create reference ..." << endl;
      CORBA::object_ptr obj = _poa->id_to_reference (oid.in());
      _poa->the_POAManager()->activate();

      // increase the reference count
      returnRoomBooking::Meeting::_narrow(CORBA::Object::_duplicate(obj));

    }
    catch( const CORBA::SystemException& excep ) {
      cerr << "System Exception occurred while creating new Meeting" <<
      endl;
      exit(1);
    }
    return newMeetingRef;
```

4.2   Meeting Factory Server

The meeting factory server follows the same pattern as the room server. We
initialize the ORB, create the meeting factory object, and follow the usual
rules to activate the object with the root POA.

```
#include "vpolicy.h"
#include "EasyNaming.h"
#include "MeetingFactoryImpl.h"

int main( int argc, char *const *argv ) {

    CORBA::String_var context_name;
    char str_name[ 256 ];

    if ( argc < 2 ) {
```

```
      cerr << "Usage: " << argv[0] << " FactoryServerName" << endl;
      exit (1);
   }

context_name =
      (const char *)"/BuildingApplications/MeetingFactories/";
try {
  // initialize ORB
  CORBA::ORB_var orb = CORBA::ORB_init( argc, argv );

  // Get the root POA object reference
  CORBA::Object_var obj =
    orb->resolve_initial_references( "RootPOA" );

  // Narrow the object reference to a POA reference
  PortableServer::POA_var root_poa =
        PortableServer::POA::_narrow( obj.in() );

  // create a persistent poa
  PortableServer::POA_var persistent_poa =
                        create_persistent_poa (root_poa);

  // create an object Id
  PortableServer::ObjectId_var =
        PortableServer::string_to_objectId(CORBA::string_dup(argv[1]));
  MeetingFactoryImplmeeting_factory(argv[1]);

  // Register servant with POA
  persistent_poa->activate_object_with_id(oid, & meeting factory);

  cout << "activating poa mgr ..." << endl;
  root_poa->the_POAManager()->activate();
```

In the meeting factory server we use the Naming Service differently from the way we use it in the room server. Instead of binding a name to the object reference, we rebind it. This means that when there is already an object bound to the name we have chosen, we override the old binding. We use the method `rebind_from_string()` of the class `EasyNaming` which calls `rebind()` on the naming context.

Note that we use rebind only to demonstrate another feature of the Naming Service; the rebind semantics are not implied by the meeting factory.

```
// register with Naming Service
// create EasyNaming object
EasyNaming *easy_naming = new EasyNaming( orb );

// Copy context_name
strcpy( str_name, context_name );

// Append logical name to be registered with Naming Service
```

```
strcat( str_name, "MeetingFactory");

// rebind str_name to meeting factory object
// overrides any previous binding
easy_naming->rebind_from_string( str_name, meeting_factoryRef );
```

We finish by calling `orb->run()` to wait for incoming invocations and then catch exceptions.

```
    // enter ORB's event loop
    orb->run();

} catch( const CORBA::SystemException& sexcep ) {
    cerr << "MeetingFactoryServer: System Exception occurred" << endl;
    cerr << sexcep << endl;
    exit(1);
} catch( const CORBA::UserException& uexcep ) {
    cerr << "MeetingFactoryServer: User Exception occurred" << endl;
    cerr << uexcep << endl;
    exit(1);
}
return(0);
}
```

5   Starting Servers

Starting the servers requires the following steps. As explained in Chapter 5, we have defined a naming domain to which all components of our application belong. We do this by setting the root context to a naming context called ROOT.

Start Naming Service

```
> CosNamingExtFactory ROOT ROOT_log > CosNaming.ior & (UNIX)
> nameextf ROOT ROOT_log > CosNaming.ior & (Windows)
```

Start meeting factory server

```
> MeetingFactoryServer MeetingFactory -SVCnameroot ROOT &
```

Start room servers

```
> RoomServer "Board Room" -SVCnameroot ROOT &
> RoomServer "Training Room" -SVCnameroot ROOT &
> RoomServer "Meeting Room" -SVCnameroot ROOT &
> RoomServer "Andreas' Office" -SVCnameroot ROOT &
> RoomServer "Keith's Office" -SVCnameroot ROOT &
```

6   *Building Clients*

Clients can be implemented as C++ applications or Java applications or Java applets. In order to build Java client applications or applets, we require the Java ORB. For further details, refer to *Java Programming with CORBA* by Andreas Vogel and Keith Duddy (1998). In this section we illustrate how to build a text-based C++ client application.

The following output shows the initial state of a client that is viewing a booking system containing four bookings made previously by other clients.

Room Booking Client Application

	AM			PM				
Rooms	*9*	*10*	*11*	*12*	*1*	*2*	*3*	*4*
Training room	Book	Book	Book	Book	View	Book	Book	Book
Keith's office	Book	Book	View	Book	Book	Book	Book	Book
Meeting room	Book	Book	Book	Book	Book	View	Book	Book
Board room	Book	View	Book	Book	Book	Book	Book	Book
Andreas's office	Book	Book	Book	Book	Book	Book	Book	Book

The following output shows a view of the booking system after a user has selected the training room's 9 A.M. time slot and the booking has been made.

Room Booking Client Application

	AM			PM				
Rooms	*9*	*10*	*11*	*12*	*1*	*2*	*3*	*4*
Training room	View	Book	Book	Book	View	Book	Book	Book
Keith's office	Book	Book	View	Book	Book	Book	Book	Book
Meeting room	Book	Book	Book	Book	Book	View	Book	Book
Board room	Book	View	Book	Book	Book	Book	Book	Book
Andreas's office	Book	Book	Book	Book	Book	Book	Book	Book

The following shows a sample output from invoking a "View" operation on the 9 A.M. slot of the training room.

```
Enter the name of the room you would like to book/cancel/view:Training Room

Enter the slot number you would like to book/cancel/view
(9,10,11,12,1,2,3,4):9

Meeting Details:
```

```
Room name: Training Room
selected slot: 9am
Purpose: C++ ORB Training
Participants: Andreas & Keith

The following operations are available:
        Cancel
        Return

To Cancel, enter 'c' or 'C'
To Return to Main menu, enter 'r' or 'R'
```

6.1   Client Application

We initialize the ORB by invoking ORB_init(). We then call init_from_ns() which obtains the meeting factory and room naming context references from the Naming Service. Then we invoke the method view() to get the booking information from each room.

```
int main( int argc, char *const *argv ) {

  try {
    orb = CORBA::ORB_init( argc, argv );
    init_from_ns();

    CORBA::Boolean quit_flag = 0;

    view();
```

Following initialization, we accept user input. The choices available to the user at this time are to view an existing booking, to book a room or to quit. Based on the user input, we take action accordingly. The method select_room_slot() allows the user to select a particular room and slot. The method meeting_details() displays the details of an existing meeting. The method display_rooms() presents a table of all the rooms with their booking status.

```
    // Accept input from the user
    // Modify internal variables accordingly
    for(;;) {
      cout << "\n\nThe following operations are available:" << endl;
      cout << "\tBook\n";
      cout << "\tView\n";
      cout << "\tQuit\n\n\n";

      cout << "To Book, enter 'b' or 'B'\n";
      cout << "To View, enter 'v' or 'V'\n";
      cout << "To Quit, enter 'q' or 'Q'\n";

      char choice;
      cin >> choice;
```

```
        switch(choice) {
        case 'v':
        case 'V':
         select_room_slot();
         meeting_details();
         display_rooms();
         break;
        case 'b':
        case 'B':
         select_room_slot();
         book();
         break;
        case 'q':
        case 'Q':
         quit();
         quit_flag = 1;
         break;
        default:
         cout << "\n\nThe choice you entered was incorrect. Please enter
         again\n";
          break;
        }
        if (quit_flag) break;
      }
    }
    catch( const CORBA::SystemException& sexcep ) {
      cerr << "RoomBookingClient: System Exception occurred" << endl;
      cerr << sexcep << endl;
      exit (1);
    }
    catch( const CORBA::UserException& uexcep ) {
      cerr << "RoomBookingClient: User Exception occurred" << endl;
      cerr << uexcep << endl;
      exit (1);
    }
    return 0;
}
```

6.2 Methods in the Client Application

In this section we explain the methods which are part of the client application.

6.2.1 Overview of Methods

The C++ client application consists of the following methods:

> void init_from_ns()—Gets the room context from the root context and obtains a reference to the meeting factory by resolving it from a predefined name.

CORBA::Boolean view()—Queries all rooms and displays the result at the user interface.

CORBA::Boolean cancel()—Cancels a selected booking.

void select_room_slot()—Processes the event of clicking a button to book or view a meeting. It decides if the room is free and a booking can be made or if the booking details should be displayed.

void meeting_details()—Queries and displays the details of a meeting. The method deals mainly with GUI programming and hence the code is only shown in the Appendix.

CORBA::Boolean book()—Creates a meeting and books it into a selected slot.

void display_rooms()—Displays all the rooms and slots in a tabular fashion along with their booking status.

void display_labels()—Helper function for display_rooms(). Displays labels.

void display_room_status()—Helper function for display_rooms(). Examines the booked array and displays View if the slot already has a booking and Book if the slot is empty.

6.2.2 Variable Declarations

We start the implementation of the class with a number of local variables.

```
// RoomBookingClient.C

#include "RoomBooking_c.hh"
#include "EasyNaming.h"

CORBA::ORB_var orb;
CORBA::String_var ior;

RoomBooking::MeetingFactory_var meeting_factory;
CosNaming::NamingContext_ptr room_context;

CORBA::String_var participants;
CORBA::String_var purpose;

CORBA::UShort **booked;

CORBA::ULong selected_room;
RoomBooking::Room::Slot selected_slot;

RoomBooking::Room_var *rooms;
RoomBooking::Meeting_var *meetings;

CORBA::String_var *r_label;
```

```
int num_rooms = 0;
const int max_slots = 8;
const int max_buf_len = 80;
```

6.2.3   init_from_ns()

We have decided on a naming convention for the room booking system illustrated in Figure 6.2. Room objects are bound to names in the context "/BuildingApplications/Rooms" and the meeting factory object is bound to the name "/BuildingApplications/MeetingFactories/MeetingFactory." The method init_from_ns() resolves the rooms context and obtains an object reference to the meeting factory using methods from the class EasyNaming, which we introduced in Chapter 5.

```cpp
// Initialize from Naming Service
void init_from_ns () {

  try {

    // Create EasyNaming Object
    EasyNaming *easynaming = new EasyNaming( orb );

    // get room context
    room_context = CosNaming::NamingContext::_narrow(
                        easynaming->resolve_from_string(
                            "/BuildingApplications/Rooms"));
    if ( room_context == CosNaming::NamingContext::_nil() ) {

      cerr << "Room Context is NULL" << endl;
      cerr << "exiting... " << endl;
      exit(1);
    }

    // get MeetingFactory from Naming Service
    meeting_factory = RoomBooking::MeetingFactory::_narrow(
                        easynaming->resolve_from_string(
                      "/BuildingApplications/MeetingFactories/Meeting
                      Factory"));
    if ( meeting_factory == RoomBooking::MeetingFactory::_nil() ) {
      cerr << "No Meeting Factory registered at Naming Service" << endl;
      cerr << "exiting..." << endl;
      exit(1);
    }
  }
  catch( const CORBA::SystemException& system_exception ) {
    cerr << "System Exception while initializing from Naming Service: "<<
    endl;
    cerr << system_exception << endl;
  }
  catch( const CORBA::UserException& naming_exception ) {
```

```
      cerr << "User Exception while initializing from Naming Service: " <<
      endl;
      cerr << naming_exception << endl;
    }
}
```

6.2.4 view()

The method view() displays information about the current availability of
rooms. Therefore it has to find out about all existing rooms and call the
View() operation on each of them.

Object references for the available rooms can be obtained from the
Naming Service. We have already initialized a room context in which,
according to our convention, room objects are bound.

We query the room context by using the method list(), defined in the
interface CosNaming::NamingContext. As explained in Chapter 6, the operation
list() has three parameters:

> in long length—The maximum length of the list returned by the second
> parameter, which is a CORBA::Ulong in C++.

> out CosNaming::BindingList—A sequence of names. Since it is an out
> parameter we declare a BindingList_var variable bl and use its
> .out() in accordance with the C++ language mapping for out
> parameters.

> out CosNaming::BindingIterator—A binding iterator, that is, an object from
> which further names can be obtained. It is also an out parameter
> and so we declare a BindingIterator_var variable bi and use its
> .out() in accordance with the C++ language mapping for out
> parameters.

In our implementation we demonstrate the use of the list as well as the
iterator. We obtain object references from the room context via the resolve()
operation. We then narrow the resulting object to the right type. We go
through the binding list as well as through the binding iterator.

```
CORBA::Boolean view() {
    try {
        // list rooms
        // initialize binding list and binding iterator
        // objects for out parameter
        CosNaming::BindingList_var       bl;
        CosNaming::BindingIterator_var bi;

        // we are lazy and consider only 20 rooms
        // although there could be more in the binding iterator

        if (room_context == CosNaming::NamingContext::_nil()) {
            cerr << "room context has become NIL" << endl;
```

```
  exit(1);
}
room_context->list(20, bl.out(), bi.out());

// create an array of Room and initialize it by resolving
// the entries in the Room context of the Naming Service
num_rooms = bl->length();

rooms = new RoomBooking::Room_var [ num_rooms ];
for( CORBA::ULong i = 0; i < num_rooms; i++ ) {
  cout << "Room " << i << ": " << bl[i].binding_name[0].id << endl;
  rooms[i] = RoomBooking::Room::_narrow(
               room_context->resolve( bl[i].binding_name ));

}

// be friendly with system resources
if (bi != CosNaming::BindingIterator::_nil())
  bi->destroy();
```

We create an array of labels, one for each room, which is eventually used to display the names of the rooms. We also create an array of type CORBA::Boolean for internal use to store information about whether each slot is already booked or not.

```
// create room labels according to the number of rooms
r_label = new CORBA::String_var[ num_rooms ];

// create booked array according to the number of rooms
booked = new CORBA::UShort*[ num_rooms ];
for( i = 0; i <= num_rooms-1; i++ )
  booked[i] = new CORBA::UShort[ max_slots ];
```

Next we initialize the elements of the label array by invoking the accessor method for the attribute name of the interface Room.

```
// show the label with the room name
for( i = 0; i < num_rooms; i++ ) {

// get the names of the rooms and store them locally
r_label[i] = rooms[i]->name();
```

For each of the rooms we invoke the operation View(), which returns an array of Meeting_var objects. For such arrays a valid object reference identifies a meeting object which is booked into the indexed slot, while a nil object reference means an empty slot. We go through the array and set the corresponding element in the booked array to 1 or 0 depending on whether the slot is empty or not.

```
      // call view operation on the i-th room object
      // and create book or free label
      cout << orb->object_to_string( rooms[i] ) << endl;
```

```
            meetings = rooms[i]->View();

            for( CORBA::ULong j = 0;
                   j < RoomBooking::Room::MaxSlots; j++ ) {
              if ( meetings[j] == RoomBooking::Meeting::_nil() )
                booked[i][j] = 0;
              else {
                booked[i][j] = 1;
                }
              }
          }

      display_rooms();
    }
    catch( const CORBA::SystemException& system_exception ) {
      cerr << system_exception << endl;
    }
    catch( const CORBA::UserException& naming_exception ) {
      cerr << naming_exception << endl;
    }
    return 1;
}
```

6.2.5   cancel()

To cancel a meeting, the method cancel() invokes the operation Cancel() on the appropriate room, providing the selected slot as an argument.

If the selected slot does not contain a meeting object reference, the operation Cancel() raises an exception of type NoMeetingInThisSlot. This can only happen when there are multiple clients running that attempt to cancel the same meeting in overlapping time intervals. A more sophisticated approach would be to use the CORBA Transaction Service.

```
CORBA::Boolean cancel() {
  try {
    room[ selected_room ]->Cancel( selected_slot );
  }
  catch( const RoomBooking::Room::NoMeetingInThisSlot& no_meeting ) {
    cerr << "Cancel: " << no_meeting << endl;
  }
  catch( const CORBA::SystemException& system_exception ) {
    cerr << "Cancel: " << system_exception << endl;
  }

  // show bookings of all rooms
  return view();
}
```

The method select_room_slot() prompts the user to enter the name of a room that he/she is interested in booking, viewing, or canceling an existing booking. It then validates the user input by comparing against the list of room names available. Following this, it prompts the user to enter a slot number and checks for its validity. At the end of this method, the variables `selected_room` and `selected_slot` contain valid values that can be further processed.

6.2.6 book()

The booking of a meeting, managed by the method book(), involves two tasks: creation of the appropriate meeting object and booking of the selected meeting.

We create the meeting object using the meeting factory. This is done by invoking the operation CreateMeeting(). Its two parameters are obtained from two text fields.

The newly created meeting is then booked by calling the operation Book() on the selected room object. It is again possible that someone else has booked the slot in the meantime. If so, we catch an exception of type SlotAlreadyTaken.

```
CORBA::Boolean book() {

  try {
    char purpose[ max_buf_len ];
    char participants[ max_buf_len ];

    cout << "Enter the purpose of the meeting:";
    cin.ignore( max_buf_len, '\n' );
    cin.get( purpose, max_buf_len );

    cout << "\nEnter the participants in the meeting:";
    cin.ignore( max_buf_len, '\n' );
    cin.get( participants, max_buf_len );

    RoomBooking::Meeting_var meeting =
      meeting_factory->CreateMeeting(purpose, participants);
    cout << "Meeting created" << endl;

    rooms[ selected_room ]->Book( selected_slot, meeting );
    cout << "Room is booked" << endl;
  }
  catch( const RoomBooking::Room::SlotAlreadyTaken& already_taken ) {
    cerr << "book: " << already_taken << endl;
    cerr << "Please select another slot or room" << endl;
  }
  catch( const CORBA::SystemException& system_exception ) {
    cerr << "book: " << system_exception << endl;
  }

  // show bookings of all rooms
  return view();
}
```

6.2.7 *meeting_details()*

The method `meeting_details()` displays the details about a meeting by invoking the `name()` method on the meeting object. To obtain the purpose and the participants in a meeting, it invokes the `View()` method on the selected room. Following this, the user is prompted for a choice regarding cancellation of the current booking.

```cpp
void meeting_details() {

  try {

    cout << "\n\nMeeting Details:\n\n";

    cout << "Room name: "
            << rooms[ selected_room ]->name() << endl;

    cout << " selected slot: " << slot_map[selected_slot] << endl;

    // Get information about this room

    meetings = rooms[ selected_room ]->View();

    RoomBooking::Meeting_var meeting = meetings[ selected_slot ];

    if ( meeting != RoomBooking::Meeting::_nil() ) {
      cout << "Purpose: " << meeting->purpose() << endl;
      cout << "Participants: " << meeting->participants() << endl;

      CORBA::Boolean valid_choice = 0;

      cout << "\n\nThe following operations are available:\n";
      cout << "\tCancel\n";
      cout << "\tReturn\n\n";

      while (!valid_choice) {

        cout << "To Cancel, enter 'c' or 'C'\n";
        cout << "To Return to Main menu, enter 'r' or 'R'\n";

        char choice;
        cin >> choice;
        switch(choice) {
        case 'c':
        case 'C':
          cancel();
          valid_choice = 1;
          break;
        case 'r':
        case 'R':
          valid_choice = 1;
```

```
        break;
      default:
        cerr << "\n\nThe choice you entered was incorrect.\n";
        break;
      }
    }
  }
  else {
    cerr << "\nThere is no meeting scheduled in the above slot and
    room!!\n" << en
  }
}
catch( const CORBA::Exception& exception ) {
  cerr << "meeting_details: " << exception << endl;
}
}
```

7 Extensions to the Example Application

The example can be extended, in particular to include various other CORBA services. We outline possible extensions below.

The Object Trading Service could be used as an alternative to the Naming Service for locating objects. The server classes would register objects with the Trading Service and a client would query the Trading Service to search for room and meeting factory objects.

The Transaction Service could be used to ensure ACID properties to booking and cancel operations. In the current implementation we do not explicitly roll back the creation of a meeting object when it cannot be booked into a particular slot.

The Security Service could be used to authenticate users and to authorize a user to execute certain operations. For example, only a user who booked a meeting originally should be allowed to cancel it.

The Event Service could be used to notify certain users that a meeting in which they are participating is now starting.

7

Advanced Features

In this chapter we explain and give examples of how to use some advanced CORBA features. The features, which are explained in detail here, have already been introduced in Chapters 3 and 4. They are:

- TypeCodes
- Any
- Interface Repository (IR)
- Dynamic Invocation Interface (DII)
- Dynamic Skeleton Interface (DSI)
- Tie approach
- IDL context

1   The Extended Hello World Example

To demonstrate these advanced features we will adapt the distributed Hello World example from Chapter 1.

1.1   Interface Specification

The IDL for the extended example will look as follows:

```
module HelloWorld {

 interface GoodDay {
    string hello( out short hour, out short minute );
 };

};
```

In the IDL above, we again specify an interface GoodDay with an operation hello(). The module is again called HelloWorld. However, we have changed the signature of the operation specification. Its result is still a string, but this time the operation has parameters and it returns the description of the server's location. The parameters are tagged as out, meaning that their values will be supplied by the invoked object. They are both of type short and their intended meaning is that they hold the current time at the server's location: hour holds the hour and minute the minute.

An out parameter in an IDL operation has pass-by-result semantics. This means that a value for this parameter will be supplied by the invoked object. The value will be available to the client after the invocation is completed.

1.2   A Client

The main difference between the client in this example and the simple Hello World example introduced earlier is that we now declare two CORBA::Short variables, hour and minute, and pass references to these variables during the invocation of the hello() method.

```
// HelloWorldClient.C
#include "HelloWorld_c.hh"

int main(int argc, char* const* argv) {
  CORBA::String_var ior;
  CORBA::Short      minute;
  CORBA::Short      hour;
  char              *location;

  // get stringified IOR from command line
  if ( argc >=2 )
    ior = (const char *) argv[1];
  else {
    cerr << argv[0] << ": Missing IOR, specify IOR of server" << endl;
    return 1;
  }

  cout << "IOR: " << ior << endl;
```

```
try {
  // Initialize the ORB
  CORBA::ORB_var orb = CORBA::ORB_init(argc, argv);

  // get object reference from the command line
  CORBA::Object_var obj = orb->string_to_object( ior );

  // narrow it down to GoodDay
  HelloWorld::GoodDay_var goodDay =
        HelloWorld::GoodDay::_narrow( obj );

  // check if object reference is NIL
  if ( goodDay == HelloWorld::GoodDay::_nil () ) {
    cerr << "Could not narrow object
              reference to HelloWorld::GoodDay\n";
    exit(1);
  }
```

1.2.1   Invoking the Operation

After we initialize the ORB and obtain a narrowed object reference, we
invoke the operation. We assign the result of the operation to a string location. After the successful return of the invocation, the variables named hour
and minute will carry the values set by the invoked object.

```
  // invoke the operation
  location = goodDay->hello( hour, minute );
  // print location and time obtained
  cout << "Hello World!" << endl;
  if ( minute < 10 )
    cout << "The local time in " << location << " is "
         << hour << ":0" << minute << "." << endl;
  else
    cout << "The local time in " << location << " is "
         << hour << ":" << minute << "." << endl;
} // Catch CORBA system exceptions
  catch (const CORBA::Exception& e) {
  cerr << e << endl;
  return(1);
  }
  return(0);
}
```

When we print out the results we obtain the time at the remote location
from the variables hour and minute. We compile the client as before and execute the client. The stringified object reference must refer to an object that
provides the extended Hello World interface. The following is a typical result.

```
$ HelloWorldClient 'cat HelloWorld.ior'
IOR:012020201b00000049444c3a48656c6c6f576f726c642f476f6f644461793a31
2e3000200200000001534956640000000101012009000006672616e6b6c696e00202
020fe040000010000003d00000001504d43000000001b00000049444c3a48656c6c6c6
f576f726c642f476f6f644461793a12e3000201100000048656c6c6f576f726c6453
6572766572200202020000000000000000059000000010100200e0000003230362e36
342e31352e3232370056113d00000001504d43000000001b00000049444c3a48656c6c
6c6f576f726c642f476f6f644461793a312e3000201100000048656c6c6f576f726c6c
6453657276657200
Hello World!
The local time in San Mateo is 22:25.
```

1.3   Servant Implementation

The servant, GoodDayImpl, derives from the skeleton class POA_HelloWorld::POA_GoodDay which is generated by the IDL compiler. The variable declarations and the constructor are as in the class GoodDayImpl of the simple Hello World example, but the signature of the method hello() has changed this time. There are now two references to short variables as parameters to the hello() method. We create an object localtime of type Localtime which holds the time information of the system. The convenience class Localtime is defined in Localtime.h, supplied with the examples. We retrieve the hour and minute by invoking the methods hour() and minute() on the localtime object. We assign the values to the corresponding short variables passed in by reference. We also return the location as in the earlier example.

```
// HelloWorldServer.C

#include "HelloWorld_s.hh"
#include "Localtime.h"

class GoodDayImpl : public POA_HelloWorld::POA_GoodDay {

  private:
    CORBA::String_var _location;

  public:
    GoodDayImpl( const char *location,
                 const char *object_name = NULL) :
                             _location( location ) {
        PortableServer_ServantBase::_object_name( object_name )
    }

    char *hello( short &hour,
             short &minute ) {

        // use the Localtime class to get
        // location and time of the server
        Localtime localtime;
```

```
      hour = localtime.hour();
      minute = localtime.minute();

      return CORBA::strdup(_location);
   }

};
```

The server implementation uses the servant class `GoodDayImpl`. Once the ORB is initialized, we create an instance of the servant class `GoodDayImpl`. We then obtain a reference to the root POA by invoking `resolve_initial_references` on the ORB and narrow it to a POA reference. The argument Inprise_TPool_Persistent makes the operation return a POA with pre-set threading and lifespan policy.

```
int main(int argc, char* const* argv)
{
  CORBA::String_var location;

  location = ( argc < 2 ) ?
      (const char *) "some place" : (const char *) argv[1];

  try {
    // Initialize the ORB
    CORBA::ORB_var orb = CORBA::ORB_init(argc, argv);

    // Create a new GoodDay object.
    GoodDayImpl goodDayImpl( "HelloWorldServer", location );

    // Get the Root POA object reference with pre-set policies
    CORBA::Object_var obj =
          orb->resolve_initial_references(
                  "Inprise_Tpool_Persistent" );

    // Narrow the object reference to a POA reference
    PortableServer::POA_var root_poa =
          PortableServer::POA::_narrow( obj.in() );
```

We then invoke the `activate_object()` method on the POA. This causes the `goodDayImpl` object to be registered with the POA and activates it. To activate the POA, we invoke the `activate()` method on the POAManager.

```
cout << "Activating the GoodDay object …" << endl;
PortableServer::ObjectId_var oid =
      root_poa->activate_object( &goodDayImpl );

cout << "Activating the POA to wait for requests …" << endl;
root_poa->the_POAManager()->activate();
```

We then create an object reference corresponding to the activated object by invoking `id_to_reference()` on the POA. This creates an object reference from the activated object which we then stringify by invoking `object_to_string()` and then export to clients.

```
cout << "Create Object Reference …" << endl;
CORBA::Object_var goodDayRef =
      root_poa->id_to_reference( oid );

// Stringify the object
cout << orb->object_to_string( goodDayRef ) << endl;
```

We finally enter the ORB's event loop.

```
// Enter ORB Event loop
   orb->run();

 } // catch CORBA system exceptions
   catch(const CORBA::Exception& e) {
   cerr << e << endl;
   return(1);
 }

 return(0);
 }
```

2 The Any Type and TypeCodes

In this section we demonstrate the use of Anys as parameters of IDL-defined operations. We use a variant of the distributed Hello World example introduced previously.

2.1 Interface Specification

In the IDL following, although we have changed the signature of the interface specification, we retain the semantics of the hello() operation. Both the result of the operation and the only parameter are of type any. As before, the operation will return the location of the object implementation as a string, this time contained in an Any. This is an example of the use of a predefined datatype within an Any.

The any_time parameter is an example of passing a user-defined datatype in an Any. The parameter will contain a structure with two fields, both short integers, representing the minute and hour of the local time at the object implementation. Although this structure is not directly used in the specification of the operation, its definition needs to be available to the client and the server. Hence we define the Time structure within the module.

```
module HelloWorld{

struct Time{
    short hour;
    short minute;
};

interface GoodDay{
    any hello( out any any_time );
};
}
```

2.2   Object Implementation

The object implementation class GoodDayImpl derives from the skeleton base class POA_HelloWorld::POA_GoodDay which is generated by the IDL compiler. We also keep the same private variable _location and the constructor.

```
// HelloWorldServer.C

#include "HelloWorld_s.hh"
#include "Localtime.h"

class GoodDayImpl: public POA_HelloWorld::POA_GoodDay {

private:
  CORBA::String_var _location;

public:
  // constructor
  GoodDayImpl( const char *object_name,
          const char *location )
          : _location( location ) {
    POA_HelloWorld::POA_GoodDay::_object_name( object_name );
}
```

The signature of the method hello() corresponds to the IDL mapping for Anys, as explained in Chapter 3. We have an Any for the result and declare a variable of type CORBA::Any_ptr for the out parameter.

We make use of the Localtime class to obtain the local time at the server's location, as in the original example. In the next step we create an object of the class HelloWorld::Time, which is the C++ representation of the IDL type definition struct Time. There is no default constructor generated for this class, so we obtain the hour and minute from invoking _localtime.hour() and _localtime.minute() and assign the hour and minute fields of struct_time.

We declare a CORBA::Any variable any_time, to return the time over to the client. Now we have to insert the value of the time variable into the Any. The CORBA::Any class provides an entire range of methods overloading the insertion operator <<= and the extraction operator >>=. However, these methods are available only for primitive datatypes and for CORBA-specific datatypes. For user-defined datatypes, such as HelloWorld::Time in our example, the IDL compiler needs to be instructed specifically (with VisiBroker for C++ 3.x IDL compiler idl2cpp, using the -type_code_info command line option) to generate code that we can use for inserting a variable of type HelloWorld::Time to a CORBA::Any and for extracting a variable of type HelloWorld::Time from a CORBA::Any. Using the insertion operator <<= that was generated by the IDL compiler, now the Any object any_time contains the value of struct_time.

```
// method
CORBA::Any_ptr hello( CORBA::Any_ptr& any_time ) {
  // use the Localtime class to get
  // location and time of the server
  Localtime localtime;

  // create time-structure assign hour and minute to it
  HelloWorld::Time struct_time;

  struct_time.hour = localtime.hour();
  struct_time.minute = localtime.minute();

  // create an any and shuffle structure into it
  any_time = new CORBA::Any();
  *any_time <<= struct_time;

  // create an any and shuffle location into it
  CORBA::Any_ptr any_location = new CORBA::Any();
  *any_location <<= CORBA::strdup(_location);
    return any_location;
  }
};
```

The operation result is stored in the variable any_location, an Any holding a string value. Since the class CORBA::Any provides us with an insertion operator <<= for strings, we insert the value of _location by calling the method operator <<= on the Any object. There are similar methods, listed in Chapter 3, defined in the class CORBA::Any for the other predefined datatypes.

The last task of the implementation is to return the Any_ptr any_location. The server class implementation is the same as above and in Chapter 1.

2.3   Client Implementation

The client implementation follows the same structure that we used before.

2.3.1   *Initialization and Invocation*

We declare two variables `any_location` and `any_time` of type `CORBA::Any` for the method's result and its parameter, respectively.

```
// HelloWorldClient.C

#include "HelloWorld_c.hh"

int main(int argc, char * const *argv) {

  CORBA::String_var ior;

  // get stringified IOR from command line
  if ( argc >= 2 )
    ior = (const char *)argv[1];
  else {
    cerr << argv[0] << ": Missing IOR, specify IOR of server" << endl;
    return 1;
  }
  try {
    // initialize the ORB
    CORBA::ORB_var orb = CORBA::ORB_init( argc, argv );

    // get object reference
    CORBA::Object_var obj = orb->string_to_object( ior );

    // and narrow it to GoodDay
    HelloWorld::GoodDay_var goodDay = HelloWorld::GoodDay::_narrow(obj );

    // check if object reference is NIL
    if ( goodDay == HelloWorld::GoodDay::_nil() ) {
      cerr << "Could not narrow object reference to HelloWorld::GoodDay\n";
      exit(1);
    }

    // invoke the operation

    CORBA::Any_var any_location, any_time;
    any_location = goodDay->hello( any_time.out() );
```

We initialize the ORB, convert the command line argument into an object reference, and narrow it to the right type. Then we invoke the method `hello()` with the argument `any_time.out()` and assign the result to `any_location`.

Note that we pass `any_time.out()` in accordance with the IDL/C++ mapping for out parameters. Note that the `out()` is specified by the IDL/C++ mapping.

2.3.2 Obtaining TypeCodes

TypeCodes are a runtime representation of IDL types. They are explained in detail in Chapter 4. In the following example we obtain type information about the values contained in the Anys. First we declare a variable `tc` of type `CORBA::TypeCode_var`. The type `CORBA::TypeCode_var` is a variant of `CORBA::TypeCode` and provides automatic memory management. It is useful to make use of the `_var` classes whenever possible to avoid memory leaks in applications. Then we obtain the TypeCode of the value held in the container variable `any_time`. The Any object referred to by `any_time` has a method `type()`, which returns the TypeCode of the stored value. In this example the value is a C++ object representing an IDL struct.

A TypeCode represents an attributed type tree. It provides various methods to obtain the values of the attributes. For example, we query the Interface Repository identifier of the type by calling the method `id()` on the TypeCode object. Similarly, we get the name of the type by invoking the method `name()`.

Since we are expecting the Any to contain an IDL structure, we need to traverse the type tree to obtain type information about the fields of the struct. The method `member_count()` returns the number of fields and `member_name()` returns the name of the indexed field.

Because type definitions differ in their structure, operations on TypeCode objects are only valid for particular kinds of TypeCodes. If an inappropriate method is invoked, the exception `CORBA::TypeCode::BadKind` is raised. The method `member_name()` raises the exception `CORBA::TypeCode::Bounds` when the index is out of bounds.

```
// declare a type code object
CORBA::TypeCode_var tc;

// get type of any_time and print type information
tc = any_time->type();
try {
  cout << "IfRepId of any_time: " << tc->id() << endl;
  cout << "Type Code of any_time: " << tc->name() << endl;
  for( int i = 0; i < tc->member_count(); i++ )
    cout << "\tname: " << tc->member_name(i) << endl;
}
catch(const CORBA::TypeCode::BadKind ex_bk) {
  cerr << "any_time: " << ex_bk << endl;
}
catch(const CORBA::TypeCode::Bounds ex_b) {
  cerr << "any_time: " << ex_b << endl;
}
```

In the following code, we check if the value of `any_location` is of the expected kind, `CORBA::tk_string`, and if so we query for its length. Note that the length refers to the type definition and not the current value. The method `length()` returns the maximum size of a bounded string, sequence, or array. If the type is unbounded it returns zero. We must again catch the exception `CORBA::TypeCode::BadKind`.

```
// get length of any_location
tc = any_location->type();
try {
  if ( tc->kind() == CORBA::tk_string )
    cout << "length of any_location: " << tc->length() << endl << endl;
  else
    cout << "any_location does NOT contain a string." << endl << endl;
}
catch( CORBA::TypeCode::BadKind ex_bt) {
  cerr << "any_location: " << ex_bt << endl;
}
```

When executing the client, the preceding code will produce the following result:

```
IfRepId of any_time: IDL:HelloWorld/Time:1.0
Type Code of any_time: Time
     name: hour
     name: minute
length of any_location: 0
```

2.3.3 Unpacking the Results

Now we proceed to the normal behavior of the client; that is, we obtain the results and print them. We can print the Anys directly by using their overloaded `<<` operator method or we could obtain the contained value and print them in a customized manner. We show both possibilities.

First we print the Anys `any_location` and `any_time` in the default format. Then we obtain the string from `any_location` by invoking the overloaded method for the extraction `operator>>=`. To get the time object from the Any `any_time` we call the extract method provided by the generated code. Once we have the values in the usual types, we print the message in the same way as in the original example.

```
// get String from any_location
char *location = (char *)NULL;
*any_location >>= location;
```

```
      // get Struct from any_time
      HelloWorld::Time  time;
      *any_time >>= time;

      // print results to stdout
      cout << "Print Anys: " << endl;
      cout << "any_location: " << endl << any_location << endl << endl;
      cout << "any_time: " << endl << any_time << endl << endl;
      // print results to stdout

      cout << "Hello World!" << endl;
      if ( time.minute < 10 )
        cout << "The local time in " << location << " is " << time.hour
             << ":0" << time.minute << "." << endl;
      else
        cout << "The local time in " << location << " is " << time.hour
             << ":" << time.minute << "." << endl;
    }
    catch(const CORBA::Exception& ex) {
      cerr << ex << endl;
      return 1;
    }
```

When the client is invoked, it prints the results in the following form:

```
Print Anys:
any_location:
TypeCode:
CORBA::TCKind:tk_string
Parameter Number: 0
TypeCode:
CORBA::TCKind:tk_ulong
Value:
0
Value:
SanMateo

any_time:
TypeCode:
Repository id: IDL:HelloWorld/Time:1.0
CORBA::TCKind:tk_struct
Parameter Number: 0
TypeCode:
CORBA::TCKind:tk_string
Parameter Number: 0
TypeCode:
CORBA::TCKind:tk_ulong
Value:
0
Value:
Time
Parameter Number: 1
```

```
TypeCode:
CORBA::TCKind:tk_string
Parameter Number: 0
TypeCode:
CORBA::TCKind:tk_ulong
Value:
0
Value:
hour
Parameter Number: 2
TypeCode:
CORBA::TCKind:tk_TypeCode
Value:
2
Parameter Number: 3
TypeCode:
CORBA::TCKind:tk_string
Parameter Number: 0
TypeCode:
CORBA::TCKind:tk_ulong
Value:
0
Value:
minute
Parameter Number: 4
TypeCode:
CORBA::TCKind:tk_TypeCode
Value:
2
Value:
22 25

Hello World!
The local time in San Mateo is 22:25.
```

3 *Interface Repository and Dynamic Invocation Interface*

In this section we present a client that is capable of invoking operations on an object whose type was unknown to the client at compile time. So far, clients have used stub code generated by an IDL compiler to create a proxy object on which they have invoked methods corresponding to each operation.

The structure of the example is

- ♦ Initialize the ORB (section 3.1)
- ♦ Browse the Interface Repository (section 3.2).
- ♦ Unparse and print the type information obtained from the Interface Repository (section 3.3).

- ♦ Create a Request object (sections 3.4–3.6).
- ♦ Invoke an operation using the Dynamic Invocation Interface (section 3.7).
- ♦ Obtain and print results (section 3.8).

To make invocations on objects without having access to IDL-generated code we have to

- ♦ Obtain information about the interface type of the object
- ♦ Invoke a method without an IDL-generated client-side proxy class (stub)

The first task is carried out using the Interface Repository, which contains type information about interfaces. Typically the Interface Repository is populated by the IDL compiler. Our client will query the Interface Repository using a standard method on the object reference, defined in CORBA::Object. This returns a reference to an Interface Repository object that represents the target object's interface type. The object is part of a type tree which the client can traverse.

The second task is carried out using the Dynamic Invocation Interface (DII). It provides a Request object which can be used for the invocation of methods on arbitrary objects. The DII's interface Request is defined in the CORBA module using pseudo-IDL. It is the programmer's responsibility to initialize a Request pseudo-object with all the necessary information (a target object reference, an operation name, argument types and values) in order to make an invocation.

Figure 7.1 illustrates the process by which interface information is obtained and used to invoke the object implementation. The IDL compiler creates the skeleton code for the server side as usual and populates the Interface Repository with the types specified in the IDL file. The client can then query the Interface Repository about the type of any object reference it obtains.

3.1   Initializing the ORB

The client obtains an object reference from, for example, a stringified object reference or from the Naming or Trading Service. For simplicity, we use stringified object references in our example. Note that we cannot narrow the object reference to its particular interface type because we do not know its type and do not have access to the _narrow() method, which is part of the code generated by the IDL compiler.

```
// DiiClient.C

#include "corba.h"
```

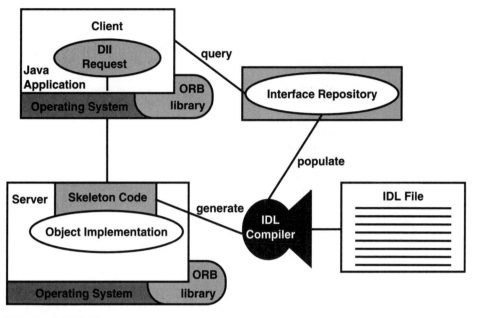

FIGURE 7.1 DII client.

```
int main(int argc, char * const *argv) {

  CORBA::String_var ior;

  // get stringified IOR from command line
  if ( argc >= 2 )
    ior = (const char *)argv[1];
  else {
    cerr << argv[0] << ": Missing IOR, specify IOR of the server" << endl;
    return 1;
  }

  cout << "IOR: " << ior << endl;

  try {

    // initialize the ORB
    CORBA::ORB_var orb = CORBA::ORB_init( argc, argv );

    // get object reference
    CORBA::Object_var obj = orb->string_to_object( ior );
```

We call the method `_get_interface()` on our new object reference. This is a standard method, provided by the class CORBA::Object, which returns a pointer to an object of type InterfaceDef. Note that we make use of the convenience class `InterfaceDef_var` to store the return value. This class takes care of freeing allocated memory. The InterfaceDef interface is defined in the Interface Repository specification. The interfaces of the Interface Repository are explained in Chapter 2.

```
// get interface definition from Interface Repository
   CORBA::InterfaceDef_var if_def = obj->_get_interface();
```

3.2   Browsing the Interface Repository

The InterfaceDef interface has an operation, describe_interface(), which returns a pointer to a structure FullInterfaceDescription. It contains a number of nested structures which represent the operations and attributes contained in the interface. One of the nested structures, OperationDescription, describing an operation, also contains nested structures describing the operation's parameters.

The structure FullInterfaceDescription represents a flattening of the objects in the Interface Repository to provide all the necessary type information in a single data structure without the need to make further calls to the Interface Repository objects to query their types. Alternatively, traversal of the Interface Repository can be done by obtaining object references to OperationDef objects and AttributeDef objects that can be queried to discover their component definitions.

```
// get full interface description
   CORBA_InterfaceDef::FullInterfaceDescription_var full_if_desc =
                        if_def->describe_interface();
```

In our client we store the interface description in a variable `full_if _desc`. The type is defined in IDL as the following struct. We only show the type definitions we use in the example.

```
typedef string Identifier;
typedef sequence <OperationDescription> OpDescriptionSeq;

struct FullInterfaceDescription {
   Identifier          name;
   RepositoryId        id;
   RepositoryId        defined_in;
   VersionSpec         version;
   OpDescriptionSeq    operations;
   AttrDescriptionSeq  attributes;
   RepositoryIdSeq     base_interfaces;
   TypeCode            type;
}
```

We use the members name and operations, which is a sequence of OperationDescription structs:

```
typedef sequence < ParameterDescription > ParDescriptionSeq;
typedef sequence < ExceptionDescription > ExcDescriptionSeq;

struct OperationDescription{
    Identifier name;
    RepositoryId id;
    RepositoryId defined_in;
    VersionSpec version;
    TypeCode result;
    OperationMode mode;
    ContextIdSeq contexts;
    ParDescriptionSeq parameters;
    ExcDescriptionSeq exceptions;
};
```

In turn, parameters and exceptions that are part of an operation are described by structures.

3.3 A Simple Unparser

The following code traverses the nested structures and prints all operations of the interface in a simplified version in OMG IDL syntax. We go through all the operations that are defined in the interface, obtaining the result type in the form of a CORBA::TypeCode, the operation name which is a string, and the parameters. We invoke the method kind() on the result to obtain the value of the typecode. Note that we use a helper function print_tk2idl() that takes as input a CORBA::TCKind and prints the corresponding IDL type to cout.

```
int no_of_parameters = 0;

// print various information
cout << "Querying the Interface Repository" << endl;
cout << "interface " << full_if_desc->name << "{" << endl;

for( int i = 0; i < full_if_desc->operations.length(); i++ ) {
  no_of_parameters =
      full_if_desc>operations[i].parameters.length();

  cout << " ";

  // print the type code of the operation's result
  print_tk2idl (full_if_desc->operations[i].result->kind());

  // print the name of the operation
  cout << " " << full_if_desc->operations[i].name << " (" << endl;
```

The parameters are described by a sequence of structures of type ParamDescription: enum ParameterMode {PARAM_IN, PARAM_OUT, PARAM_INOUT};

```
struct ParamDescription{
    Identifier    name;
    TypeCode      type;
    IDLType       type_def;
    ParameterMode mode;
};
```

The parameter's type member is of type TypeCode and its name is an Identifier, which is an alias of string. The parameter mode is an integer, and its values are defined in the enumerated type CORBA::ParameterMode. We have to convert the mode value into strings.

```
// define and initialize text representations
// for parameter modes
CORBA::String_var mode, in, inout, out;
in = (const char *)"in";
inout = (const char *)"inout";
out = (const char *)"out";

char last_char = ',';

// print parameters of the operations
for( int j = 0; j < no_of_parameters; j++ ) {

  // set the right text for the parameter mode
  switch (full_if_desc->operations[i].parameters[j].mode) {
  case CORBA::PARAM_IN:
    mode = in; break;
  case CORBA::PARAM_INOUT:
    mode = inout; break;
  case CORBA::PARAM_OUT:
    mode = out; break;
  default:
    mode = (const char *)"unknown mode";
    }

  // deal with separating commas
  if( j == no_of_parameters - 1 )
    last_char = ' ';
  // print mode, type and name of the parameter
  cout << "     " << mode << " ";
  print_tk2idl(
    full_if_desc->operations[i].parameters[j].type->kind()
  );
    cout << " " <<
  full_if_desc->operations[i].parameters[j].name;
 cout << last_char << endl;
 }
 cout << "  );" << endl;
}
cout << "};" << endl
```

3.4 Initializing Requests

Now that we have discovered the type of the object, we want to invoke an operation on it. We will need the DII to do this. This requires the creation of a Request object, as illustrated in Figure 7.2. A Request has three components:

- string—carries the name of the operation to be invoked
- NamedValue—carries the type and value of the operation's result
- NVList—carries the mode, type, and value of the operation's parameters

3.5 Creating Supporting Objects

We now create and initialize the NamedValue for the result and the NVList containing the arguments to the operation. A NamedValue is a datatype defined in pseudo-IDL in the module CORBA. It is a triple of a name of type CORBA::String, a typed value of type Any, and a mode of type int. Appropriate constants are defined in the enum CORBA::ParameterMode. An

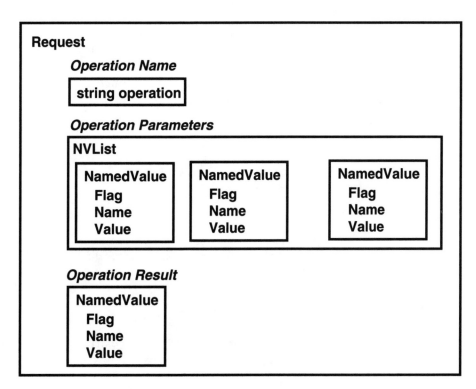

FIGURE 7.2   Request object.

NVList is an object containing a list of NamedValue objects. See Chapter 4 for details.

To initialize an operation result we only need to set the type we expect by initializing the value with a dummy value of the right type. After the invocation, the value will hold the result of the operation.

We create an NVList result_list of length one and insert a single element later using the method add_value(). This method has three parameters, one for each of the components of a NamedValue.

The tricky part is to create an Any which carries the type and the value of an argument. For out parameters we only need to put the type information into the Any. The class Any provides overloaded insertion and extraction operators for all primitive datatypes which take care of filling in the appropriate typecode information (see Chapter 3). So we just create a new Any object.

We need to be able to only set the types of Any objects but not their values. This is needed for parameters which are tagged as in or inout. The IDL/C++ language mapping provides us with overloaded insertion and extraction operators to solve this problem. If you look at the code generated for IDL-defined types you will find examples of the use of output streams. While these streams are standardized in the IDL/Java mapping and are used as a portability layer, this is not the case in C++.

The following code shows the implementation of the overloaded insertion operator <<= defined in the class HelloWorld::Time which has been generated by the IDL compiler. It is the generated class for the struct Time that we defined for the previous example.

```
inline friend void operator<<=(CORBA::Any& _a, const Time& _val) {
  CORBA::MarshalOutBuffer _mbuf;
  _mbuf << _val;
  _a.replace(_tc_Time_get(), _mbuf);
}
inline friend CORBA::Boolean operator>>=(const CORBA::Any& _a, Time&
_val) {
  CORBA::TypeCode_var _tc(_a.type());
  if ( !_tc->equal(_tc_Time_get()) ) return 0;
    CORBA::MarshalInBuffer _mbuf((char *)_a.value(),
    (CORBA::ULong)_a.len());
    _mbuf >> _val;
    return 1;
}
```

The overloaded method operator>>=() extracts val which is of type Time& from an Any. The previous methods use typecodes to ensure the type safety of the insertion.

3.6   Using the Supporting Objects

We now return to our DII client class. For simplicity we have chosen to invoke the first operation of the interface specification, `full_if_desc.opera-tions[0]`. This is the interface specification for the object whose object reference we obtained from a string when initializing the client.

We create two NVLists, one for the operation result, `result_list`, and the other for the operation's parameter list, `arg_list`. For the operation result, we only have to set the type which we expect the operation to return. We get an Any object of the right type for the result by creating a `CORBA::Any` variable with the right TypeCode and an initial value of zero. The list is populated using the `NVList` method `add_value()`.

```
// using the DII to make an invocation
cout << "Make a DII call" << endl;

// create and initialize result
CORBA::NVList_ptr result_list = new CORBA::NVList();

result_list->add_value( "",
                          CORBA::Any(
                             full_if_desc->operations[0].result,
                             0
                          ),
                        0 );

// create and initialize arg_list
CORBA::NVList_ptr arg_list = new CORBA::NVList();
no_of_parameters = full_if_desc->operations[0].parameters.length();
for( i = 0; i < no_of_parameters; i++ ) {

  // add empty value
  arg_list->add_value(
              full_if_desc->operations[0].parameters[i].name,
              CORBA::Any(
                  full_if_desc->operations[0].parameters[i].type,
                    0),
              full_if_desc->operations[0].parameters[i].mode + 1 );
}

cout << "operation: " << full_if_desc->operations[0].name << endl;
```

For the argument list we use a for loop over the parameter specifications from the interface description and add corresponding values for each argument with the `add_value()` method. The values are Any objects of the right type, obtained by invoking the constructor for `CORBA::Any` that takes as a parameter a TypeCode and an initial value. The argument list must contain values for in and inout arguments. Note that this method only deals properly with out parameters.

3.7 Creating and Invoking a Request Object

Once we have initialized the result and the arguments, we can create and initialize a Request object by calling `_create_request()` on the object reference on which we want to invoke the operation. The method `_create_request()` has the following parameters:

Context—which we do not use and hence initialize to `CORBA::Context::_nil()`.

Operation name—which we obtain from the interface description.

Arguments—which we have created in NVList `arg_list`.

Result—which is the first element of the NVList `result_list`.

Request object—which is the request object being constructed by this method. We use the `out()` method since the request object is an out parameter to this method.

Flags—which we do not use and hence initialize to zero.

```
// create request
CORBA::Request_var request;
obj->_create_request(
        CORBA::Context::_nil(),      // context - not used
        full_if_desc->operations[0].name,  // operation name
        arg_list,                    // NVList with arguments
        result_list->item(0),        // NamedValue for result
        request.out(),               // created request
                                     // object
        0                            // Flags
        );

// invoke request
request->invoke();
```

Now we can call the method `invoke()` on the Request object. This results in an invocation on the object reference from which we obtained the Request. Once the call is completed the Request object will place the result of the operation and the values for the inout and out parameters into the NVLists provided to its constructor.

3.8 Getting Results

Next we print the value of the result and the values of the out parameters of the operation. We use the overloaded method for the extraction operator

<<= on the Any objects, which allows us to print the value of Any objects directly using cout, as shown below. Note that if the Any contains another Any, indicated by its TypeCode kind CORBA::tk_any, then we have to extract the contained Any as shown in the code snippet below.

```
// get result
CORBA::Any_var res_any_var = request->result()->value();
cout << "result: " << endl;

// Check typecode of result
CORBA::TypeCode_var tc = res_any_var->type();

// If typecode kind is CORBA::tk_any, need to extract
// the contained Any
if ( tc->kind() != CORBA::tk_any ) {
  cout << *(res_any_var) << endl;
}
else {
  CORBA::Any res_any;
  * (res_any_var) >>= res_any;
  cout << res_any << endl << endl;
}

// get out parameters
CORBA::NVList_ptr nv_list = request->arguments();
for( i = 0; i < no_of_parameters; i++ ) {
  cout << nv_list->item( i )->name() << ":" << endl;
  CORBA::Any_var nv_any_var = nv_list->item( i )->value();

  // Check the typecode of the Named Value
  CORBA::TypeCode_var tc = nv_any_var->type();

  // If typecode kind is CORBA::tk_any, need to extract the
  // contained Any
  if ( tc->kind() != CORBA::tk_any )
    cout << (*nv_any_var) << endl;
  else {
    CORBA::Any nv_any;
    (*nv_any_var) >>= nv_any;
    cout << nv_any << endl;
  }
 }
}
// catch exceptions
catch( const CORBA::TypeCode::Bounds& bex ) {
  cerr << bex << endl;
  return 1;
}
catch( const CORBA::SystemException& ex ) {
  cerr << ex << endl;
  return 1;
```

```
        }
      catch(const CORBA::Exception& ex) {
        cerr << ex << endl;
        return 1;
      }
```

3.9   Executing the Client

When executing the DII client we can invoke operations on arbitrary objects. In our example we invoke the first operation defined in the interface. The following output is produced when the object reference used refers to an object supporting the extended Hello World interface.

```
.../dii> DiiClient IOR:012020201b00000049444c3a48656c6c6...

Querying the Interface Repository
interface GoodDay{
  string hello (
      out short hour,
      out short minute
  );
};
Make a DII call
operation: hello

result: TypeCode:
CORBA::TCKind:tk_string
Parameter Number: 0
TypeCode:
CORBA::TCKind:tk_ulong
Value:
0
Value:
SanMateo,California,USA

hour:
TypeCode:
CORBA::TCKind:tk_ushort
Value:
22
minute:
TypeCode:
CORBA::TCKind:tk_ushort
Value:
33
```

As another example, we use the DII client program to invoke the AnyHelloWorld object from the previous section. Again the client queries the Interface Repository and prints the interface specification in OMG IDL syntax. As in the previous section, the interface GoodDay again provides an operation hello(). However, this time the result and the only parameter are both of type Any. The client creates the corresponding Request object and invokes it. In this example, however, notice that the return type is an Any and the out parameter is also an Any. In this case, we will encounter CORBA::tk_any in the typecode kind of the return value and the out values, thus causing an additional extraction of the contained Any.

```
.../dii > DiiClient IOR:012020201b00000049444c3a48656c6c6f57...

Querying the Interface Repository
interface GoodDay{
  any hello (
     out any     any_time
  );
};
Make a DII call
operation: hello

result:
TypeCode:
CORBA::TCKind:tk_string
Parameter Number: 0
TypeCode:
CORBA::TCKind:tk_ulong
Value:
0
Value:
SanMateo,California,USA

any_time:
TypeCode:
Repository id: IDL:HelloWorld/Time:1.0
CORBA::TCKind:tk_struct
Parameter Number: 0
TypeCode:
CORBA::TCKind:tk_string
Parameter Number: 0
TypeCode:
CORBA::TCKind:tk_ulong
Value:
0
Value:
Time
Parameter Number: 1
TypeCode:
CORBA::TCKind:tk_string
Parameter Number: 0
TypeCode:
CORBA::TCKind:tk_ulong
```

```
Value:
0
Value:
hour
Parameter Number: 2
TypeCode:
CORBA::TCKind:tk_TypeCode
Value:
2
Parameter Number: 3
TypeCode:
CORBA::TCKind:tk_string
Parameter Number: 0
TypeCode:
CORBA::TCKind:tk_ulong
Value:
0
Value:
minute
Parameter Number: 4
TypeCode:
CORBA::TCKind:tk_TypeCode
Value:
2
Value:
22 28
```

4   *Dynamic Skeleton Interface*

Similar to the DII on the client side, the Dynamic Skeleton Interface (DSI) provides an interface on the server side which allows the invocation of methods on objects without compiler-generated skeletons. We introduced the CORBA specification of the DSI in Chapter 2 and explained its mapping to C++ in Chapter 4. In this section we demonstrate how to program with the DSI. Once again we use a modified Hello World example to illustrate it.

The implementation of the server is the same as usual, only we provide a different implementation of the GoodDay interface. The interface is implemented by a C++ class called GoodDayImpl, which represents the servant in POA terminology.

```
// HelloWorldServer.C

#include "corba.h"
#include "Localtime.h"

class GoodDayImpl: public PortableServer_DynamicImplementation {
```

The implementation class extends the class PortableServer_Dynamic-Implementation. As with the static implementation class we declare a private field _location. The constructor of the GoodDayImpl class implicitly calls the constructor of the base class.

We describe the interface type in the form of an Interface Repository identifier. These identifiers are strings with the following syntax (in EBNF):

"IDL:" {module_name "/"} interface_name ":" major "." minor

The major/minor pair are currently always 1 and 0, as the use of versioning in the Interface Repository is not well defined.

Repository identifiers can be easily created. In our example we just hard-code them into the class. More flexible and sophisticated solutions could look them up from the Interface Repository or receive them from a third party.

```
private:
  CORBA::String_var _location;

public:


  // constructor
  GoodDayImpl( const char *location,
               const char *object_name ) :
          _location( location ),
          PortableServer_ServantBase::_object_name( object_name );
}
```

The class PortableServer_DynamicImplementation defines the abstract methods invoke() and _primary_interface(). The invoke() method is called whenever an invocation is made on the dynamic implementation object. The method has one parameter which is of class CORBA::ServerRequest, which is very similar to the corresponding class Request in the DII in structure, but different in signature. The class CORBA::ServerRequest is defined in C++ as

```
class CORBA::ServerRequest {
  ...
    public:
    const char *op_name() const { ... }
    CORBA::Context_ptr ctx() { ... }
    void params( CORBA::NVList_ptr );
    void result( CORBA::Any_ptr );
    void exception( CORBA::Any_ptr exception );
    const char *operation() const { ... }
    void arguments( CORBA::NVList_ptr param) { ... }
    void set_result( const CORBA::Any& a) { ... }
    void set_exception( const CORBA::Any& a) { ... }
    ...
}
```

Within the implementation of the method `invoke()` we need to analyze the server request object to determine which operation has been invoked. The DSI is typically used to dynamically delegate incoming requests for operations that were not defined at the time the server was written. Of course, the server must be able to interpret the semantics of the request, or forward the request somewhere where it is understood. Examples of this sort of behavior can be found in generic wrappers whose clients define IDL in a particular pattern that is understood by the server, which identifies the corresponding legacy functionality to perform the required task, and in bridges that simply pass on the request uninterpreted. The recently adopted CORBA-DCE interworking specification explains the use of the DSI in a dynamic bridge.

In our example we provide one operation as a demonstration of dealing with the ServerRequest. This is implemented directly in the `invoke()` method. If the operation name of an incoming request is not "hello" we throw the CORBA system exception CORBA::BAD_OPERATION.

```
// methods
void invoke( CORBA::ServerRequest_ptr request ) {

  cout << "DSI: invoke() called" << endl;
  cout << "operation: " << request->op_name() << endl;
  cout << "if def: " << this->_get_interface() << endl;

  // check operation name
  if ( strcmp( request->op_name(), "hello" ) != 0 ) {
  throw CORBA::BAD_OPERATION();
}
```

The `_primary_interface()` method should return the Repository ID of the object being implemented. This is required to provide the necessary type information to the dynamic skeleton. In the static case, this information would be contained in the skeleton class generated from the IDL. Following is the implementation of the `_primary_interface()` method:

```
CORBA::RepositoryId _primary_interface(
                    const PortableServer::ObjectId& oid,
                    PortableServer::POA_ptr poa ) {
    return CORBA::string_dup( "IDL:HelloWorld/GoodDay:1.0" );
```

Otherwise we proceed with the implementation of the hello() operation by making use of the `Localtime` class to get the current time. To return the result and the out parameters we have to wrap the values in Any objects and put them into the ServerRequest object. This needs to be done earlier when we are expecting some arguments to our operation, as the ServerRequest requires us to pass an NVList with all the parameter names and types initialized into which it places the values that came from the client. In our case, we are only passing out parameters, so we can create the NVList after the processing is done.

We create the Any objects in the usual way and insert our values using the appropriate overloaded methods for the insertion operator <<= on the Any object. For user-defined datatypes we would use the overloaded method for the insertion operator <<= generated by the IDL compiler, as described in the previous section.

```
// get local time of the server
Localtime localtime;
CORBA::Short hour, minute;

hour = localtime.hour();
minute = localtime.minute();

// create anys for hour, minute and location
CORBA::Any any_hour;
CORBA::Any any_minute;

any_hour <<= hour;
any_minute <<= minute;
```

We now create a NameValue list for the arguments to which we add two elements: the two Any objects we have created for the out parameters. Then we set the parameters and the result of the ServerRequest object.

```
    CORBA::NVList_ptr parameters = new CORBA::NVList();
    parameters->add_value("hour", any_hour, CORBA::ARG_OUT);
    parameters->add_value("minute", any_minute, CORBA::ARG_OUT);

    request->params( parameters );

    // create an any and shuffle location into it
    CORBA::Any_ptr any_location = new CORBA::Any();
    *any_location <<= CORBA::strdup(_location);
    request->result( any_location );
  }
};
```

When a client invokes methods on an object implemented with the DSI, it does not notice any difference to invoking an object implemented with an IDL-generated skeleton.

5 *Tie Mechanism*

So far we have constructed statically typed object implementations by inheritance of skeleton classes generated by the IDL compiler. These skeletons implement the marshaling and incoming request delegation of the CORBA object. They are then extended to provide methods that support the operations in the IDL interface. The inheritance approach forces an implementation to inherit from a skeleton class. There are occasions when there are existing classes which cannot be modified to inherit from the skeleton class.

A solution to the problem is to use delegation instead of inheritance. This is achieved by generating a pseudo-implementation or Tie class which inherits the skeleton. However, rather than implementing the operations, this pseudo-implementation class calls methods on another object that actually implements the operations' semantics. The delegation approach is also known as the Tie mechanism.

We use the Hello World example as introduced in Chapter 1 to demonstrate the Tie approach. We have to modify both the server class and the object implementation class, and introduce the pseudo-implementation class. Let's start with the implementation class. The only difference from the inheritance approach is in the declaration of class GoodDayImpl.

```
// HelloWorldServer.C

#include "HelloWorld_s.hh"
#include "Localtime.h"

class GoodDayImpl {
```

While the implementation class extends the skeleton class in the inheritance approach, in the Tie approach it does not.

The class GoodDayImpl implements the methods corresponding to the IDL. The Tie class serves as a wrapper around this real implementation class and delegates incoming requests to it.

```
class GoodDayImpl {

private:
  CORBA::String_var _location;

public:

  // constructor
  GoodDayImpl( const char *location ) : _location( location ) {}
  // method
  CORBA::Any_ptr hello( CORBA::Any_ptr& any_time ) {
```

In the server implementation, we initialize the ORB. Then we create an instance of the GoodDayImpl class, called goodDayImpl, and supply it as a parameter to the constructor of the Tie object goodDayPseudoImpl. As usual, we obtain a reference to the root POA, register the servant with the root POA, and activate the object. Following this, we activate the POA, have the POA manufacture the object reference, write out the object reference to be exported to clients, and enter the ORB's event loop.

```cpp
int main( int argc, char * const *argv ) {

  CORBA::String_var location;

  location = ( argc < 2 ) ?
    (const char *) "some place" : (const char *) argv[1];

  try {
    // initialize the ORB
    CORBA::ORB_ptr  orb = CORBA::ORB_init( argc, argv );

    // create a GoodDay object
    GoodDayImpl goodDayImpl( location );

    // create a Tie Object
    HelloWorldPOA_tie_GoodDay<GoodDayImpl>
      goodDayPseudoImpl( goodDayImpl );

    // Get the Root POA object reference
    CORBA::Object_var obj =
      orb->resolve_initial_references( "Inprise_TPool_Persistent" );

    // Narrow the object reference to a POA reference
    PortableServer::POA_var root_poa =
      PortableServer::POA::_narrow(obj.in() );

    cout << "Activating the GoodDay object …" << endl;
PortableServer::ObjectId_var oid = root_poa->activate_object(
&goodDayPseudoImpl );

    cout << "Activating the POA to wait for requests …" << endl;
    root_poa->the_POAManager()->activate();

    cout << "Create Object Reference …" << endl;
    CORBA::Object_var goodDayRef = root_poa->id_to_reference( oid );

    // print stringified object reference
    cout << "IOR: " << orb->object_to_string( goodDayRef ) << endl;

    // start ORB's Event loop
    orb->run();

  }
  catch( const CORBA::Exception& e ) {
```

```
      cerr << e << endl;
      return 1;
  }
  return 0;
}
```

To understand what is happening behind the scenes, let's have a look at the class `HelloWorldPOA_tie_GoodDay`. This is the Tie, or pseudo-implementation, class.

The Tie class inherits from the class `POA_HelloWorld::POA_GoodDay`, which connects it with the ORB runtime system. The class is a templated C++ class and contains a private variable named `_ptr` which represents the real implementation class. This variable will be initialized by each of the constructors. As we have already seen in the server class, the implementation class is provided as a parameter to the constructor.

```
template <class T>
class HelloWorldPOA_tie_GoodDay : public POA_HelloWorld::POA_GoodDay
{
private:
  CORBA::Boolean _rel
  PortableServer::POA_ptr _poa;
  T* _ptr

  HelloWorldPOA_GoodDay_tie(const HelloWorldPOA_GoodDay_tie&) {}
  void operator=(const HelloWorldPOA_GoodDay_tie&) {}
public:
  HelloWorldPOA_GoodDay_tie(T& t)
    : _ptr(&t), _poa(0), _rel(0) {}
  HelloWorldPOA_GoodDay_tie(T& t, PortableServer::POA_ptr poa)
    : _ptr(&t),
    _poa(PortableServer::_duplicate(poa)), _rel(0) {}
  HelloWorldPOA_GoodDay_tie(T* p, CORBA::Boolean release= 1)
    : _ptr(p), _poa(0), _rel(release) {}
  HelloWorldPOA_GoodDay_tie(T *p, PortableServer::POA_ptr poa,
    CORBA::Boolean release=1)
    : _ptr(p), _poa(PortableServer::_duplicate(poa)),
    _rel(release) {}
  virtual ~HelloWorldPOA_GoodDay_tie() {
    CORBA::release(_poa);
    if (_rel) delete _ptr;
  }

  CORBA::Any* hello(
      CORBA::Any*& any_time) {
    return _ptr->hello(
        any_time);
  }

};
```

Once a method is invoked by a client, the pseudo-implementation object calls the method `hello()` on the real implementation object `ptr` and returns the result from this invocation back to the client. Note that the out parameter is also set by the pseudo-implementation.

6 IDL Context

This section describes IDL-specified context. A Context can be used to supply optional context information associated with a method invocation, such as the value of an environment variable. In this section we show how to pass information using IDL context by extending the Hello World example introduced earlier.

In the IDL below, the operation hello() now has a context associated with it called MY_VALUE.

```
module HelloWorld{

interface GoodDay{
 string hello( out short hour, out short minute) context("MY_VALUE");
};

};
```

The code generated from this IDL will contain the following signature.

```
virtual char* hello(
        CORBA::Short& _hour,
        CORBA::Short& _minute,
        CORBA::Context_ptr _context
      );
```

This code shows an additional parameter generated for the method `hello()`. This parameter is of type `Context_ptr`. The ORB provides methods to create a context, obtain the default context, set values to a context, and get values from a context.

6.1 Creating a Context

The code below shows a portion from the client program in the Context example. We obtain the default context from the ORB and create a child from the default context called CONTEXT. We again obtain the default context of the child created. We then create an Any variable, insert a string `"Test"` into the Any and associate it with MY_VALUE using the `set_one_value()` method. Note that MY_VALUE is actually the context specified in IDL.

```
// obtain default context from the ORB
CORBA::Context_ptr default_ctx;
CORBA::Context_ptr ctx;

orb->get_default_context(default_ctx);
default_ctx->create_child("CONTEXT",ctx);
orb->get_default_context(ctx);

// set value to the context created
CORBA::Any any;
any <<= (const char *) "Test";
ctx->set_one_value("MY_VALUE",any)
```

6.2   Invoking the Method

To match the signature of the `hello()` method in the generated code, we invoke the `hello()` method using an additional parameter `ctx` that was created above:

```
// invoke the operation
location = goodDay->hello( hour, minute, ctx );
```

6.3   Getting Values from the Context

Similarly, to extract the information carried in a context, we use the `get_values()` method. The server program of the context example shows how to retrieve the information received from a context.

```
// method
char *hello( short &hour,
             short &minute,
             CORBA::Context_ptr context ) {

  // Obtain context information
  if ( !CORBA::is_nil(context) ) {

    CORBA::Flags flags = 0;
    CORBA::NVList_var nv_list;

    context->get_values("", flags, "MY_VALUE", nv_list.out());
    char *value;
     for( CORBA::ULong i = 0; i < nv_list->count(); i++ ) {
       CORBA::NamedValue_var named_value = nv_list->item(i);
       *(named_value->value()) >>= value;
       cout << "HelloWorldServer: context value [" << i << "] = ";
       cout << value << endl;
     }
  }
```

```
else {
    cout << "The context information passed by the " << endl;
    cout << "client for this method invocation is NIL" << endl;
}
```

In the previous code, we first check if the incoming context is NIL. If not, we use the get_values() method to retrieve the information contained in the IDL context MY_VALUE. The get_values() method takes in an empty NVList and fills in the values. We then obtain the individual elements from the NVList.

G L O S S A R Y

Acronyms

AB: Architecture Board.

API: Application Programming Interface.

BOA: Basic Object Adapter.

CGI: Common Gateway Interface.

CORBA: Common Object Request Broker Architecture.

DCE: Distributed Computing Environment.

DCE-CIOP: DCE Common Inter-ORB Protocol.

DII: Dynamic Invocation Interface.

DIS: Draft International Standard.

DSI: Dynamic Skeleton Interface.

DTC: Domain Technology Committee.

ESIOP: Environment-Specific Inter-ORB Protocols.

EUSIG: End User Special Interest Group.

FDTF: Financial Domain Task Force.

GIOP: General Inter-ORB Protocol.

IDL: Interface Definition Language.

IIOP: Internet Inter-ORB Protocol.

IMCDTF: Interactive Multimedia and Electronic Commerce Domain Task Force.

IOR: Interoperable Object Reference.

IR: Interface Repository.

ISIG: Internet Special Interest Group.

ISO: International Standards Organization.

JSIG: Japan Special Interest Group.

MDTF: Manufacturing Domain Task Force.

ODP: Open Distributed Processing.

OMA: Object Management Architecture.

OMG: Object Management Group.

ORB: Object Request Broker.

PIDL: Pseudo-IDL.

POA: Portable Object Adapter.

PTC: Platform Technology Committee.

RFI: Request For Information.

RFP: Request For Proposal.

RMI: Remote Method Invocation.

RTSIG: Real Time Special Interest Group.

SIG: Special Interest Group.

SSL: Secure Socket Layer.

TSIG: Transportation Special Interest Group.

UUID: Universal Unique Identifier.

Terms

Any: Pre-defined data type in OMG IDL which can contain self-describing values of *any* type.

Architecture Board: An OMG board that reviews proposals and technology for conformance to the OMA.

Auditing: Keeping records of which principals perform which invocations on secured objects.

Authentication: Verifing that principals are who they claim to be.

Basic Object Adapter: The first specification of an object adapter in the CORBA standard. Its interface is considered incomplete, and ORB vendors have used divergent implementations to complete its functionality.

Byte-code: Intermediate representation of programming language code. The Java byte-code is very popular and virtual machines which can execute Java byte-code are available for most hardware platforms and operating systems.

Common Facilities: See CORBA facilities.

Common Gateway Interface: Interface at HTTP servers which allows access to resources, e.g., databases or programs outside the server.

Common Object Request Broker Architecture: Architecture for distributed object systems defined by the OMG.

Common Object Services: See CORBA services.

CORBAfacilities: A set of published specifications for application-level object services that are applicable across industry domains, e.g., Printing Facility, Systems Management Facility.

CORBAnet: Permanent showcase to demonstrate IIOP-based ORB interoperability sponsored by the OMG and most ORB vendors. CORBAnet is hosted by the Distributed Systems Technology Centre in Brisbane, Australia. CORBAnet can be accessed at http://www.corba.net.

CORBAservices: Set of published specifications for fundamental services assisting all object implementations, e.g., Naming Service, Event Service, Object Trading Service.

Core Object Model: The fundamental object-oriented model in the OMA which defines the basic concepts on which CORBA is based.

Credential: An encapsulation of a principal's identity and security attributes.

DCE Common Inter-ORB Protocol. Environment Specific Interoperability Protocol based on DCE. The first ESIOP adopted by the OMG.

Distributed Computing Environment. Distributed middleware developed under the control of the Open Group, formerly Open Software Foundation (OSF).

Domain Task Force: Group in the OMG responsible for specifying technologies relevant to a particular industry sector. They report to the Domain Technical Committee.

Domain Technology Committee: OMG Committee which supervises several Domain Task Forces concerned with technology specification for particular domains.

Draft International Standard: ISO defines phases through which a potential International Standard must pass. Draft International Standard is the penultimate phase.

Dynamic Invocation Interface: Interface defined in CORBA which allows the invocation of operations on object references without compile-time knowledge of the objects' interface types.

Dynamic Skeleton Interface: Interface defined in CORBA which allows servers to dynamically interpret incoming invocation requests of arbitrary operations.

Environment-Specific Inter-ORB Protocols: CORBA interoperability protocols which use data formats other than the ones specified in the GIOP. See also DCE ESIOP.

Firewall: Networking software that prevents certain types of network connections and traffic for security reasons.

General Inter-ORB Protocol: Protocol which belongs to the mandatory CORBA Interoperability protocol specifications. It defines the format of the protocol data units which can be sent via any transport. Currently there is only one transport protocol defined, namely, IIOP.

Interface Definition Language: Language to specify interfaces of objects independent of particular programming language representations. OMG has defined OMG IDL.

Interface Repository. Component of CORBA which stores type information and makes it available through standard interfaces at run time. Typically, an Interface Repository is populated by an IDL compiler when processing IDL specifications.

Interoperable Object Reference: Object reference which identifies objects independent of the ORB environment in which they have been created.

JavaBean: A Java class that supports certain conventions to allow it to be inspected and used as a component by visual application builder environments.

Marshal: Conversion of data into a programming-language and architecture-independent format.

Non-repudiation: Creation, transmission, and storage of irrefutable evidence that a principal performed an action.

Object Adapter: The ORB component which at invocation time locates the correct method in the correct programming language object based on an object reference. It is also informed by servers when objects are ready to be invoked.

Object Management Architecture: This is the overall architecture and roadmap of the OMG, of which CORBA forms a part.

Object Management Group: An international industry consortium with over 600 members which specifies an object-oriented framework for distributed computing, including CORBA.

Object Reference: Opaque data structure which identifies a single CORBA object, and enables clients to invoke operations on it, regardless of the object's location. Objects can have multiple object references.

Object Request Broker: The central component of the OMA which transmits operation invocation requests to distributed objects and returns the results to the requester.

Object Services: See CORBAservices.

OMA Reference Model: The structural model defining roles for the various components taking part in the OMA. It identifies five groups of objects to be specified: Object Request Broker, Object Services, Common Facilities, Domain Objects and Application Objects.

Open Distributed Processing: Group within ISO which is concerned with the standardization of open distributed systems.

Platform Technology Committee: OMG Committee which supervises several Task Forces concerned with specifying the ORB platform infrastructure.

Portable Object Adapter: An object adapter with standard interfaces to associate CORBA object references to programming language object instances. It is considered to be a replacement for the Basic Object Adapter.

Principal: A user or system component with a verifiable identity deprecated since CORBA 2.2.

Pseudo-IDL: Interface definitions for components of ORB infrastructure that will not be implemented as CORBA objects.

Request For Information: A formal request from an OMG body for submissions of information relating to a specific technology area.

Request For Proposal: A formal request from an OMG body for a submission of a technology specification in IDL with English semantics.

Secure IIOP: An extension of the IIOP protocol that includes security information and provides optional encryption of request data.

Secure Socket Layer: A protocol that extends TCP/IP sockets by providing authentication and encryption of communications.

Servant: Term used in the context of the POA for the implementation of an IDL interface.

Special Interest Group: Member group in the OMG that has a topic of interest in common. These groups report findings to Committees within the OMG, or the Architecture Board.

TypeCode: A run-time representation of an IDL type.

Universal Unique Identifier. Used in DCE to identify an entity.

Unmarshal: The inverse of marshaling.

I N D E X